THE BEST GOLF TIPS EVER

THE BEST
GOLF
TIPS
EVER

NICK WRIGHT
FOREWORD BY DAVID TOMS

Thomas Allen Publishers
Toronto

First published in Canada
2003 by Thomas Allen Publishers
a division of Thomas Allen & Son Limited
145 Front Street East, Suite 209
Toronto, Ontario M5A 1E3

National Library of Canada Cataloguing in Publication

Wright, Nick, 1967-
The best golf tips ever / Nick Wright.

Includes index.
ISBN 0-88762-116-3

1. Golf. I. Title.

GV965.W75 2003   796.352'3   C2002-905745-0

This book was conceived, designed, and produced by
Planet Books Ltd
Suite 330, 30 Great Guildford Street
London SE1 0HS, UK
planetpub@btinternet.com

Publisher: Stephen Paul
Project Manager: Anne McDowall
Art Director: Mark Roberts
Designer: Andrew Easton
Editorial: Andy Armitage & John Watson
Illustrator: Graham Gaches
Photographer: Mark Newcombe/Visions in Golf

Color origination: PDQ Ltd, Suffolk
Printed in Singapore by Star Standard Industries (Pte) Ltd

Foreword, David Toms

 As a PGA Tour professional, one of my regular commitments is taking part in the Pro-Am played before each regular event on the Tour schedule. I do enjoy those days and try and help my playing partners feel at ease while having a good time. As one might imagine, amateur golfers often use that time to ask questions on a variety of topics ranging from life on Tour, winning a major championship, insight on the latest equipment, and, of course, what it's like to compete against Tiger Woods. However, the most common questions are centered on how to play better golf.

The most effective way to improve your game in the long term is by taking lessons from a PGA professional and then practice what you learn over and over. However, all golfers, no matter what level of play, love quick tips. Even professionals like me, who make a living playing this great game, sometimes find it hard to resist a quick piece of advice from a fellow competitor or instructor. In that respect, we are no different from amateurs in that we are always looking for something that will help us hit the ball farther and straighter or more consistently or sink every putt we look at. If we can achieve that without having to spend more hours on the practice range or putting green, then all the better!

If you love tips, you'll enjoy this book. Each area of the game is covered in depth, with advice from top players and coaches throughout history. Players such as Lee Trevino and Arnold Palmer to Nick Faldo, Seve Ballesteros, and Tiger have made a contribution in some form or another. You might even find a couple of thoughts from me as well. In addition to providing an easy-to-read resource for improving your game, this collection of tips provides insight into the minds of some of golf's greatest champions. The fact that each player has a slightly different approach to the game is what makes golf such a unique and popular sport around the world.

Enjoy the book and good luck with lowering your handicap!

Best regards,

David Toms
2001 PGA Champion
Member, 2001 US Ryder Cup Team

contents

HOW TO FIND THOSE SHOT-SAVING TIPS
Use the at-a-glance cross-referencing icons to
pick up tips for all aspects of your game.

Accuracy &
distance

Setup

Club selection

Strategy

Equipment

Swing theory

INTRODUCTION

Casting an eye across the entire sporting spectrum, there can be very few games that boast as many self-professed experts as golf. One only has to pay a visit to the local driving range in the evening to witness a whole host of wannabe David Leadbetters and Butch Harmons casually dispensing quick tips and nuggets of advice to any suffering golfer within earshot. It is ironic, not to mention rather amusing, that most of these well-intended words of wisdom are delivered by amateur golfers with very limited knowledge of the technicalities of the game and whose swing flaws, in many instances, are even worse than those of the poor soul they are trying to assist.

But that's neither here nor there. The point is that all golfers, from the weekend hacker to the accomplished low handicapper, are searching for that one snippet of information that will transform their game overnight. Almost every single person who has struggled with the incomprehensible inconsistency of golf, genuinely believes that they are just one simple swing thought away from mastering the game for good. Not only will this magical swing key instantly transform them from a golfing equivalent of Mr Bean into a reincarnation of Ben Hogan, it will do so without them even having to suffer the inconvenience of actually having to practice.

This quick-fix mentality is not restricted solely to the amateur game, however. Even at the professional level, there is not a single player—with the exception perhaps of Tiger Woods—who has not experienced the frustration of a temporary dip in form and the accompanying desperation that will drive them to grasp at straws and try absolutely anything, no matter how ridiculous or futile it may seem, in the hope that it will bring their game back. More often than not, it is a fellow player or rival who comes up with the solution after spotting a swing flaw on the range or a quirk in the putting stroke on the practice green. It is this free exchange of advice within the "family of golfers" that makes the sport so great.

We are also very fortunate in golf in that so many of the game's great champions of past and present have chosen to write so eloquently and openly about their swing secrets and techniques over the years. It is a fact that more magazine articles and books have been written on the subject of golf instruction and swing theory than any other physical motion, so there is clearly no shortage of information available to the aspiring golfer.

This book is a collection of some of the best tips and advice published within many of the most popular and best-selling golf instruction books during the last century. Think of it as a compendium of the collected wisdom of the people who have felt, and overcome, the fear of intense competition, figured out the best way to play bunker shots, and devised the most successful methods of reading greens and holing those tricky four-foot putts. It is, without a shadow of a doubt, a unique compilation.

If you take the time to read this book from cover to cover, you will unearth truths about the game that you never realized existed, glean a valuable insight to the way in which the world's best golfers and coaches approach the game, and discover tips on all areas of the game that will improve your scores immediately. It's still a good idea to go out and practice, though!

Good luck and enjoy the book.

Nick Wright
London, England

Equipment

Throughout the history of golf, the players' swings and techniques have continually evolved in response to the advancements in golf club design and technology. In the early days, golf was played using whippy, hickory-shafted golf clubs that required considerable hand action during the swing and especially through impact to square the clubface, while golf balls were originally made from pouches of leather stitched together and stuffed with feathers. Today, space-age materials, such as titanium and carbon graphite alloys, are utilized to ensure that clubs are as lightweight, forgiving and hard-wearing as possible, while modern golf balls feature intricate, computer-generated dimple patterns to ensure that they hold their line and remain in the air for as long as possible to produce maximum distance.

Invest in your golf clubs

You may never be able to hit a power drive or a towering long iron like a professional golfer, but one area of the game where you can match the top players is in the selection of your equipment. Modern technology has enabled manufacturers to produce a wide range of golf clubs and golf balls suitable for all standards, while the custom clubfitting process enables you to match your equipment to your height, build, and individual swing characteristics.

KEEP YOUR CLUBS CLEAN
The grooves on the clubface help you to obtain spin from good and bad lies. If they are clogged with mud, dirt, or grass, you reduce the effectiveness of the club. Regularly rinse off your clubfaces after a round of golf in warm, soapy water, and clean out the grooves with a golf tee or pocket knife.

CHOOSE CLUBS THAT SUIT YOUR GAME
When you're selecting a driver—or any club, come to think of it—always choose one that suits your game. Many men select stiff-shafted drivers when they don't really generate enough clubhead speed to warrant using such an inflexible shaft. In fact, most men would be better off taking advantage of the extra flex of a women's shaft to help generate distance. Colin Montgomerie won several European Orders of Merit using a driver fitted with a women's shaft.

INVEST IN YOUR EQUIPMENT
"Buying cheap clubs is a poor investment," says Dick Mayer in *How To Think and Swing Like a Golf Champion*. "Choosing clubs that don't fit you and your game is like buying the wrong tools for a do-it-yourself project."

IF IT WORKS, USE IT!
Tony Johnstone says in *Master Your Short Game*: "I have just one golden rule when it comes to choosing a putter—if it works, use it. Don't worry about whether or not you think it looks the part; if it gives you the inspiration and the confidence to get the ball into the hole on a regular basis, that's all that really matters."

A SOFT BALL WILL HELP YOUR APPROACH SHOTS
If you play on a course where the greens are very receptive, small, and well-guarded by bunkers, it is a good idea to play a soft-covered golf ball to help you stop your approach shots quickly on the putting surfaces. You should use a hard-covered ball when the entrance to the green is clear and the green is wider and longer. Most top professionals will use a softer ball because they prefer control over distance.

Strategy
Focus totally on the target **67**
Identify landing area then forget hole **101**
Inspect the area around the hole **130**

Swing theory
Shorter backswing, longer follow-through **105**
Keep your stroke simple **127**
Put a ball under right shoe to stop sway **178**

DETERMINING CORRECT CLUB LENGTH

" … The factor that primarily determines the length of clubs you should use is not your height," says Lee Trevino in *Swing My Way.* "A more important factor than height is the distance from your fingertips to the ground when you let your arms hang naturally."

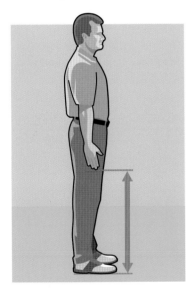

MATCH A GOLF PRO FOR EQUIPMENT CHOICE

You may never be able to swing a golf club and hit a ball like Tiger Woods or David Duval, but you can certainly devote as much attention to your golf clubs. The world's top players are meticulous about their choice of equipment and you should be just as particular.

LEAVE OUT A LONG IRON FOR AN EXTRA WEDGE

Most of the shots played during an average round of golf are played from within 70 yards of the flag. This percentage is even higher for most amateurs because they don't hit so many greens. Only a small percentage of your total shots are actually played with a long iron or fairway wood. You can improve your scoring ability and versatility around the greens by adding an extra wedge to your bag at the expense of leaving out a club that you rarely use, such as a 2-iron or 3-iron. Many of the top players, such as John Daly or Sweden's Jarmo Sandelin, will carry up to four wedges in their bag at any one time.

SWAP YOUR DRIVER FOR A FAIRWAY WOOD

One piece of advice that Greg Norman gives his amateur partners in pro-ams is to leave the driver out of their bags if they find themselves struggling with it, and to use a 3-wood or another fairway wood for their tee shots instead. He says you will get almost as much distance with your 3-wood as you do with your driver and you'll hit the ball straighter, too. The slightly shorter shaft and increased loft mean that the ball won't roll

quite so far on landing, but it's far better to lose 10 yards of distance than to struggle continually with a club.

CLUBS MUST SUIT THE PLAYER

"One of the reasons that I have a good reputation as an instructor is that I will not give a lesson to anyone whose clubs don't suit him," writes Tommy Armour, in *Tommy Armour's ABC's of Golf.*

WHY MATCHED SETS AREN'T ALWAYS THE BEST

Although most manufacturers will tell you that it is important to play with clubs that are perfectly matched, Bobby Jones won 13 major championships with a set of clubs that he acquired, one by one, from all over the world.

USE A HEAVY PUTTER ON SLOW GREENS

Using a heavy putter allows you to make a slower, smoother, and therefore more deliberate and controlled putting stroke on slow greens. If you use a very light putter on wet or slow-putting surfaces, there is a temptation to try to hit the ball too hard using a longer stroke than required. This will normally throw the putter off line and lead to pulled and pushed putts.

HAVE FAITH YOUR PUTTER

Tour pros differ in their approach to selecting and using putters. Some players will happily use the same model for their whole career, while others need to change regularly for inspiration.

THINK OF YOUR GOLF BAG AS A TOOLBOX

Many golfers carry all kinds of unnecessary items in their golf bags. Unless you have the luxury of a caddie, you should keep your golf bag as light as possible. Tony Jacklin used to think of his bag as a toolbox and avoided carrying any unnecessary items. Make sure that you have balls, tee pegs, a pencil, pitch-repair fork, glove, and ball marker as well as a towel and an umbrella. Many pros also carry a small first-aid kit, a rule book and at least one spare glove, a waterproof suit, and a woolly hat to counteract bad weather.

TRY BEFORE YOU BUY

If you are a beginner, before you commit to making an expensive purchase, sample the game with a less expensive or secondhand set of clubs. Although the clubs may not suit you perfectly, they will help you get a feel for the game until you decide whether or not you want to take it more seriously. Like cars, golf clubs depreciate quickly in value, so you should be able to pick up a very good set that is less than two years old for a reasonable price and you can always trade them in when you come to buy your first new set.

FAVOR FAIRWAY WOODS OVER LONG IRONS

Karrie Webb writes in *LPGA's Guide To Every Shot*: "When it comes to club selection and choosing, for example, between a 5-wood and a 3-iron, I would go for the 5-wood just because the woods these days are just so more forgiving. Even with a bad swing, I can get the 5-wood pretty close to the green, if not on the green. I am a fairly decent long-iron player, but they are a little bit harder to hit with than a 5-wood."

USE AS STIFF A SHAFT AS POSSIBLE

Whereas many coaches claim that most golfers would play better with a more flexible shaft in their clubs, Greg Norman has an alternative opinion. He

---

Accuracy & distance
Find maximum accurate wedge distance **89**
If length is your strength go for the green **162**
Always aim at a target in practice **186**

Club selection
Switch to a 3-wood for confidence **52**
Use your irons out the rough **81**

believes that golfers should use the stiffest shaft they can handle because this will enable them to swing a little more aggressively. Norman also claims that the assumption that a stiff shaft is to blame for pushing shots to the right is inaccurate, since many factors, including the incorrect grip size or the lie of the club, could be responsible for the inaccurate shots.

INVEST IN YOUR PUTTER

"Many golfers will willingly spend a small fortune on a new driver …" says Keith Wood, a PGA professional. "You use your driver a maximum of 13 times per round, but your putter is used at least twice as many times, so it is worth spending a little extra time and money to find a make or model that you feel comfortable using."

USE A LIGHT PUTTER ON SLICK GREENS

Slick greens can be terrifying for the amateur golfer. Whether they've been cut very low, or have been toasted by the sun or wind, slick greens can very quickly undermine your putting confidence as the ball seems to disappear out of sight even when you've administered the gentlest of touches. The answer is to invest in a light putter.

USE A SAND WEDGE TO ESCAPE FROM BUNKERS

The bounce angle on the sole of the sand wedge allows it to "ride" through the sand, says Tommy Horton. While a 9-iron is likely to dig deeply into the sand, a wedge, with a more rounded leading edge, will ensure that the clubface will not cut too deeply into the sand.

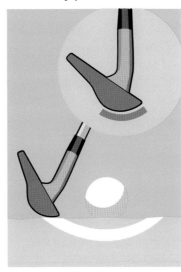

LESS IS SOMETIMES MORE

Although you are allowed a maximum of 14 clubs, you don't have to carry all of them on every single round of golf. Often, a beginner or intermediate golfer will be far better off learning to master a much smaller selection. The restricted choice of clubs also enables you to improvize and use your imagination to play half-shots and three-quarter shots. Harry Vardon won six Open Championships carrying a set of only seven clubs.

BE INSPIRED BY YOUR PUTTER

The make and style of putter that you use is a totally personal choice. According to Tiger Woods, by far the most important thing is to select a putter that feels comfortable when you hold it in your hands, and gives you plenty of confidence when you look down at the ball.

CHOOSE BETWEEN DISTANCE AND CONTROL

Choosing the correct ball for your game comes down to deciding whether you prefer distance or control. Unfortunately, the properties that give a golf ball its durability also reduce spin, while the softer cover that allows more spin to be imparted reduces distance.

THINK CAREFULLY ABOUT CLUB SELECTION

In *Go and Play Golf*, Tony Jacklin and Peter Dobereiner write: "In assembling your set of clubs you should approach the task with the care of a sultan choosing recruits for his harem. Happiness requires that the clubs are in harmony with each other and with you."

SLOT A SMALL COIN UNDER THE CLUB TOE

The PGA professional Luther Blacklock has this advice: "Check the lie of your clubs by addressing the ball on a flat surface. Ideally, there should be just enough room under the toe end of the club to place a small coin. If there is more room, your club lie is too flat. If the heel of the club is raised in the air, the lie angle is too upright."

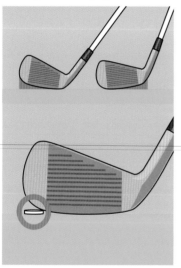

MATCH YOUR SAND WEDGE TO THE SAND

One of the main reasons why Lee Trevino is such a skilled bunker player is that he uses a variety of different sand wedges. The quality and texture of sand can vary dramatically from course to course and even from hole to hole. If you play from fluffy, fine-grained sand, use a sand wedge with more bounce on the sole to prevent the clubhead from digging in too deeply. If you play in coarse, heavy sand, which provides more resistance, you'll be better off using a sand wedge with less bounce and a lower leading edge to help the club underneath the ball.

GET CORRECT CLUBS SO YOU KNOW WHO TO BLAME

"If you say 'Eeny, meeny, miney, mo' and reach for a set off the shelves," writes Arnold Palmer in *My Game and Yours*, "you're going to wonder every time you make a bad shot whether to blame yourself or the clubs. If you know you've got the right clubs, then you know who to blame."

PERSONALIZE YOUR WEDGES AND PUTTER

Your wedges and your putter are the most personal clubs in your bag so make sure that you like the look of them as they sit behind the ball at address. If you are not totally confident with what you see, don't be afraid to change them for another make or model. Most manufacturers sell wedges individually these days, so there should be no problem at all in mixing and matching your clubs.

KEEP HEAD, HANDS, AND FEET WARM

Your head, hands, and feet are the most important body parts to keep warm during a round of golf. If you can keep the extremities of your body warm, the game can still be enjoyable in very cold weather—and your scores will improve, too.

TAKE DRIVER OUT OF THE BAG IF YOU STRUGGLE WITH IT

In his book, *Positive Practice*, David Leadbetter recommends that if you can't hit at least 50 percent of the fairways with your driver, you should remove it from your bag completely. This will remove the temptation to use the club even though you know it may well land you in deep trouble.

Setup
Aim left with everything for a fade **67**
Position shirt buttons ahead of ball **97**
Weight on front foot for better balance **126**

Swing theory
Swing better, not harder **58**
Think "stomach and buttons" for pitching **89**
Throw right palm to the hole **122**

CAVITY-BACKED CLUBS ARE MORE FORGIVING

Most modern golf clubs are more forgiving and allow you to achieve good results even if you do not hit the ball perfectly. These clubs are known as cavity-backed or perimeter-weighted because the weight is removed from the center of the club and redistributed around the edges to enlarge the sweet spot and provide straighter shots. Nick Faldo once shot a round of 62 using Ping cavity-backed irons and handed them back to the rep, saying that he hit them too straight!

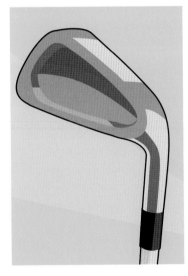

MATCH YOUR PUTTER TO YOUR STROKE

The PGA professional Denis Pugh tells us that there are two key types of putter design: the face-balanced putter and the blade. "A face-balanced putter has an equal amount of weight in the toe and the heel to keep the putter face square during the stroke. The blade is not weighted in any particular way and the hosel of the shaft connects to the heel of the club. A face-balanced putter will suit a player like Nick Price, who controls his straight back and through stroke with his shoulders, while the blade putter will suit a player like Phil Mickelson, who controls the putter more with the arms and likes to fan the face open and closed on the backswing and through swing during the stroke."

KEEP GRIPS TACKY

Scrub your grips often with soapy water to keep them clean and tacky and lengthen their life. Try to replace your grips at the beginning of each season if you are a frequent player.

SWING A WEIGHTED CLUB

In *Harvey Penick's Little Red Golf Book,* Harvey Penick writes: "Every golfer from the young adult through to Seasoned Citizens should own a heavy practice club that weighs at least 22 ounces. Swinging a weighted club with your regular grip and stance is the best exercise I know to build the golf muscles. Squeezing a tennis ball and similar exercises might be all right but I'd be afraid the wrong muscles might get developed … Swing the weighted club the night before a round, not in the morning before you tee off. Save your strength for the golf course."

CLEAN PUTTER FACE BEFORE EACH STROKE

Always wipe the face of your putter before you make your stroke; particles of sand, grass, dirt, or dust can prevent you making clean contact and so reduce the distance you hit the ball.

GREASE THE THREAD OF YOUR SPIKES

After purchasing a new pair of golf shoes, apply grease or WD-40 to the thread of the spikes to ensure that they can be removed easily when necessary.

DON'T LEAN ON YOUR CLUBS

Avoid leaning on your golf clubs and placing your golf bag against a support where the weight rests on the clubs instead of the bag. The extra strain placed on the shafts of the clubs may weaken them and cause them to snap or break earlier than they should.

The Ocean Course Kiawah Island, South Carolina

17TH HOLE, PAR-3, 197 YARDS

THE MODERN BREED OF GOLF COURSE

The Ocean Course at Kiawah Island, designed by Pete Dye, is one of the world's most spectacular. The superlatives to endorse its beauty and challenge are infinite. Built to stage the Ryder Cup in 1991, it opened just a few years after Hurricane Hugo had flattened the landscape and only a few months before the matches were due to start. Seldom has a new course achieved such eminence—or notoriety—so quickly.

The Ocean Course at Kiawah Island in South Carolina is known throughout the world for its spectacular scenery and its difficulty. It was built specially for the Ryder Cup in 1991, and players complained that it was too tough—many suffered at the hands of its length. The powers that be obviously listened; when the World Cup was staged in 1997, the course played some 800 yards shorter.

At almost 7,700 yards off the tips, it is a fearsome prospect for most amateurs—and for many pros, too—but, from the 6,031-yard white tees, it is playable and enjoyable. The well-known golf course architect Tom Doak once remarked: "If you play this course from the tips, you'll spend a week in traction."

One of the most interesting features is that the course follows a figure-eight pattern. Because of its seaside location, the wind is generally a factor and, because it changes direction so often, Dye had no knowledge of the normal prevailing wind when he penciled his provisional layout. Consequently, the course changes character daily and players have to consider their club selection very carefully.

PRO-FILE
ARNOLD PALMER

Pay attention to your golf clubs

In the early era of competitive golf, up until the late 1950s, many of the world's top golfers were also clubmakers, most of whom were resident club professionals, teaching and repairing clubs for a living. It is difficult to imagine Tiger Woods and Ernie Els taking green fees in a pro shop during their weeks off, but many of their predecessors had to juggle playing and work commitments.

Arnold Palmer grew up at the Latrobe Country Club, Pennsylvania, where he worked long hours in the pro shop, altering the specification of his clubs. It was not uncommon for Palmer to grind down the soles of his wedges so that they would cut through the rough more effectively, experiment with the swing weight of his irons, and continually adjust the lie of his putter. Although most modern sets are of the highest quality, it is still advisable to take the time to have your clubs custom-fitted. The club shafts can be individually tailored to your swing speed and swing characteristics, while the loft and lie angles of the clubface can be altered to ensure that the club rests on the ground at the perfect angle. Even grips can be perfectly tailored to match the size of your own hands.

The course takes its name from its proximity to the Atlantic and the elevated fairways provide spectacular views of the coast. Highlights from the front nine include the second hole, where the tee shot plays across the marsh. The fourth hole, rated in the world's top 500 holes, demands two carries over marshland. The ninth, a 464-yard monster, is a tremendous par-4 to finish the front nine.

The signature hole at Kiawah Island, however, is undoubtedly the par-3 17th, which gained its notorious reputation during the 1991 Ryder Cup when numerous players failed to find the green and saw their tee shots splash into the lake. At 197 yards long off the back tees, length is clearly not this hole's main defence. The challenge for every level of golfer is carrying the ball all the way over the water and then being able to stop the ball on a thin slither of a green that is angled away from the tee and protected on the right once again by the lake and on the left by two large bunkers and deep rough.

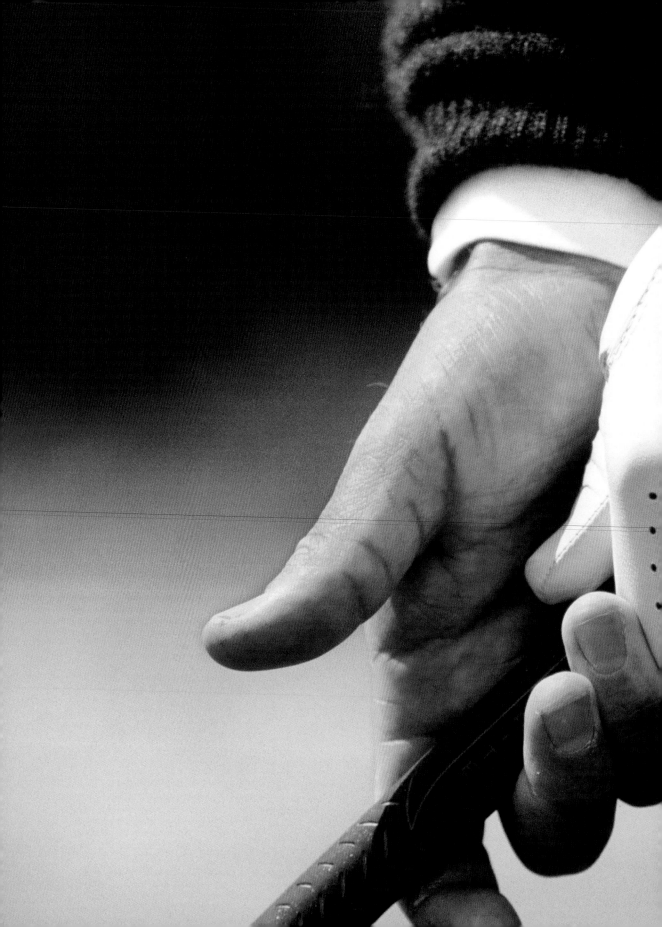

2

Swing Fundamentals

The world's top golfers, unlike most amateurs, appreciate the importance of good basic fundamentals. Without a solid grip, an athletic posture, good alignment, ball position, and balance, the golf swing is simply a disaster waiting to happen. Tour professionals are meticulous in their preparation to the point that they spend more time working on the quality of their address position than any part of the game. At the very top level, when a golfer starts to play badly, more often than not the problem can be traced back to a flaw in the setup or the initial stages of the swing. Good basics take a little while to master and to feel natural—particularly if you have been holding the club and addressing the ball in an unorthodox style for a while, but the long-term benefits to your handicap are well worth a little dedication.

Work on the fundamentals

Good basic fundamentals are the first link in an orthodox and consistent golf swing. You should regularly check all of your basics, including your grip, stance, alignment, and posture, when practicing, because bad habits can easily creep into your setup over a period of time and begin to affect the quality of your swing and your ball-striking. If you pay careful attention to your fundamentals, your swing is less likely to go off track.

KEEP GRIP PRESSURE CONSTANT

Maintaining a constant grip pressure throughout the whole swing right up until the follow-through is one of the keys to consistent ball-striking. Jack Nicklaus warns against the habit of allowing your hands to loosen on the grip after impact because there is a real danger and a strong possibility that you will eventually begin to loosen your hands before you strike the ball, which will cause problems with your power and accuracy.

SET WEIGHT TOWARD THE HEELS OF YOUR FEET

"The combination of flexed knees and weight somewhat back on the heels gives you a solid feeling," writes Dick Mayer in *How To Think and Swing Like a Golf Champion*. "You should feel confident that if someone suddenly tapped you from any side, you wouldn't fall over."

ADDRESS THE BALL ATHLETICALLY

Gary Player's Golf Secrets tells us: "On the tee the woman golfer should address that ball with knees bent and hips ready to swivel. The woman who daintily stands up to the ball, with back and legs stiff like a crusty old schoolmarm, is just asking for a rough time from the men in the next foursome."

SLAP HANDS TOGETHER ON THE GRIP

The purpose of the grip is to place your hands on the club in such a way that they create a single unit. Sandy Lyle says that he achieves this feeling of unity by placing his hands on the grip as if he was slapping his palms together. This ensures that neither hand dominates and that both are square to the target.

IT PAYS TO BE ORTHODOX

Golfers who address the ball in an unorthodox fashion have to rely heavily on their flexibility, hand-eye coordination and feel for the clubhead in order to strike the ball cleanly. They must be able to improvise and compensate for their faults so that they can return to an orthodox and powerful position at impact. But players such as the Japanese Senior Tour star Isao Aoki and former PGA tour professional Lanny Wadkins,

Strategy
Tee it up on the side of the trouble **61**
Pitch over water—focus on back fringe **88**

Setup
Move ball back in the stance to hit it low **73**
Point left elbow towards hole at address **126**

who both have a rounded posture and almost straight legs at address, are very rare indeed at the top level of the game.

◉ SQUEEZE A TUBE OF TOOTHPASTE

Stuart Dowsett, a PGA professional, has some gripping advice: "A good way to work out the correct grip pressure is to imagine holding a new tube of toothpaste. You want to hold it fairly firmly, but without squeezing any of the paste out the tube. That's the correct grip pressure."

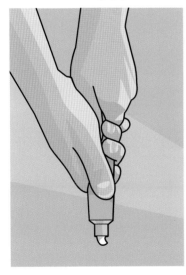

◉ HOW A BAD GRIP COSTS YOU ACCURACY

Take a handy tip from the PGA professional Gary Smith, who says: "A neutral grip is the best way of returning the clubface square to the target at impact,

which is why 99 percent of the world's top golfers hold the club in an almost identical way. A neutral grip enables you to keep the natural shape of your forearms when you place your hands on the club. If you stand with your arms hanging by your sides and then bring your hands together, that is what your grip should look like. If your grip is too weak, with your right hand too far over, you will inevitably slice the ball to the right. If your grip is too strong, with your right hand too much underneath the club, you will be prone to hitting the ball left."

◉ COUNTDOWN TO THE START OF YOUR SWING

A consistent preshot routine breeds consistency in your swing and shot making. If you timed many of the world's top players from the moment they take the club out of the bag until they are ready to start their swing, their whole routine will vary by less than a second each time. Many players, such as Greg Norman, have a checklist of preparatory movements that make up their routine, while other players, such as Colin Montgomerie, spend very little time over the ball. The key is not the length and content of your routine, but its consistency. This will pay dividends under pressure.

◉ CENTER WEIGHT BETWEEN HEEL AND BALL OF FEET

The perfect position to support the weight of the body is to set your weight directly between the heel and the toe of each foot.

◉ GRIP CLUB AT 45-DEGREE ANGLE

"Because your hands turn inward when your arms hang by your sides," says Nick Bradley, a PGA professional, "it's easier to grip the club correctly if you hold the club at a 45-degree angle to the right rather than straight in front of you."

◉ RAISE CHIN AWAY FROM CHEST AT ADDRESS

One of Tiger Woods's key swing thoughts is to keep his chin away from his chest so that he has room to turn his shoulders.

DEVOTE FIVE MINUTES A DAY TO YOUR GRIP

Changing your grip can be a difficult process for many golfers. One way to accelerate the process is to practice forming and re-forming your grip as often as you can. Nick Faldo claims that even if you can devote just five minutes a day—either at home sitting in front of the television or in your office—to working on your new grip, your game will improve dramatically.

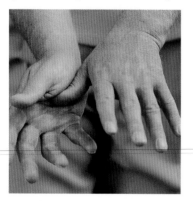

GOOD ADDRESS LEADS TO GOOD IMPACT

To get into the correct position at impact, you must first get into the correct position at setup.

TAKE A SNAPSHOT OF YOUR BALL POSITION

Unless you play often, it can be difficult to groove a consistent address position, and your ball position. Greg Norman says that a good way to help you stand

correctly each time is to take a "picture" of the correct setup in your mind's eye. "Set up for a shot and take careful note of the view you have through your hands to the ball," he says in his *100 Instant Golf Lessons*. In Norman's case, the back of his left thumb pad covers the arch of his left foot.

KEEP GRIP PRESSURE CONSISTENT

Regardless of whether you naturally hold the club gently or tightly, the most important thing is to ensure that the pressure remains consistent. Tiger Woods says that, if you tighten your grip pressure at any time during the swing, you will lose control of the club and reduce your clubhead speed.

PRESHOT PREPARATION IS KEY TO GOOD GOLF

"The more I teach, play, and watch golf, the more convinced I become that the decisive factor in good shot making is preparation: shot assessment, club selection, grip, aim, stance, posture," asserts John Jacobs in *Play Better Golf with John Jacobs*. "If you can master these departments you have every chance of playing golf to the best of your capabilities, whatever they may be."

TAKE DEAD AIM

The legendary golf teacher Harvey Penick, who taught Tom Kite, Ben Crenshaw, and Davis Love III, had one key catchphrase: "Take dead aim." He always instructed his pupils to ensure that they took the time to aim both the clubface and their body carefully to the target every time and on every shot.

DON'T SIT ON YOUR HEELS

"If there's one key fault to avoid when standing to the ball it's adopting what I call a 'sitting' position where you bend your knees and allow your weight to fall back onto your heels," says Keith Wood, a PGA professional. "Tilt forward from your hips so that your bottom sticks out, but not so much that it causes your legs to straighten

Accuracy & distance
Get your big muscles involved in the swing **36**
Avoid excessive backspin on pitch shots **86**

Club selection
Leave out a long iron for an extra wedge **13**
Choose the club that will hit the green **72**
Keep the ball low and under control **98**

and feel that your knees 'settle' comfortably without overflexing. A general guideline is that with a midiron, if you drew a line vertically down from your shoulders, it would pass through your knee caps and the balls of your feet."

SPEND MORE TIME REVIEWING BASICS

"The harder I work on my swing," says Nick Faldo in *A Swing for Life*, "the more I appreciate the fundamentals that shape it. I probably spend more time fine-tuning the quality of my grip and setup position than I do checking anything else."

PALMS FACE EACH OTHER ON THE GRIP

Jose Maria Olazabal is an example of a player who has achieved great success playing with a comparatively "weak" grip, while Tom Lehman and David Duval have both won major championships with slightly "strong" grips. Although there are many examples of unorthodox grips on tour, it is advisable to grip the club in a neutral fashion. Butch Harmon, one of the world's top coaches, believes that all good grips obey one fundamental principle: that the palms of your hands must face each other as they hold the club. If they don't face each other, one hand takes over to dominate the grip, producing inaccurate shots.

LIE OF THE CLUB INFLUENCES THE SETUP

"The lie of the club at address determines the height of your hands, your posture and how far you stand from the ball," says Luther Blacklock. "Set the club behind the ball with your right hand and then build your stance around the club."

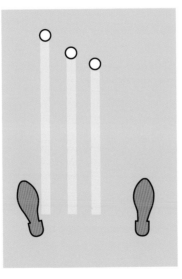

BALL POSITION IS TO BLAME

Greg Norman has always maintained that, if he encounters a bad spell of form, the root cause of the problem is invariably a flaw in his ball position.

POOR GRIP LEADS TO A TIGHT GRIP

There are many reasons why many amateur golfers grip the club too tightly but, according to Tiger Woods, one of the main reasons is because the hands aren't placed on the club correctly at the outset and the player is then forced to increase his or her grip pressure to prevent the club from twisting in the hands during the swing.

DON'T SWING UNTIL YOU'RE READY

Less depends on the quality of your opening tee shot than any other shot you play during the whole round. Tommy Armour's approach was to hit his tee shot on the first hole using a swing that replicated his loosest possible practice swing.

LEFT LITTLE FINGER GRIPS TIGHTLY

The famous Tommy Armour always believed that the key to a good grip was keeping the middle two fingers on the left hand nice and firm. He said that if the left little finger was prevented from loosening then the other fingers would remain secure, too. These two middle fingers apply the pressure on the club, which remains consistent throughout the swing.

VISUALIZE THE EIFFEL TOWER AT ADDRESS

Golfers use all kinds of mental pictures and images to help them adopt the correct positions at address and during the swing. Nick Faldo, for example, likes to visualize the structure of the Eiffel Tower to remind himself of the need to build a solid and stable base with his lower body. The former US Open champion, Dick Mayer, used to think of forming a tripod shape at address to prevent him from swaying during the backswing.

FEEL THE CLUBHEAD WITH YOUR HANDS

"To master control," advises Tommy Armour in *Tommy Armour's ABC's of Golf*, "you've got to have the grip that allows you to feel the clubhead. You

must know that it is getting neither loose nor locked, but is always held so that you can instinctively guide it."

FOCUS ON SWING BASICS AND SHORT GAME

Nick Faldo once calculated that more than 75 percent of his practice time was devoted to either sharpening his short game or refining the small details of his address position. Faldo believes that focusing on the short game and the swing basics is the key to consistent ball striking and low scoring.

SOLID GRIP PLUS ABILITY EQUALS GOOD GOLF

In his book *Natural Golf*, Sam Snead writes: "If you have a lot of inherent ability, you can take any sort of a grip and still play the game well. Unfortunately, the average golfer doesn't have that kind of inherent ability … A golfer with an inherent ability to play the game, plus a foolproof grip, is on his way to topflight golf."

USE THIGHS TO CHECK ALIGNMENT

One of Harvey Penick's favorite alignment exercises was to ask pupils to take their normal stance and then to hold a club shaft across the top of their

thighs. This shows exactly where the club and the body are aiming.

VARYING STANCE WIDTH AND BALL POSITION

Most top golfers will vary their ball position to play different types of shots. Justin Leonard, for example, starts with a default ball position for his driver, midirons and wedges, but then he will vary these positions for almost every shot. Leonard will play the ball well forward, just inside his left instep, to hit a high fade or opposite his right foot to hit a low draw. He will also take a wider stance to hit the ball lower, and narrow his stance in order to hit a higher shot.

Strategy
Split the green into quarters **89**
Look to hole every putt **125**

Setup
Good address leads to good impact **24**
Left hip pocket toward the target **59**

USE A MIRROR TO CHECK YOUR SETUP

"The best professionals can deal with their grip and stance unconsciously because they recognize their importance and they practice them, sometimes more than they practice hitting golf balls," says Dr Bob Rotella in *Golf Is Not a Game of Perfect*. "Many of them have full-length mirrors at home on which they have placed tape to indicate where their hands, shoulders, and other checkpoints should be when they set up properly."

FORM A "Y" SHAPE AT ADDRESS

The PGA professional Keith Wood says: "I like to see a "y" shape, where the stalk of the letter is the club forming an extension of the left arm. The early benefit

of this position is width in the takeaway. Later in the swing, keeping the club shaft in line with the left arm allows the wrists to hinge correctly and set the club on the correct plane."

RELAXED LEGS ALLOW EFFECTIVE BODY WORK

The legs play a crucial role in generating and delivering power during the swing. Walter Hagen always said that as long as he kept his legs relaxed he didn't worry. He believed that, if he could keep his legs nice and relaxed, the rest of his body—and in turn his swing—would take care of itself.

AIM CLUBFACE FIRST, THEN BODY

"I don't even try to align my body to the target until after I have aligned my clubface," writes Greg Norman in his *100 Instant Golf Lessons*. "Holding the club in my right hand only, I approach the ball from behind. While I do this, I sight up and down the line that extends from the ball to my target, looking for a spot a few yards in front of my ball and on that line. Once I find that, I set the clubface behind the ball, and swivel it minutely back and forth until it is pointing directly at the spot. Only after the clubface is squarely in

position do I assume my grip and align my body in the address position." Norman's routine ensures that his body alignment matches the angle of the clubface at address.

LEFT ARM AND CLUB SHAFT FORM A ROD

The shaft of the club and the left arm create a lever with the left wrist forming the only hinge. When placing the right hand on the club, Ben Hogan always made sure that his right arm was very soft and the right elbow was pointing down.

REST TEE PEG ON BASE OF SPINE

"An image that I use to keep my lower back straight is to picture a tee peg resting on the base of my spine without it rolling off," says Nick Dougherty, a PGA European Tour professional.

WHY YOUR INITIAL SWING INSTINCTS ARE WRONG

The correct grip can be very difficult to master, as it is a totally unnatural process. Ben Hogan maintained that, when a person picks up a club for the first time with the intention of hitting a ball, the natural instinct to hold the club in a way that will enable them to hit the ball powerfully is invariably wrong.

FORM A "Y" AT ADDRESS FOR A FLEXIBLE SWING

In *The Mechanics of Golf*, PGA professional Alex Hay utilizes the letter "y" again: "It is used to describe approximately the line of the arms to the shaft when a more flexible or wristy type of swing is required … Weaker persons creating a Y shape should realize that, whilst a left-side dominated setup is not for them, their necessary Y shape has its limitations and is vulnerable."

STANCE COMES LAST

"One area in which it is especially important to have a set pattern is in setting up to the ball," says Arnold Palmer in *The Arnold Palmer Method*. "I have a three-step pattern that brings me up to the point when I'm ready to start waggling the club. First, I size up the shot from behind and to the side of the ball. At the time I check the best line to the target and consider the proposed flight of the ball. Next I place the clubhead squarely behind the ball so that the clubface looks down the target line. Finally I assume my stance."

NARROWER STANCE REDUCES TENSION

"One of the first points to notice in Bobby Jones's play is the closeness with which he holds his feet together, even on the full shots," observes Grantland Rice in *A Close-Up of Bobby Jones: Explaining a Few of the Simpler Details That Make Up His Game*. "Even on the drive I don't believe his feet are more than a foot apart, certainly not more than fourteen inches … The matter of bringing the feet closer together than most golfers has two distinct values. In the first place, it reduces tension throughout the body … In the second place, there is a feeling of better and easier balance. There is less tendency to hit with the body, a fault that has driven several million golfers into the borderland of melancholy depression, year after year."

LIFT LEFT ARM TO CHECK YOUR ALIGNMENT

The PGA professional, Mark Arnold, says: "Keeping track of your alignment is difficult since it's difficult to see exactly where your feet and shoulders are aiming when you are standing over the ball. A good way to double-check your aim is to take your address position then take your left hand off the club and lift your arm straight up in the air to the side of you. If you're aligned correctly, your arm should point in a direction parallel left of your intended target. Unfortunately, most golfers aim too far right of the target with their upper body. If that's the case, when you lift your left arm, it will aim either at the target or to the right."

FOCUS ON AIMING CLUBFACE SQUARELY

One of golf's great debates is whether you should grip the club and then aim it, or vice versa. It doesn't really matter. Ernie Els, for example, sets the club behind the ball before taking his grip, while Tiger Woods forms his grip while holding the club out in front of him. The key is to aim the clubface squarely to the target and then aim your feet, knees, hips, and shoulders parallel left of that line.

Equipment
Organize the contents of your golf bag **153**
Play in several thin layers of clothing **211**

Accuracy & distance
Hit down on your irons **69**
Visualize the whole line **129**

28

○ SPINE TILTS AWAY FROM
THE TARGET AT ADDRESS
Butch Harmon claims that your
spine should tilt away from the
target with your right shoulder
set lower than your left and your
head behind the ball. From this
position and with your weight
distributed evenly between both
feet, a simple turn shifts your
weight correctly and permits a
powerful coil.

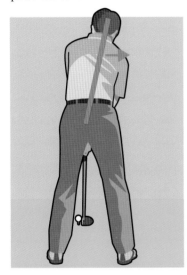

○ YOU CAN'T STAND TOO
CLOSE TO THE BALL
"If you start reaching
perceptively for the ball," writes
Byron Nelson in *Winning Golf*,
"the arc of your swing will
become too flat. The prominent
fault is standing too far from the
ball, rather than too close too it.
It is next to impossible to stand
too close to the ball."

○ LAST THREE FINGERS
CONTROL SWING
The American golfer, Bobby
Jones, advises: "It is never
necessary to squeeze the
clubhead with any part of the
hand. When you ground the
club behind the ball, you should
merely be conscious that you
are holding it, that you feel it.
When you begin to move it, your
grip will tighten naturally. But
when you begin to move, start
the action with the left hand,
and feel the pressure in the
three smaller fingers of that
hand, and then keep the feeling
all the way through that these
three fingers keep the club
under control."

○ PLACE A SHORT LEFT
THUMB ON THE GRIP
Like many of the world's top
players, big-hitting John Daly
grips the club with a short left
thumb. When he places his left
hand on the grip, instead of
extending the thumb as far down
the shaft as possible, he will
"inch" it upward so that it is
level with the knuckle on his left
index finger. This minor
adjustment allows him to make a
full wrist cock at the top of his
backswing while maintaining full
control. Keeping the left thumb
extended can lead to an open
clubface at the top of the swing.

○ CHECK WEAR AND TEAR
ON YOUR GLOVE
One of the first signs of a poor
grip is wearing a hole in your
golf glove. According to David
Leadbetter, this is a sure sign
that you are holding the club too
much in the palm of your hands
rather than in the fingers.
Ideally, the grip club should run
diagonally across the left hand,
from the knuckle on the left
index finger to the base of the
little finger.

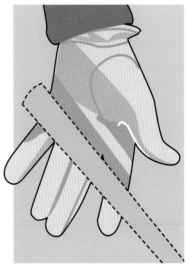

○ CREATE A BUTTERFLY
SHAPE WITH YOUR GRIP
PGA professional, Denis Pugh,
advises: "To form a neutral grip,
form a butterfly shape with your
hands. This will ensure that your
forearms maintain their natural
shape and that neither hand
dominates on the club."

Pebble Beach California

17TH HOLE, PAR-3, 178 YARDS

GOOD ALIGNMENT BREEDS ACCURACY

Designed in 1919 by two amateur golfers, Jack Neville and Douglas Grant, the Pebble Beach Golf Links, on the spectacular Monterey peninsular in California, is America's best-known golf resort and the country's equivalent to St. Andrews, boasting several fine courses in its portfolio. It has staged the US Open four times and annually hosts the AT&T International Pro-Am, one of the most popular events on the PGA Tour.

The 17th hole at Pebble Beach is one of the most spectacular short holes in the world. With the Atlantic Ocean as its backdrop, this challenging par-3 can play as two distinctly different holes depending on the pin placement. A back left flag will play at least one club longer into what is normally a significant headwind. The player also has to contend with the sprawling bunker that cuts into the front edge of the green and the ocean that lies just beyond it. The right side of the green is an easier target to aim at but, regardless of the pin location, an accurate tee shot is essential, since many flags are virtually inaccessible from the wrong side of the green.

The US Open has been held at Pebble Beach four times—1972, 1982, 1992, and 2000. On each occasion, the 17th has been a pivotal hole. In 1972 Jack Nicklaus hit one of the most famous shots in history. Leading by three shots, he selected his 1-iron but the wind closed his clubface and he had to make a split-second adjustment at impact to prevent a severe pull. His tee shot drilled through the wind, hit the flagstick and stopped within six inches of the cup to set up a

PRO-FILE
NICK FALDO

Build your swing on solid fundamentals

During the early 1980s, Nick Faldo emerged as one of Europe's leading golfers and almost won the Open Championship at St. Andrews in 1984, when he was in contention, but fell away over the closing holes. It was Faldo's final-round performance that prompted his decision to overhaul his game. Although pleasing to the eye, Faldo's old swing was long and willowy, and relied on a big hip and leg drive to generate power. Consequently, he relied on exceptional hand-eye coordination to square the clubface at impact. In short, his swing looked good, but was unreliable.

Under the tutelage of his coach, David Leadbetter, Faldo went back to basics, adjusting his setup to develop a swing where the muscles in the torso were responsible for creating and releasing the power.

After two years, the end result was a more consistent swing that was able to secure 18 straight pars in the final round of the 1987 Open Championship, at Muirfield, Scotland, to secure his first major championship. In addition to winning the Masters in 1989, 1990 and 1996, Faldo also won the Open Championship again in 1990 at St. Andrews and again at Muirfield in 1992.

birdie that guaranteed his victory.

In the 1982 US Open, Nicklaus was involved in yet more drama at the 17th hole, but this time on the receiving end. Tom Watson began the day tied for the lead with Nicklaus three shots behind. However, by the time Nicklaus had finished his round, the pair were tied. Watson's 2-iron drifted into the rough left of the 17th green, 15 feet from the hole and in a seemingly impossible lie. Watson then pitched the ball up into the air with his sand wedge and into the hole for a birdie. Another on the par-5 18th hole sealed his victory.

However, the 17th hole has also seen its fair share of disaster stories. In the Crosby Pro-Am in 1963, Arnold Palmer's tee shot sailed over the back of the green and disappeared into what he thought was the ocean. Palmer teed up a new ball, but, when he found his original lying on the rocks, he played it onto the green. The PGA later decided that Palmer had effectively abandoned his first ball by hitting the second, and disqualified the great man, ending his streak of 47 consecutive tournaments without missing a cut.

3

The Swing Lesson

With such a vast number of instructional books, magazine articles, and videos devoted to this particular subject, one could be forgiven for thinking that the golf swing must be an extremely difficult technique to master. Although there is plenty of scope for error when you are swinging a club through an arc of about 25 feet and attempting to strike an object about an inch wide with a thin strip of metal, broken down to its simplest form, the golf swing is really nothing more than a combination of the turning of your body with the swinging of your arms. Many top professionals will, however, use a couple of simple swing thoughts to help keep their swing on the right track, particularly if they are susceptible to specific swing flaws that can damage their game.

Two turns and a swish

The 1991 Masters champion, Ian Woosnam, once described the golf swing as nothing more than two turns and a swish. By this, Woosnam meant that during the swing the upper body turns back and through while the hands and arms release the club through impact to send the ball flying toward the target. Unfortunately, many golfers are guilty of over-complicating and over-analyzing the swing and, subsequently, lose their natural flair.

STOP HEAD BOBBING

Although moving the head laterally from side to side during the swing is a dangerous swing flaw, Jack Nicklaus believes that allowing the head to bob up and down is equally damaging. An easy way to see if you lose your height during the swing is to hit some shots while a friend holds the grip end of a driver lightly on top of your head.

FLARE BOTH FEET SLIGHTLY FOR EXTRA CONTROL

How you position your feet at address will affect how efficiently and effectively you turn on the backswing and through swing. Tiger Woods likes to flare his right foot away from the target slightly to help him turn his hips without straining his knee or thigh. He flares his left foot toward the target slightly to prevent him from overturning his hips on the backswing, while giving him a little extra freedom in the downswing to rotate powerfully through the ball.

LET YOUR LEFT HEEL RISE

Many amateur golfers mistakenly believe that keeping the left heel planted on the ground will enable them to make a more consistent swing. Unfortunately, this is not the case because a golfer will inevitably lose height and balance on the backswing. Another bad side effect of keeping the left heel down, according to Alex Hay is that the left leg will straighten, causing the momentum and force of the swing to pull the body to the right, leading to a lateral sway.

THINK "THUMBS UP" FOR A BETTER STRIKE

To improve your wrist action during the swing, think about pointing your thumbs upward in your backswing and follow-through. This will enable you to create a 90-degree wrist hinge and also set the club on the correct plane. It will also improve your release through impact, giving your swing extra power.

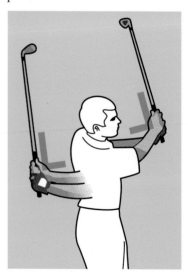

Setup
Set weight towards the heels of your feet **22**
You can't stand too close to the ball **29**

Strategy
A soft ball will help your approach shots **12**
Leave yourself an uphill putt **98**

⦿ SET WRISTS EARLY, THEN TURN TO THE TOP

Many golfers, such as Nick Faldo, David Frost, and Nick Price, work on what is known as an early wrist set, whereby they expect their wrists to be fully hinged with the club on the correct plane by the time their hands reach waist height. From this point on, all they need to do to complete their backswing is complete their shoulder turn.

⦿ ROTATE RIGHT FOREARM IN TAKEAWAY

"I've always had a 'handsy' takeaway and swung the club to the inside too early," says PGA European Tour professional Nick Dougherty. "Now I focus on rotating my right forearm in the takeaway to keep the club in front of me for longer in the back swing."

⦿ HANDS COVER CLUBHEAD AT 9 O'CLOCK

Justin Rose, a PGA European Tour professional, advises: "Looking down the target line, one of my key swing checkpoints is to ensure that my hands completely cover the clubhead at the 9 o'clock position in the backswing when the shaft is parallel to the ground and square to the target." This stops his swing becoming flat.

⦿ TILT HEAD TO RIGHT AND KEEP EYE ON BALL

Chi Chi Rodriguez gives us this advice in *The Secrets of Power Golf*: "I always keep my head about six inches in back of the ball at address and tilted slightly to the right. I concentrate on looking at the ball with my left eye and I keep this eye on the ball throughout my entire backswing and downswing."

⦿ SYNCHRONIZE YOUR ARMS AND BODY

Robin Boretti writes in the December 2001 issue of *Golf for Women*: "Golfers often swing their arms independently of the rest of their body, which weakens their shots. Your goal is to keep the two connected to maximize your power at impact."

⦿ DON'T KEEP YOUR HEAD DOWN

"One of the most misleading bits of advice in golf is the phrase "keep your head down"," says Ernie Els in *How To Build a Classic Golf Swing*. "It really does make me want to cringe when I hear someone say this to their playing partner and I reckon it does ten times more harm than good. In my experience, when someone is told to keep their head down, they tend to bury their chin into their chest at address. From there, they can't possibly make a good turn in the backswing as there's no room for the left shoulder to turn into … Keeping your chin up gives your left shoulder power in your golf swing."

⦿ REMEMBER THE CLUBHEAD STRIKES THE BALL

The eminent golf coach, John Jacobs, has this advice in *Play Better Golf with John Jacobs*: "I would like to ask you always to remember with what you hit a golf ball. It is not your shoulder pivot, your straight left arm, your bent right arm, your knees, your hips, nor even your hands. It is the head of the golf club. In the last analysis, what golf is all about is applying the head of the club to the ball as fast and flush as possible."

◉ HOVER CLUBHEAD OFF THE GROUND AT ADDRESS

To prevent the club from snagging or catching in the grass on the takeaway, many top players like to hover the clubhead slightly off the ground at address. Jack Nicklaus and Greg Norman are among many top players who believe that doing this not only improves their first move away from the ball, but also their swing rhythm.

◉ COMPLETE THE BACKSWING

"Short backswings and quick tempo go hand in hand," maintains Colin Montgomerie, the PGA European Tour professional. "One of my key swing thoughts is to complete my backswing. If I do this, I know that my swing tempo is just about right."

◉ TURN AROUND YOUR SPINE

"Try to imagine your spine as a central column, with your upper body rotating around it," urges Ernie Els in *How To Build a Classic Golf Swing*. "That's the essence of maintaining a constant spine angle. You don't want to be wavering too much from side to side and certainly not moving up and down. The spine stays fixed from the moment you address the ball to the moment it fizzes into the distance."

◉ HEAD CONTROLS BALANCE

"The head is the gyroscope of the entire swing, so far as balance is concerned," asserts the former PGA Tour professional Cary Middlecoff.

◉ USE YOUR FEEL TO SQUARE THE BLADE AT IMPACT

The legendary Henry Cotton maintains that there is no secret to squaring the clubface at impact. It is purely feel.

◉ SWING WITHIN YOURSELF

"You will never meet a top tournament pro who swings as hard as he could physically, other than in exceptional circumstances for an occasional recovery shot," says John Jacobs in his book *Play Better Golf with John Jacobs*.

◉ SAME RHYTHM WITH EVERY CLUB

Regardless of whichever club he is using—from a driver to a pitching wedge—Nick Faldo always tries to make the same relaxed and unhurried swing and trust the club to do its job.

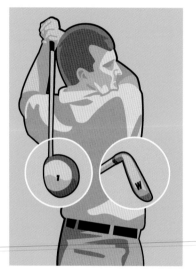

◉ GET YOUR BIG MUSCLES INVOLVED IN THE SWING

"There are three sources of power in the golf swing—your hands and wrists, your arm swing, and your body—and that's all," says Tom Kite, a PGA senior Tour professional and the 1994 US Open Champion. "You can probably generate about 70 or 80 percent of your power just with your hands and arms, not using the body at all. But to hit the ball that extra distance, you have to get the body involved."

STRENGTH IS A MATCH FOR BEAUTY

Strength in the fingers at impact, according to Henry Cotton, is far more important than a graceful-looking swing.

CONTROL YOUR RHYTHM

"Rhythm is easier to experience than define," writes W. Timothy Gallwey in *The Inner Game of Golf*. "When your golf swing is rhythmic you know it, and when it's not you can tell immediately if you are at all aware. Because we can feel rhythm we can increase control over it."

THE MAGIC MOVE OF THE GOLF SWING

If there is a magical swing thought, move, or special swing secret, Harvey Penick believes that it is allowing your weight to shift onto your front foot as your right elbow returns to the side of your body at the start of your downswing. However, these two movements should be done simultaneously.

GOOD BALANCE MAKES GOOD SWINGS

In *Tommy Armour's ABC's of Golf*, the author advises: "In good balance you make a good-looking swing; when you are out of balance your swing is grotesque and ineffective."

EXTEND BUTT OF CLUB AWAY FROM RIGHT HIP

Creating width in the backswing is a key to longer and more powerful hitting. To create maximum extension in his takeaway, Tiger Woods likes to extend the butt end of the shaft as far away from his right hip as possible as he turns his shoulders.

LET RIGHT SHOULDER LAG BEHIND IN DOWNSWING

To help you hit the ball farther and straighter, Butch Harmon has a routine that concentrates on the movement the rear shoulder makes through the downswing. When you start the downswing with your weight transferring and your hips beginning to uncoil, concentrate on keeping your rear shoulder lagging behind so that it doesn't uncoil at the same speed as your hips. Obviously it helps if you have the suppleness and strength to control this, but the bonus is that you will get into a better position at the point of impact.

IMPROVE QUALITY OF YOUR MISTIMED SHOTS

One of the secrets of Lee Trevino's seemingly unorthodox technique was that he kept the clubface travelling square to the target line for a long period of time. Trevino figured that if he could keep his clubhead on the flight path for three inches while other golfers could manage to do so for only two inches, he would have a 50 percent performance advantage—on good and bad shots.

SWING THE BUCKET TO START THE TAKEAWAY

Many golfers have a trigger to start their swing. Harvey Penick would ask pupils to assume their normal stance and imagine they were holding a bucket of water with their hands on either side of the bucket. To swing the bucket back like a golf swing, you won't attempt it from a stationary position. Your whole body rocks toward the target a little to provide the momentum that starts the move away.

HIT THE SECOND BALL FOR FULL EXTENSION

"If you tend to "quit" at impact, or if your wrists sometime break down and you pull the club quickly to the inside, then pretend that you're hitting not one ball, but two," says Greg Norman in his *100 Instant Golf Lessons*. "Imagine a second ball, approximately 19 inches forward of the actual ball and on a straight line from the actual ball to your target. Then, try to 'hit' that second ball as well as the real one. This exercise will ensure that you extend your arms and club properly through impact."

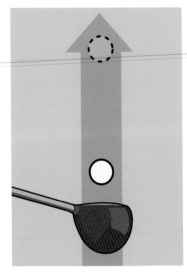

SET RIGHT WRIST BACK ON ITSELF FOR POWER

"The wrists can hinge in two ways in the backswing," Nick Faldo maintains in *Golf—The Winning Formula*. "The right wrist can be hinged or cupped upward against the thumb. This in itself does not create power. The movement is fairly limited and weak. It can also be set backward to a right angle—the wrist set used to create power and leverage."

FUNCTIONAL IS BETTER THAN PRETTY

Your swing doesn't have to look good in order to be effective, according to Lee Trevino in *Swing My Way*. He says: "I developed a swing that isn't the prettiest thing you'll ever see, but I think it's the most functional golf swing around."

TURN YOUR LEFT SHOULDER BEHIND THE BALL

Tom Kite, a senior PGA Tour professional, gives us this advice: "After you set up with good posture and are in balance, I encourage you to try to make a big shoulder turn … What I try to do is turn my left shoulder behind the ball. Picture a pane of glass coming straight up from the ball vertically, then at the top of the swing you want to have your entire left shoulder back behind that pane of glass. Don't be afraid to let your shoulder get behind that ball."

SWING THROUGH HANDS NOT WITH THEM

Sandy Lyle has a neat visualization that helps him with his swing. Rather than feeling as though he is swinging the club *with* his hands, Lyle likes to think of himself swinging the club *through* his hands. This helps him focus on using his hands to do nothing more than hold the club correctly.

LIFT LEFT HEEL IF TURN IS RESTRICTED

Many golfers experience the sensation that their turn is restricted if they try and keep their left heel firmly planted on the ground. By letting the left heel lift naturally on the backswing you will improve your ability to turn. But the keyword here is "naturally".

Strategy
Imagine you're still on the range **53**
Chip or pitch? **89**

Accuracy & distance
Use a heavy putter on slow greens **14**
Tee it low to hit it straight **61**

38

◉ KICK LEFT KNEE TO TARGET TO START DOWNSWING

Most amateur golfers fail to use their legs properly, particularly in the downswing. According to Rodger Davis, the best way to activate your legs in the downswing is to kick the left knee toward the target as you start down. This automatically gets your weight moving onto your left side through the ball.

◉ LET THE WRISTS HINGE A LITTLE FOR WIDTH

Butch Harmon believes that two of his star pupils—Tiger Woods and Davis Love III—run into trouble when their swing arc becomes too wide in the takeaway. Harmon maintains that while you should push your right hand as far as possible from your head at the top of the backswing, with your right elbow bent about 90 degrees, this is easier to achieve if you have a gentle wrist hinge on the backswing.

◉ USE YOUR NATURAL BEAT

"The golf stroke, like the tennis stroke, is basically a two-beat rhythm: back and forth," writes W. Timothy Gallwey in *The Inner Game of Golf*. "These two beats are fundamental to most movement—the rhythm of breathing, for example. We don't have to force it: it is there."

◉ HANDS LEVEL WITH BALL, WRISTS COCKED

In *Tommy Armour's ABC's of Golf*, the author lets us in on a secret: "The glorious trick is to get the hands just about even with the line of the ball in the downswing, while your wrists are completely cocked and the shaft of the club is at the same right angle with your straight left arm as it was at the top of the backswing."

◉ LEFT ARM GUIDES, RIGHT HAND HITS

According to the legendary Tommy Armour, the left arm and hand control and guide the swing, while the right hand is used to apply the power in the downswing and through impact.

◉ DON'T WATCH THE CLUBHEAD

Harvey Penick used to say that any technical swing flaw during the takeaway was nowhere near as disastrous as actually watching the clubhead move away from the ball in the first few feet of the backswing.

◉ SLIDE HIPS TO LEFT TO START DOWNSWING

"The one fifth of a second it takes to reach the point of impact (in the downswing) allows only one constructive swing thought," say Bernard Gallacher and Mark Wilson in *Teach Yourself Golf*. "We suggest that this should be concerned with starting the downswing with a slight lateral movement of the hips—a slide of about two to three inches to the left, parallel to the target line, and a tugging down of the arms."

◉ LAUNCH OFF RIGHT FOOT IN THE DOWNSWING

You should feel a certain amount of tension on the inside of your back thigh and the inside of your back foot at the top of your backswing position, claims Butch Harmon. If you keep your right foot totally grounded at the top of the backswing, you have a firm platform that you can push against to start your downswing.

POINT SHAFT AT BALL IN DOWNSWING

Johnny Miller has a neat practice routine to help groove your swing. Visualize a line travelling down the shaft of the club and out through the grip. Half way back on your backswing, align the shaft so that it is pointing directly at the ball. Release and then repeat the routine. Hit a bucket of balls following this routine and feel how you relax and get into a grooved routine.

KEEP A STEADY HEAD

Tommy Armour said that you could place a glass of water on top of Bobby Jones's head while he was hitting a shot and he wouldn't spill a drop—such was the gracefulness of his balance and rhythm.

BUILD UP TO YOUR IDEAL RHYTHM

"To find your ideal rhythm, tee up five balls in a row," advises Simon Hotham, a PGA professional. "Hit the first ball at about 40 percent of your full power, then immediately step up to the next ball and hit it at half your speed and power. Continue down the line and gradually increase your swing speed until you're swinging flat out on the last ball. You'll probably find that you get the best results with the third or fourth ball. All you need to do then is recreate that same swing speed when you hit shots for real out on the course."

TIMING BEATS BRAWN

In his book, *Bedrock Principles of Golf*, W. W. Lowe explains the relative merits of timing and strength: "Try to remember that golf is not all a matter of brawn, though strength and build play a great part in the game. A player, however, may have all the necessary adjuncts as to build and strength, yet never be able to apply them. A player of fourteen stones using clubs weighing sixteen ounces may be outdriven by a youth of ten stones using a club of thirteen ounces, simply owing to the fact that the latter is timing his shots."

MATCH YOUR "WAGGLE" TO THE SHOT

Many top golfers like to "waggle" the club to remove tension before they start their backswing. The game's greatest ever player Jack Nicklaus takes this philosophy one step further and actually waggles the clubhead along his intended swing path so that he has a rehearsal of the actual shot he wants to play.

KNOW AND CONTROL YOUR BAD SHOTS

"We all succeed at golf for one big reason: we all found a way to control our bad shots," says Lee Trevino in *Swing My Way*. "I know if I hadn't done that I'd still be living on beans and beer. You'd still be thinking "Trevino" is Italian."

Setup
Grip club at 45-degree angle **23**
Stance comes last **28**

Strategy
Warm up hitting chip shots if short on time **53**
Chip close enough to one putt **95**

LOWER BODY CONTROLS SHAPE OF THE SHOT

Lee Trevino learned how to shape his shots by watching Ben Hogan practice in Texas. He noticed how Hogan controlled the shots with his lower body and, in particular, the way in which he would lead the downswing with his hips and legs in order to fade the ball from left to right in the air.

BECOME A GOOD SWING COPIER

There are many good players, such as Laura Davies, who claim to have never taken a lesson in their lives, while Retief Goosen says that he learned his swing from reading instruction articles in books and magazines. Imitation of good players is one of the best ways to learn the swing techniques.

SHAFT RESTS ON COLLAR AT THE FINISH

A good follow-through is symptomatic of all the preceding movements in the swing. Nick Faldo likes to finish in a position where the shaft of the club rests on his shirt collar, almost as though he were wrapping the club around his neck. When he practices, Faldo holds his finish position until the ball he has just hit has landed.

COORDINATE SHOULDER AND CHIN IN THE SWING

"Practice getting the right relationship of shoulders and chin—your left shoulder should cover the chin in the backswing and the right one cover it in the follow-through," says Vivien Saunders in *The Golf Handbook for Women*. "Practice swinging back and through to feel the relationship of chin and shoulders—and do it with your mouth open. This gives an even more definite feeling to chin and shoulder. Remember that this is a woman's problem. Men just don't do it."

CHECK YOUR RIGHT ARM DURING THE SWING

One of the key swing checkpoints that Tiger Woods regularly reviews is the position of his right arm at the top of the backswing. He likes to keep his right arm close to his side and in front of his body as he completes his coil.

KEEP BELT LEVEL FOR A BETTER TURN

This good advice comes from Frank Nobilo, a PGA Tour professional: "To avoid a reverse pivot in your swing, think about keeping your belt buckle level with the ground at all points during the swing."

KNOW YOUR OWN SWING

Most of the world's top golfers have video tuition, but this professional style analysis is available to everyone nowadays. In *Golf Tips from the Stars*, Jose Maria Olazabal recommends that every amateur golfer should watch their swing on video and become aware of their flaws so that they have a chance to put things right if they start playing badly on the course.

UNWIND HIPS, KEEP SHOULDERS SQUARE

Although it is widely known that a clearing of the hips initiates the downswing, Henry Cotton always believed that the world's best players kept their shoulders square to the target until they had struck the ball.

START DOWNSWING FROM THE GROUND UP

Butch Harmon has a very neat visualization for getting your downswing started, and which will help you hit the ball longer and straighter. A common mistake is to try and start your downswing with your hands, shoulders, or upper body. This will most likely result in sliced or pulled shots. To address this, try and think about starting your downswing from the ground up. Make that focus on transferring your weight to your left foot with a little nudge to the left through your hips and left knee, and then uncoiling your left hip in advance of your shoulders. This sequence will automatically bring your arms and hands along, and therefore get you in to a good position at point of impact.

STICK TO YOUR NATURAL TEMPO

Everybody has a different natural tempo. Nick Price and Lee Trevino, for example, both walk and talk very quickly, so it's only natural that their swing rhythm will be quicker than, say, that of an Ernie Els or a Retief Goosen, who both walk and talk more slowly and deliberately. One of the keys to a consistent swing is to find your natural "beat" and stick to it.

NAIL YOUR RIGHT SIDE

Clearing the right side out of the way on the backswing permits a full shoulder turn. Seve Ballesteros will often visualize a nail being hammered through his right buttock at address. This prevents it from moving more than two inches backward, but is enough to encourage a full and smooth turn.

STRAIGHT LEFT ARM CAN CAUSE PROBLEMS

"I think there is often too much emphasis placed on the left arm being kept straight through impact," says Nick Faldo in *Golf —The Winning Formula*. "This tends to produce an action where the arms stay fairly firm and the wrists release with a kind of throwing action through impact, which closes the clubface."

KEEP ELBOWS SAME DISTANCE APART THROUGHOUT

One of Arnold Palmer's key swing principles is to maintain the gap between his elbows from address until the finish of the swing. He believes that this leads to an efficient and compact swing. When the elbows move further apart than they were at address, it is easy to lose control of the swing and play inconsistently.

DON'T MOVE HEAD FORWARD IN DOWNSWING

"If you move your head forward during your downswing or through impact, you will hit a weak, ugly shot, probably a pulled slice …" writes Harvey Penick in *Harvey Penick's Little Red Golf Book*. "Before you can stay behind the ball, you must get behind it. I mean set up with your head behind the ball and keep your head behind the ball."

DOMINANT HAND CONTROLS THE TAKEAWAY

Many golfers like to control their takeaway and backswing with their left arm. Seve Ballesteros, on the other hand, has always maintained that you should use your dominant side to start the backswing, so he takes the club away from the ball with his right arm and hand.

Swing
See clubhead out of corner of left eye **61**
A forward defence stroke for solid contact **100**
Polish your building blocks **123**

⬤ FINISH WITH BELT BUCKLE
FACING THE TARGET
To hit the ball toward your
intended target, your body
must finish facing the target.
Check where your belt buckle
points in your follow-through
position. If it aims right of the
target, you need to improve
your hip and leg action through
the ball.

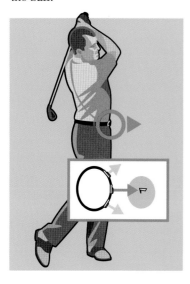

⬤ MINIMIZE WEIGHT
TRANSFER TO TURN CORRECTLY
According to Gary Smith, a PGA
professional, you should feel
very little weight transference
when you turn your upper
body—a maximum of 20
percent. "However, that doesn't
mean you can let your weight
fall onto your left side in the
back-swing—a reverse pivot is
equally destructive to your game.

Once you've set up to the ball
correctly, create resistance in
your right knee and then focus
hard on coiling your upper body
so that your shoulders turn
through at least 90 degrees
while you remain centered
over the ball."

⬤ FEEL THE CLUBHEAD TO
IMPROVE RHYTHM
"Feeling the weight of the
clubhead against the tension of
the shaft helps me to swing
rhythmically," says Jack
Nicklaus in *Golf My Way*. "As
the backswing progresses I like
to feel the clubhead's weight
'pulling' my hands and arms
back and up. Starting down, I
like to feel the weight of the
clubhead lagging back—
resisting—as my thrusting legs
and hips pull my arms and
hands down."

⬤ PUSH LEFT HAND DOWN
FOR EXTENSION
"The suggestion of a downward
push by the left hand in this
club positioning phase [the
takeaway] together with
centrifugal pull of the clubhead
takes care of all the left arm
extension the player needs,"
writes Joe Novak in *Par Golf In
Eight Steps*. In other words, it is
not necessary to create a wide
swing arc.

⬤ IF YOU CAN DANCE YOU
CAN SWING
The rhythm, coordination and
nimble footwork required to be a
good dancer are useful in the
golf swing. Marlene Floyd claims
that any woman who can dance
will be able to master the
footwork involved in hitting a
golf ball. The weight shifts from
the left heel to the right heel on
the backswing and from the right
heel to the left foot in the
downswing.

⬤ PRACTICE SWING IN
BETWEEN SHOTS
Use your time in between shots
to hone your swing and improve
your hand action through impact.
Henry Cotton would carry a club
in his hands and clip the heads
off daisies and swish the grass as
he walked to his ball.

Cypress Point California

16TH HOLE, PAR-3, 223 YARDS

TIME TO TRUST YOUR SWING

Situated in a secluded setting on the Monterey Peninsular in southern California, Cypress Point is arguably the world's most spectacular and most difficult golf course. The course, which cohosts the AT&T pro-am in conjunction with its more illustrious neighbors, Pebble Beach and Spyglass Hill, constantly features in the toughest holes on Tour seasonal statistics and has become a Mecca for golf enthusiasts the world over.

If ever there is a time when you want to have resounding and unquestionable faith in your swing, standing on the tee of the 16th hole at Cypress Point looking out over the crashing surf of the Pacific Ocean is almost certainly it. It's a spellbinding and spectacular par-3, which plays from one peninsular extremity to another, and you simply cannot avoid hitting your tee shot out over the high bay to a green situated on a craggy outcrop over 200 yards in the distance. Even on a calm day the shot is intimidating enough, but, when the wind gets up, it can be nigh on impossible to reach dry land. It's the ultimate matchplay hole, and, to make matters worse, the only realistic bailout area is accessible only to a well-struck mid-to-long iron off the tee. Even so, there are many professionals who elect to play the hole this way each time and refuse even to contemplate the do-or-die tee shot.

Named after the tree that inhabits the region, Cypress Point stemmed from the creative imagination of Dr. Alister MacKenzie in 1928 and it was his work here that prompted Bobby Jones to invite the Scottish doctor to assist him in

PRO-FILE
SAM SNEAD

Rhythm rules OK

Sam Snead had the sweetest swing in golf. His natural, freewheeling motion was so fluid and graceful that many fellow competitors back in the 1940s and 1950s predicted that he would win tournaments when he was 60. How close they were! Snead won his last PGA Tour title in 1965 at the age of 52 and he finished third in the USPGA Championship in 1974 at the age of 62. In total he won seven majors and posted 46 top-10 finishes in the grand-slam events—a record surpassed only by Jack Nicklaus. One of Snead's key thoughts was to create a "package" backswing, where the hands, arms, shoulders, and hips flow back in one controlled movement. Snead was one of the first players to refer to the takeaway as a one-piece motion and he was particular about his balance and footwork as he believed them to be the framework of his whole swing.

Snead believed that the secret of powerful, straight hitting is to accelerate the downswing gradually and delay the unhinging of the wrists until the hands pass the belt buckle. He very rarely swung at anything like full effort, preferring to use only about 85 percent of his power.

the layout of Augusta National. Cypress is often referred to as "the Sistine Chapel of golf" for its sheer beauty, and the layout traverses through a stunning and delightful combination of seaside, cliff top, wooded hillside, and almost heathland-type terrain.

The club itself is very private and is open only to members and guests. A small and privileged membership ensures that the course is rarely crowded or overplayed and is therefore usually in immaculate condition. The course is littered throughout with risk/reward-type shot options to tempt the more proficient golfer, yet MacKenzie deliberately built in safer routes on each hole so that the amateur golfer could enjoy an equal challenge. The theme of tempting and rewarding the adventurous golfer with a par or birdie, while still allowing the more conservative player to make his score via a longer approach, is continual, and even the par-3 16th hole was intended as such, starting out in MacKenzie's mind originally as a par-4.

4

The First Tee

It's a fact of life that every single golfer, regardless of whether a once-a-week high-handicapper or the multiple major championship winner Tiger Woods, gets a little nervous standing on the first tee. Cold, tight muscles and an expectant gallery can combine to make the situation even more daunting. The key to overcoming your apprehension on the opening hole is to use these nerves to your advantage by channeling them to focus your attention and concentration, and not let them turn you into a quivering wreck. Establishing a solid preround routine, and taking the time to loosen your muscles before you head to the first tee, will prepare you more thoroughly for the experience.

Beat your first-tee nerves

Many golfers allow their first-tee nerves to ruin their enjoyment of the game. It is important to remember that your nerves are perfectly normal. Always bear in mind that, when you consider your total round of golf, your tee shot on the opening hole is of no more importance than, say, your tee shot on the 8th hole or a two-foot putt on the 15th hole. If you can keep a sense of perspective, the opening tee shot becomes far less daunting.

● TAKE YOUR HOT STREAK TO THE FIRST TEE

Most players encounter a hot streak of form in the middle of their round. However, Dr Bob Rotella says that there's no reason why you shouldn't be able to start you round full of confidence. To get your round off to a fast start, replicate the state of mind that you experience when "in the zone" straightaway on the first tee.

● SWITCH TO A 3-WOOD FOR CONFIDENCE

Splitting the fairway with a solid drive is guaranteed to give you a huge confidence boost, but, if you hit the ball into the trees or the rough, you can set the tone for the day. Don't feel that you have to reach for your driver. Nick Faldo advised Colin Montgomerie to take a 3-wood off the first tee in a Ryder Cup match in 1993. Take the club with which you feel most confident.

● FOCUS ON A TEMPO THOUGHT

Even the world's top players get nervous standing on the first tee. Nick Faldo likes to focus on a key tempo and take a couple of deep breaths before making his first swing of the day.

● SLOW DOWN YOUR ROUTINE AND STICK TO IT

One of the side effects of nerves is that you instinctively speed up. Compensate for this by slowing your routine. It's also important to adhere to your normal preshot routine. Going through the same series of prerehearsed motions will provide a comfort zone and lessen the effects of your nerves.

● WARM UP BEFORE YOU GET TO THE FIRST TEE

Nothing is guaranteed to kick-start the mental gremlins more than standing on the first tee without having warmed up.

Ideally, you should spend about 15 to 20 minutes gently hitting balls and loosening your muscles so that you are prepared for the opening tee shot. If you don't have time for that, some simple aerobic exercises like jogging on the spot will get the blood pumping through your veins. Alternatively, gently swing a couple of clubs together to stretch the muscles in your upper body.

Swing theory
Stop head bobbing **34**
Hands level with ball, wrists cocked **39**
Repetition is th name of the game **43**

Accuracy & distance
How a bad grip costs you accuracy **23**
Short putting **137**

Setup
Address the ball athletically **22**
Narrower stance reduces tension **28**

52

WARM UP HITTING CHIP SHOTS IF SHORT ON TIME
Harvey Penick's Little Red Golf Book has some timely advice: "If you arrive at the course with just a few minutes to warm up before a round, use that time to hit chip shots. The chip shot ... tells your muscles and your golfing brain to get ready to play. Most average golfers with only a few minutes to warm up will rush to the range and try to hit balls fast. This may loosen up the grease, but it can also ruin your tempo for the day and perhaps implant negative thoughts."

FOCUS ON WHAT YOU WANT TO ACHIEVE
Rather than think about all the things that could go wrong, channel your thoughts positively and focus on what you want to achieve rather than what you don't. It can be difficult to block negative thoughts out of your mind completely, but, if they do creep in, don't allow them to settle—and immediately replace them with a more constructive and positive thought.

TRICK YOURSELF INTO FEELING CONFIDENT
The golf psychologist, David Norman, says: "You can trick your brain into feeling confident by projecting a positive body language. Stand tall and proud and use your time on the tee while others hit their drives to visualize the perfect shot you want to play."

TAKE DEEP BREATHS BEFORE AN IMPORTANT SHOT
"Before you step up to any shot from deep trouble, especially in a tight match, make it a point to take a couple of deep breaths," advises Fred Couples in *Total Shotmaking*. "There is a tendency to get more anxious than normal when playing from tough course situations that you're not used to. Ironically, this is when you need to stay especially cool."

STAY IN THE PRESENT
Harvey Penick claims that your mind determines how well you will play in an important match and in a pressure situation. He says that you should avoid trying out new or different things that will distract you from your normal routine. He also recommends that you should resist the temptation to think about the result of a match in advance. Stay in the present.

IMAGINE YOU'RE STILL ON THE RANGE
In order to help amateurs cope with their first-tee nerves, Fred Couples believes that you should stand on the tee and imagine that you're a on a wide-open practice range. After taking a couple of deep breaths, make the same relaxed swing that you normally make on the range. This simple ploy will improve your confidence over the ball.

Muirfield Scotland

1ST HOLE, PAR-4, 448 YARDS

TAME THE FIRST-TEE TRAUMA

Muirfield, on the outskirts of Edinburgh, Scotland, is widely regarded as the best course on the Open Championship rota. The home of the Honourable Company of Edinburgh Golfers, it is also the oldest golf club in the world with records dating back to 1744. In conjunction with the Royal & Ancient, which was formed just a decade later, Muirfield, Prestwick, and St. Andrews took it in turns to host the Open Championship from 1872 until 1894.

Although undoubtedly not as tough in benign conditions as Royal St. George's, Royal Lytham & St. Annes, or even Royal Birkdale, Muirfield is without doubt the fairest test of golf in the Open Championship, and testimony to the quality of the golf course is its role call of illustrious champions, including Walter Hagen, Henry Cotton, Jack Nicklaus, Nick Faldo, and Ernie Els.

The opening hole at Muirfield is a long par-4 of 448 yards that doglegs slightly to the right. Ordinarily, neither the length nor the shape of the hole should cause the modern top players too many problems, but, as the golfing world witnessed at the Open Championship in 2002, the combination of first-tee nerves and the high rough that bordered the fairway combined to "shrink" the landing area, and, consequently, many players found the trouble and several amassed disastrous openings to their rounds.

During that particular Open Championship and also during those staged previously at Muirfield, it was interesting to note that the majority of the players decided to take either a long iron or a lofted fairway wood off the first tee instead of

PRO-FILE
PHIL MICKELSON

Read the architect's mind

Although he is one of the longest hitters in the game, Phil Mickelson is not really regarded as one of the best drivers. However, his philosophy on tee shots is one that golfers of all levels would do well to emulate. The first thing that Mickelson does as he walks onto the tee of a par-4 or a par-5 is to work out how the architect wants him to play the hole. This strategy also inevitably involves looking at where the architect doesn't want him to hit the ball.

In almost all instances, there will be more than one way to play a hole successfully. If this is the case, the deciding factor on whether he should take on the more adventurous or aggressive route to the green, according to Mickelson, is how well he has played the previous holes. If he is confident and the hole suits his preferred shape of shot, he may play more aggressively, but if he has been striking the ball indifferently, he will adopt a more conservative strategy. The key lesson to learn is that focusing your attention on analyzing the hole will take your mind off your nerves and give you something positive to focus on, while matching your state of mind allows you to take advantage of your confidence.

the driver. One of the reasons behind this strategy was that the course was dry and fast-running, but another was simply that the players wanted to get off to a safe start using a club with which they felt confident of hitting the fairway. Although this option left most competitors with a long-iron approach into the first green, this was deemed a far more preferable option compared to hacking out of the rough sideways and still facing a lengthy third shot to the green under pressure. Another contributing factor in the players' decision-making process is that the width of the fairway narrows as it nears the green, making a driver a particularly risky choice of club, especially for the long hitters in the game.

Driving

While a sharp, short game and a hot putter will often bail you out of trouble or help you on your way to a low score, the fact remains that it is difficult to play really good golf if you struggle with your driving. The driver is the longest and least forgiving club in the bag, and it is therefore the most dangerous. In order to take advantage of the club's power, your swing basics will need to be sound and your swing solid and consistent—otherwise the lack of loft on the clubface and the length of the shaft will ruthlessly expose any flaws in your technique.

The most important shot

The drive, or the tee shot, is the most important on any hole. A long, straight tee shot benefits your whole game and makes each subsequent shot a little easier. A longer drive will enable you to hit a shorter approach shot into the green, which is likely to enable you to hit the ball closer to the hole and sink more putts. The statistics show that the longest and most accurate golfers on Tour shoot the lowest scores.

GET YOUR TEE HEIGHT RIGHT
"For a regular drive, tee the ball so that the top of the clubface is level with the manufacturer's logo on the ball," says the LPGA professional Claire Waite.

CLEAR YOUR HIPS FOR LONG DRIVES
John Daly counsels in *The Killer Swing*: "Since a tee shot demands that you hit with a sweeping action, you must create a shallow angle of attack by rotating your hips to your left at the start of the downswing. This clearing action of the hips allows your arms to swing away from your body and whip the club powerfully through the ball."

SWING BETTER, NOT HARDER
When asked his opinion on how to hit the ball further, PGA Tour professional Davis Love III usually replies that he tries to make a perfect swing rather than swing harder, in order to ensure that he delivers the ball to the clubface in the middle of the sweet spot.

REACH MAXIMUM SWING SPEED JUST AFTER IMPACT
"Most amateur golfers deliver the power at the wrong stage in their swing," says Catrin Nilsmark, an LPGA Tour professional. "In most cases, they generate the power too early—at the start of the downswing in an effort to lunge at the ball. However, by the time the clubhead reaches impact it is actually slowing down and transmits less power to the ball. On the contrary, I'm looking to achieve my maximum swing speed just after impact. That way, I am certain that the clubhead will be accelerating as it passes through the hitting area."

STRETCH UPPER BODY AGAINST KNEE RESISTANCE
One of Nick Faldo's key driving thoughts is to stretch and turn the larger muscles in his upper body against the resistance of his knees and hips. This maximizes his coil.

STRAIGHTEN LEFT LEG FOR 20 MORE YARDS
You won't find this tip in any textbook of the golf swing, but when Tiger Woods wants to

---

Accuracy & distance
Swap your driver for a fairway wood 13
Create resistance and power, then let go! 46
Find your best yardage with your wedges 89

Swing theory
Let your left heel rise 34
The magic move of the golf swing 37
The game begins and ends from hips down 45

Club selection
Favor fairway woods over long irons 14
Never use long club if short one will do 68

generate an extra few yards of distance off the tee, he snaps his left leg straight just before impact. This enables his hips to clear faster and increases the speed of his shoulders, arms, and legs.

TEE THE BALL AS HIGH AS YOU CAN

Many club golfers slice their tee shots because they tee the ball too low and therefore have to hit down too steeply to get the ball in the air. To reduce your chances of slicing, tee the ball a little higher. This will force you to swing the club more around yourself on a slightly flatter plane in order to strike the ball powerfully.

LEFT HIP POCKET TOWARD THE TARGET

"To feel the correct driver setup stand to the ball and imagine that someone is tugging your left hip pocket towards the target and your right shoulder away from it," says Gary Smith, a PGA professional.

DRAW YOUR RIGHT FOOT BACK FOR A DRAW

Sam Snead writes in *The Game I Love*: "On my normal driver swing, I would always drop my right foot back a little, giving me more room to turn and promoting an aggressive inside attack. With this alignment I could play a nice draw and feel a nice easy turn."

REHEARSE DRIVER SWING WITH 3-WOOD FIRST

To regain his confidence with the driver, PGA Tour professional, Brad Faxon, used to practice his key driving-swing thoughts with his 3-wood. When confident enough to hit the ball correctly with the fairway wood, he would do the same with the driver. If he had practiced those thoughts with the driver, he could easily have lost confidence.

THINK "R.P.B." FOR EXTRA DISTANCE

"When my mission is to get maximum distance on a tee shot, in order to reach a par-5 in two, I'll tell myself: 'R.P.B.'," writes Greg Norman in his *100 Instant Golf Lessons*. "Those initials stand for 'right pocket back' a reminder for me to make a full hip turn in which my right front trouser pocket rotates around toward my back as far as possible."

KEEP DRIVER LOW TO THE GROUND IN TAKEAWAY

In order to ensure that as much of the clubface as possible makes contact with the ball at impact, Chi Chi Rodriguez keeps the driver low to the ground at the beginning of the backswing.

MAKE SAME SWING WITH YOUR DRIVER

Although the swing for a driver is different from that for an iron, you should not swing differently. Playing the ball forward in your stance and setting extra weight on your right side at address will create a more rounded plane.

BETTER LONG THAN SHORT

According to John Daly, it's better to be long and inaccurate than short and inaccurate.

LET MOMENTUM KICK-START YOUR COIL

Many top pros make driving look easy. Taking a nice, wide stance to ensure they have good balance, they ease the club back from the ball, slowly and low to the ground, almost as though they were letting the gathering momentum of the club pull them into the backswing. Carrying on in to the top of the backswing, this pulling motion creates the upper body coil necessary for power in the shot. Again, on the downswing the momentum of their uncoiling body seems to pull the club back down to meet the ball.

SHAKE HANDS WITH THE FLAG STICK

"Every time I hit a shot, I feel like I am shaking hands with the flag stick," says Moe Norman at www.moenorman.com.

KEEP DOWNSWING LOW TO THE GROUND

One visualization that helps generate extra clubhead speed, as well as a more solid contact with the ball, is to focus on keeping the clubhead low to the ground on both the takeaway and on the downswing.

THINK "SAM SNEAD" TO IMPROVE DRIVING

Nick Dougherty tells us in *Golf Monthly*, October 2002: "I went along with Nick Faldo when he visited Sam Snead at his home in Virginia and it was a real eye-opener and a breath of fresh air for both of us. Sam was very nontechnical in his approach … His only swing thought was to keep his rhythm the same as he turned back and through. He told us that to help him focus on his tempo, he would say "Sam" on the backswing and "Snead" on the downswing."

KEEP RIGHT ARM INSIDE LINE OF LEFT

Writing in *Golf Tips* magazine Marshall Smith tells us: "To create the most power, your turn sequence should be hips, shoulders, hands. The best way to keep from coming over the top and swinging out of sequence is to set up with your right arm positioned inside your left.

When you do, you'll establish a power-rich swing plane and keep that right shoulder from swinging out of turn."

ACCELERATE GRADUALLY

"One of the easiest and most effective ways to strengthen your body action is to hold a driver out at around waist-height and swish the clubhead baseball style," writes Nick Faldo in *A Swing for Life*. "Feel your shoulders turn fully back and through, and stir up a storm. Make the wind whistle through impact, then recreate that sound with your regular swing. The beauty of this exercise is that it teaches you the discipline of building acceleration gradually, and that's the key to maximizing clubhead speed."

DON'T KEEP YOUR HEAD DOWN

Rather than try to keep your head down—which leads to stiffness and lack of flexibility in the swing—a better swing thought is to keep your head steady. Not one top professional ever sees the club strike the ball on a full swing. Although players such as David Duval and Annika Sorenstam are looking down the fairway at the point of impact, their head position has not moved.

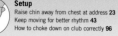

Setup
Raise chin away from chest at address **23**
Keep moving for better rhythm **43**
How to choke down on club correctly **96**

Strategy
Less is sometimes more **15**
Chip or pitch? **89**
Master variable factors for better chipping **103**

Swing theory
Choose clubs that suit your game **12**
Turn around your spine **36**

TEE IT UP ON THE SIDE OF THE TROUBLE

"As a general rule," says the author of *Tommy Armour's ABC's of Golf*, "it is wise to tee the ball on that side of the tee that is nearest trouble—out of bounds, a bunker you can reach, trees, water, or bad rough. From that teed location, not only is it almost instinctive for you to aim away from trouble, but you have a wider area into which you can let your shot fly."

BUILD UP YOUR STRENGTH

Jason Zuback, the Canadian world long-drive champion, suggests that you tape a golf ball to the face of the golf club to increase its weight. Now make some normal swings with the weighted club to develop and build up your "golf" muscles.

WORK YOUR WAY UP TO FULL POWER

One of the world's longest hitters, Davis Love III, used to perform a drill recommended by his father, whereby you use your full swing to hit the ball different distances. Start the drill by using your full swing to hit the ball only about 25 percent of its full distance. Once you can strike the ball solidly and consistently, increase your swing speed so that the ball travels 50 percent of its full distance with that club. Repeat this process until you can control the ball with each increase in swing speed and you finally reach full power.

LONGER ARC EQUALS LONGER DRIVES

In order to make up for his lack of height, Gary Player used to have all of his clubs made half-an-inch longer than standard. Longer clubs create a longer swing arc and more power and distance.

TEE THE BALL HIGH FOR DISTANCE

Jack Nicklaus believes that teeing the ball too low with the driver will sap your power and distance because you are forced to hit down on the ball, rather than sweep through it. If your attack into the ball is too steep you will deliver only a glancing blow and impart too much of the unwanted backswing that causes the ball to slice in the air.

TEE IT LOW TO HIT IT STRAIGHT

When Tiger Woods needs an especially accurate drive, he will tee the ball a little lower than normal to reduce the sidespin on the ball through impact.

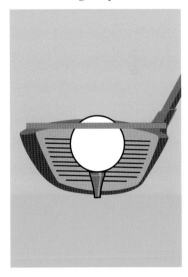

SEE CLUBHEAD OUT OF CORNER OF LEFT EYE

One of Colin Montgomerie's key driving thoughts is to make sure that he completes his backswing. To ensure that he makes a full and fluent backswing, Montgomerie will wait until he can see the clubhead out of the corner of his left eye before starting his downswing.

Carnoustie Scotland

6TH HOLE, PAR-5, 520 YARDS

THE DRIVING CHALLENGE

If a golf course is judged by its ability to confirm the greatest golfer of the day, then historically Carnoustie, on the east coast of Scotland, has no equal as an Open Championship venue, having produced an eminent array of victors that includes Tommy Armour, Henry Cotton, Gary Player, Ben Hogan, and Tom Watson. The course, which really bared its teeth in the 1999 championship, is noted for its length, difficulty, and, in particular, the brutality of its closing holes.

The renowned golf-course architect Donald Ross once said that a long iron was the ultimate test of a golfer's technique. If this is the case, then Carnoustie surely presents the ultimate challenge. A tough and uncompromising links, Carnoustie, situated on the east coast of Scotland, is regarded as the toughest venue on the Open Championship, protected by its sheer length, winding burns, pot bunkers, undulating fairways, and, in the case of the 1999 Open, knee-high rough as well.

From the opening drive, the golfer is pitched into a headlong and unrelenting battle. Anything right of center in the fairway leaves a semiblind approach that takes in an enormous sand hill. The second, a particularly impressive hole, plays uphill through a valley towards a long thin green. A succession of long and demanding par-4s and -5s follow, setting the theme for the remainder of the round.

One of the most renowned holes is the 520-yard par-5 sixth, which features a narrow strip of fairway between the out-of-bounds and the fairway bunkers, which is known as Hogan's Alley, owing to the fact that the great man was the only competitor during the 1953

PRO-FILE
COLIN MONTGOMERIE

Use the whole fairway

Colin Montgomerie is regarded as one of the game's best drivers, not because of his length off the tee, but because he hits so many fairways. Although he is not a short hitter by any stretch of the imagination, his strength lies in his ability to make full use of the fairway to his advantage. Monty likes to work the ball slightly from left to right in the air. With this in mind, he will usually aim at the left edge of the fairway, knowing that the ball will curve gently back to the center. Monty is an intelligent golfer, however, and, knowing that he will not strike every shot perfectly, he has built in some safety measures to his driving philosophy. If he aims at the left edge of the fairway and hits the shot straight, he will still be on the fairway. If he hits the shot perfectly as planned, his ball will find the center of the fairway, while even if his fade turns into a slice, his ball will probably still find the right edge of the fairway or, at worst, the first cut of semirough. So driving isn't all about brute force and power: it's about strategy and planning, too. One of the main reasons why Monty hits so many greens so regularly is because his tee shots invariably find the fairway.

Open with the nerve to aim deliberately for the narrow landing area. Hogan eschewed the safe line to the right off the tee, preferring to start the ball out over the out-of-bounds before cutting it back to land on a strip of fairway less than 10 yards wide between the bunkers and the fence. The locals who saw him play the hole twice on the final day still swear he played his second in the afternoon from the divot he left in the morning! Either way the result was the same, a clinical brassie shot to the heart of the green and two putts for a birdie.

Hogan's victory at Carnoustie meant that he had won three of the four majors in the season, a feat that remained unequalled until Tiger Woods won the US Open, the Open, and the USPGA in 2000. The Scottish spectators took the American pro to their hearts and called him the "Wee Ice Mon" for his ability to focus completely on his game. It's said that Hogan asked his wife, after he'd won a tournament, what she'd done that day. "I've been at your side," she replied!

6

From the Fairway

Once your ball has found the fairway off the tee, there are many variable factors that will affect your decision making for your next shot. The lie of the ball, the pin position, the strength and direction of the wind, the characteristics of the hole, and the positioning of any potential hazards, not to mention how well you are playing on the day, all play a key role in determining your choice of club and shot for your approach into the green. The world's best golfers are masters at computing that information quickly and efficiently and then deciding on a strategy that will give them the best possible opportunity to get the ball close to the flag while avoiding the trouble.

Master your approach play

With the almost infinite amount of variables that affect each golf shot, such as the strength and direction of the wind, the exact yardage to the hole, the pin position on the green, and the lie of the ball, it is obvious that no two shots into the green will be exactly the same. Much of the skill involved in playing accurate approach shots is possessing the ability to be able to adapt your setup and your swing to the shot in question.

REHEARSE YOUR SWING AFTER A GOOD SHOT

"Usually when a player makes a really bad stroke you see him trying the swing over again—without the ball—wondering what went wrong," says Harry Vardon in *The Complete Golfer*. "It would pay him much better to do the good strokes over again in the same way every time he makes them, as to impress the method of execution firmly in his mind."

BUILD GOOD ALIGNMENT INTO PRESHOT ROUTINE

"An imaginary shot with target awareness is a practice swing and much more," Byron Huff tells us in *Be the Target*. "It's a practice swing married to a target picture; it's a preparatory swing for your real shot. You may want to include one in your preshot routine, as it can be very useful."

CHANGE YOUR GRIP TO HIT SLICES AND HOOKS

"When I face a trouble shot where I have to slice or hook the ball a lot, I will change my grip," advises Tom Watson in *Teach Yourself Strategic Golf*. "Actually, it's probably the easiest way for most players to stop slicing and start to hook the ball. And changing your grip in practice is an excellent way to learn about spin and train yourself in trouble shots. To hit a major slice, rotate your hands counterclockwise on the grip. To hit a large hook, rotate your hands clockwise. Do not rotate the clubhead as you rotate your hands."

CHOKE DOWN ON IRONS FOR ULTIMATE CONTROL

If you are struggling to control your iron shots, think about gripping further down the shaft. Tiger Woods says that when he chokes down on the grip he hits the ball a little straighter, a little lower and with a little less backspin.

NEVER GIVE UP

A hallmark of a great player is the refusal to give up and the determination to apply 100 percent effort on each and every shot, no matter how unfavorable the circumstances may appear. Indeed, most top golfers are of the opinion that one good shot can turn everything around and nobody wins or loses until the final putt is holed.

Club selection
Use sand wedge to excape from bunkers **15**
Club carefully on large greens **71**
Keep the ball low and under control **98**

Setup
Take dead aim **24**
Tilt head to right and keep eye on ball **35**

Accuracy & distance
Lift left arm to check your alignment **28**
Select small targets to aim at **146**

◉ FOCUS TOTALLY ON THE TARGET

According to Annika Sorenstam the only thing you should focus on when preparing to play a shot is the target. She calls it "eye concentration" and the only thing she is thinking about at that moment is what she is trying to do with the golf ball. Most amateurs spend too much time thinking about where they don't want to hit the ball.

◉ THINK ABOUT THE STATE OF THE GREENS

"The condition of the greens plays a very important role in your club selection," says Per-Ulrik Johansson. "If the greens are wet and receptive, you can fly your 7-iron 150 yards through the air and it will stop stone dead. If the greens are as hard as concrete, you may need to use an 8-iron or even a 9-iron to get the ball to travel the same distance since it will bounce forward and run 10 to 20 yards on landing. Think about the state of the greens, plus the wind and even the temperature when you evaluate your shots. The ball flies considerably further in warm air than in the cold."

◉ HIT A FOREHAND WINNER TO DRAW THE BALL

Try to visualize that you are hitting a sizzling forehand winner when you're trying to put a big draw on the ball.

◉ AIM LEFT WITH EVERYTHING FOR A FADE

In *Golf Masterclass*, Christy O'Connor Jr. says: "To fade the ball, aim left of the green, your shoulders a little open, but don't overdo it. I would rather see you stand square and then just turn slightly to your left aiming everything that way. The club will now move back slightly outside the target line and come across the ball, spinning it to the right, fighting the right-to-left wind."

◉ CLOSE STANCE SLIGHTLY ON LONGER SHOTS

Most golf instruction books that you are likely to come across will advocate that you should

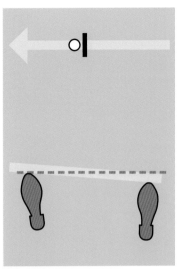

play regular shots with a square stance, but Ben Hogan used to close his stance slightly for all of the longer clubs from 4-iron to driver. Hogan claimed that this gave him better balance and traction as well as the freedom to turn his body in the backswing and downswing.

◉ REDUCE BACKSWING FOR GOOD IRON PLAY

Swedish Ryder Cup player Pierre Fulke says that overswinging with your irons is the easiest way to lose control of accuracy.

◉ HIT SAME DISTANCE WITH VARIETY OF CLUBS

You will find that practicing hitting to one distance with a variety of clubs will teach you how to add and remove distance from each club.

● NEVER USE LONG CLUB IF SHORT ONE WILL DO

"Do not use a long club when a short one will answer your purpose better. It is better to be five yards short of a bunker than five yards nearer the hole, in it," writes Horace Hutchinson in *Hints on the Game of Golf.*

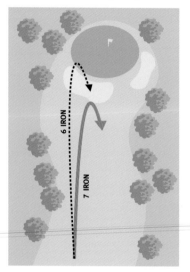

● GOLF IS ABOUT MISSES— NOT PERFECTION

"Golf is not a fair game." That, anyway, is the opinion of Bob Rotella in *Golf is Not a Game of Perfect: 365 Anecdotes and Lessons.* "A player can hit a perfect shot and have the ball end up out of bounds, or miss a shot completely and have the ball go in the hole. Golf is about how well you accept your misses much more so than it is a game of perfect shots."

● THE FASTER YOU SWING, THE LESS CHANCE OF POWER

For many golfers, the faster they try to swing the clubhead, the less chance they have of actually delivering the power right at the time when they need it most— at impact.

● NEVER SWING FLAT OUT WITH IRONS

In *Golf for Women*, Helen Alfredsson offers this advice: "Never hit your irons as hard as you can … Instead take one more club than you think you need and swing more easily. I don't do this as a rule because I'm on the range half my life. But if I'm between clubs with trouble in front of the green, or a slight wind in my face, I'll take one more club, grip down, and swing easy."

● TAKE ONE CLUB MORE THAN YOU THINK YOU NEED

Horace Hutchinson has sound advice on approach shots in *Elementary Instruction Approaching.* He says that it "cannot be repeated too often that the failing of the great majority of players is being short. For one shot that is past, you will see six that are not up. Therefore when doubtful what club to take for your approach shot, it is a good rule to always

take the longer of the two between which you are hesitating, for remember, you base your calculations on the assumption that you are going to hit the ball correctly. No accident is therefore likely to make the ball go farther than your expectation, while the accidents that may possibly curtail its distance are, alas! only too many."

● TRUST YOUR SWING AND COMMIT TO THE SHOT

Every golfer knows that feeling of planning a shot in your mind and then perfectly executing it. For this to happen, Tiger Woods says that you have to combine full commitment to the shot you are trying to hit as well as total faith in your swing. If you have one without the other, you're going to get into trouble.

● PRECISE TARGETS FOCUS THE MIND

According to the renowned golf psychologist Dr. Bob Rotella, highlighting a small target improves your focus, concentration and, most importantly, your results. A precise target helps with your alignment and also prevents unwanted distractions from entering your head while you prepare to play a shot.

Swing theory
Set wrists early, then turn to the top **35**
Turn your left shoulder behind the ball **38**
Keep elbows same distance apart throughout **42**

Strategy
Take driver out of the bag if you struggle with it **16**
Try to hole your chips **96**

Setup
Use a mirror to check your setup **27**
Close stance slightly on longer shots **67**

HIT DOWN ON YOUR IRONS

"For all iron clubs, hit down and through the ball," Julius Boros advises in *Swing Easy Hit Hard*. "In other words, your club should contact the ball first, then the turf. Consequently, the lowest point in your swing will be a half inch to two inches in front of your ball. This causes the ball to adhere to the surface of your club face long enough to impart spin … Backspin not only affects the ball when it lands but also in flight. When backspin has been applied the ball bores through the air more accurately."

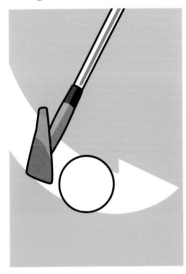

TURN HANDS TO THE RIGHT TO HIT A HOOK

"To hook the ball, turn both hands toward the right side," says Ben Hogan in *Power Golf*. "It will feel unnatural, but it will enable you to hook without altering your swing. Your hands come back to a normal position while you swing and automatically close the face of the club at impact, insuring a hook … [To fade the ball], I have turned the hands over toward the left over the shaft. During the swing they come back to a normal position, automatically opening the face of the club and giving the desired fade or slice."

LEARN TO PLAY WITH JUST ONE CLUB

In the intriguingly titled *The Snake in the Sand Trap and Other Misadventures on the Golf Tour*, Lee Trevino tells us: "Youngsters tend to emulate the players, and if they see us playing matches with one club, they'll start doing it, too. And that's really the best way to learn to play the game. If you're allowed only one club you will have to create a tremendous number of different shots with it. It's the best way for youngsters to learn finesses on the course and to develop a tremendous feel around the greens."

CONSIDER RECEPTIVENESS OF THE GREEN

There are several factors to consider when working out how best to play an approach shot. Sweden's Liselotte Neumann first checks the lie of the ball and the strength and direction of the wind and how receptive the putting surfaces are before deciding how far she wants to hit the ball.

RELEASE CLUB WITH BODY NOT HANDS

European Tour Professional Niclas Fasth believes that turning the shoulders through impact is the best way to square the clubface to the ball. He says that if your shoulders stop turning, your hands take over through impact and this makes it difficult to accurately control distance.

◉ THINK "ONE, TWO, THREE" TO IMPROVE TEMPO

The ideal state when playing golf is to have a clear mind when making your swing. However, a simple tempo thought is fairly harmless. The 2001 USPGA champion David Toms slowly counts "one, two, three" in his head to maintain his tempo.

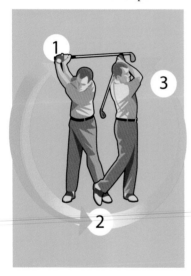

◉ ALWAYS PLAY WITHIN YOURSELF

Most amateur golfers swing at full speed on each and every shot, while the tournament pro probably swings at no more than 80 percent effort. Tony Jacklin claims that, when he won the Open Championship at Royal Lytham in 1969, he swung the club smoothly and easily with his driver on the 18th hole and hit a perfect tee shot.

◉ DISTANCE YOU HIT VARIES FROM DAY TO DAY

Arnold Palmer says he has played the Latrobe Country Club more often than any other course in America—"thousands of times, I guess," he reveals in *My Game and Yours*, "and naturally a lot of my tee shots have landed in more or less the same general area. But I don't always use the same iron for my second shot. Even if I played the same course every day and every tee shot landed in the exact same spot, I'd switch irons from time to time, depending on how I felt. Some days, when the club felt nice and light in my hands, I might use a 5-iron. The next day I might use a 4-iron, even a 3-iron."

◉ HIT BALL WITH LESS EFFORT WHEN TIRED

Every golfer gets a little tired toward the end of an 18-hole round. The best way of dealing with fatigue is not to attempt to hit the ball harder, but accept that you cannot hit the ball as far and change your club selection strategy. Arnold Palmer believes that you should reduce the length of your backswing to make it more compact and effective, while at the same time playing as though you were ten years older.

◉ THE THREE YARDAGES YOU NEED TO KNOW

"Many golf courses these days have the yardages etched onto sprinkler heads at various points in the fairway," says Per-Ulrik Johansson, a PGA Tour professional, "yet is distance to the front of the green, the middle or the back? Chances are you probably don't know. Always check in the pro shop before you go out to play to find out what the yardages refer to. The distance from the front to the back of the green can be 40 or 50 yards at times— the difference between hitting a 7-iron and a 3-iron, so it's important to know where you stand."

◉ MAXIMIZE CLUBHEAD SPEED AT RIGHT MOMENT

Lee Trevino famously once remarked that, if he could bottle

Accuracy & distance
Let youngsters hit the ball hard **44**
Land the ball on top of the flag **87**

Strategy
Safety first from pot bunkers **170**
Remove flag when chipping **199**

Swing theory
Complete the backswing **36**
Start downswing from the ground up **42**

70

clubhead speed and sell it in pro shops, he'd make more money than Mr Coca-Cola, Mr Jack Daniel's and Ms Chanel No. 5 put together. Trevino says that you can swing with enough power to launch the ball over 300 yards and still struggle to reach the end of the tee box or, alternatively, nail a drive but in the wrong direction. Clubhead speed is worthless unless the clubface is applied squarely to the ball at impact.

MOVE BALL CLOSER AT ADDRESS

When you need to hit a higher or lower shot than normal, Tom Watson says that you must move the ball an inch or so closer to your body, otherwise you'll hit the ball on the toe of the club.

DON'T OVERESTIMATE YOUR WEDGE DISTANCE

One of the main reasons why many amateurs fail to reach the greens with one of their wedges in their hands, according to Tommy Horton, is that they overestimate how far they can hit a full wedge shot.

SWING STEEPLY FROM A DIVOT

To dislodge the ball from a depressed lie such as a divot or hollow in the fairway, the club

must attack the ball from a steep angle. Arnold Palmer says that you can achieve this by keeping more weight than normal on your front foot during the whole swing. Consequently, you pick the club up steeply on the backswing and hit down steeply through impact.

HIT THE DRIVER OFF THE DECK

Many amateurs believe that hitting the driver off the fairway is a specialist shot that only pros can master. However, Phil Mickelson claims that the only amendment you need to make to your technique is to move the ball slightly forward in your stance to impart a little extra loft, and so get the ball into the air and start it rolling toward the target.

CLUB CAREFULLY ON LARGE GREENS

In *Jack Nicklaus' Playing Lessons*, the great man himself tells us: "Many amateurs regularly place themselves in three-putt territory simply by neglecting to assess pin placement in relation to the depth of the green. Big greens—and particularly long greens—seem to be a feature of modern course design, and they can make putting extremely demanding unless you pick the right club on approach shots … club yourself poorly and you'll be working on a lot of monster putts."

PLACE PRIORITY ON YOUR WOODS

Ben Hogan splits the game into three categories: woods, irons, and putts. Although he says each is equally important, if he had to single one out it would be the fairway wood and driver shots.

IMPROVE DIET TO MAINTAIN ENERGY

European Tour Professional Nick Dougherty says he used to run out of energy over the closing holes of a round of golf. He believes this was due to dehydration and poor diet. Now he eats more healthily and drinks water while playing and says that he still feels fresh when he walks off the 18th green.

MAKE YOUR PRACTICE SWING WORK FOR YOU

"A practice swing isn't just for exercise or to loosen the muscles prior to hitting a shot," says the PGA pro Keith Wood. "Its purpose is to prepare you for the real thing. In reactionary sports, such as tennis, you don't have the luxury of being able to rehearse your technique before hitting each shot, so make sure that you maximize this opportunity on the golf course. The main thing to remember is that your practice swing should have a focus. If you simply make meaningless swings, you're wasting a golden opportunity to improve your score."

HAZARDS IN FRONT OF THE GREEN

On the majority of holes, most of the trouble, such as bunkers, water hazards, ditches, and rough, are located in front of the green. In these cases, it is far better to be long than short with your approach shot, so make your club selection accordingly.

WALK IN LINE WITH THE BALL AND THE TARGET

Walk to your ball in the fairway along the ball-to-target line as soon as possible. This gives you extra time to survey the hole and assess your next shot prior to arriving at your ball. You will also benefit from the wider perspective that this gives you.

DON'T TRY TO FADE YOUR SHORT IRONS

Avoid trying to shape the ball with your short irons—anything from an 8-iron to a lob wedge—because the extra loft on the faces of these clubs will override the side spin that causes the ball to curve in the air.

CONTROL SHORT-IRON DISTANCE WITH ARMS

Tiger Woods says that, while you can squeeze extra yardage out of the longer clubs in your bag, you should never try to force an extra 10 or 20 yards out of your wedges. Tiger warns against hitting short irons with an overly aggressive swing.

STRIKE IRONS WITH BOTTOM OF CLUBFACE

To help ensure you make good contact with your irons, Johnny Miller suggests that you aim to catch the ball on the third groove up from the bottom of the club.

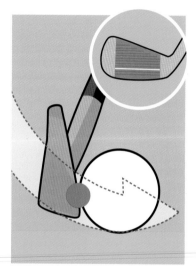

EXPECT TO MAKE MISTAKES

Walter Hagen admits that he's never played a perfect 18 holes. As he knows he will make some mistakes—he reckons on about seven a round—he doesn't worry about one bad shot.

CHOOSE THE CLUB THAT WILL HIT THE GREEN

When you're in between yardages is it better to hit the shorter club harder or the longer club more gently? Annika Sorenstam believes that the answer depends on where the

Equipment
Determining correct club length **13**
Keep ball dry for as long as possible **210**

Swing theory
Don't keep your head down **35**
Launch off right foot in the downswing **39**

flagstick is located on the green. For example, if the pin is cut on the front edge of the green, it is more sensible to take the longer club and hit past the hole. If the pin is at the back of the green, hitting the shorter club removes the risk of firing over the back of the putting surface and into trouble.

NEVER SWING FLAT OUT WITH A WEDGE

"The last club in the bag that you should ever think about hitting hard is the sand wedge," recommends Pierre Fulke, a PGA European Tour professional.

MOVE BALL BACK IN THE STANCE TO HIT IT LOW

Although you will need to move the ball back in your stance to hit a lower shot, Tom Watson urges you to remember that,

when you reduce the effective loft on the shot, the angle of the clubface changes too. Always double-check the clubface aim at address after altering your normal stance and ball position.

COMMIT, DON'T STEER

Gary Smith, another PGA professional, has this advice: "Whatever state your game is in or how nervous you are, always commit yourself to the shot and release the clubhead. Never ease up through the ball or attempt to steer it down the fairway. Golf is a game where you naturally accelerate. Slowing down rarely improves your accuracy: it just throws your timing out, creates unnecessary tension in your body and nine times out of 10 leads to even worse shots."

NEVER RELY ON BEST SHOT TO CLEAR WATER

"When a water hazard guards the front of the green, you have the option of laying up short or playing over it," says the PGA pro Keith Wood. "Regardless of which decision you make, you must know how far it is to reach the water and, also, how far it is to clear the hazard. If you're going to lay up, make sure that you don't leave the ball right at the water's edge since that will heap even more pressure on your

shoulders. If you go for the carry, don't rely on your best shot to make it. Always try to make it a comfortable shot, not one that's right at the limit of the club in your hand."

GET AS MUCH INFORMATION AS YOU CAN

During a recent Ryder Cup match, Bernhard Langer asked his playing partner Colin Montgomerie to give him the yardage to the green from a sprinkler head in the fairway. When Monty told him the yardage, Montgomerie claims that Langer asked if the yardage was from the front or back of the sprinkler head! Langer denies the story, but Montgomerie maintains that it is true.

NEVER FORCE A SHOT INTO THE WIND

Paul Foston, an English PGA professional, says that it is much easier to take two clubs more and swing very easily into the wind because the reduced swing speed keeps the ball low.

DON'T SWING AT FULL SPEED

The world's top golfers usually swing at around 80 percent of their full capacity on any given shot, including drives. This enables them to retain control of the ball for maximum accuracy.

Royal St. George's England

18TH HOLE, PAR-4, 468 YARDS

THE ULTIMATE CHALLENGE

Built on an enormous tract of land and littered with deep, cavernous bunkers, sunken sand traps, humps, hollows, and a plethora of blind approach and tee shots—not to mention testing prevailing winds—Royal St. George's at Sandwich, Kent, on the south coast of England is a tough and uncompromising links that doesn't give an inch in any quarter. Alongside Carnoustie, it is regarded by many observers as one of the toughest challenges in championship golf.

If there is one course that fits the image of a classic windswept and foreboding links, Royal St. George's has to be it. With undulating fairways, massive sand hills, heavy rough, and numerous blind shots, every stroke has to be carefully calculated and executed. The setting is superb, occupying a huge tract of land and enjoying a luxurious sense of spaciousness. As you progress around the course, you are often isolated from the rest of the golfers, hidden away in your own private valley of dunes and hollows.

Even the game's top players have struggled to come to terms with the demands that this often brutal golf course places on a player's technique and mental resilience. In the 1981 Open Championship, Jack Nicklaus shot an 83—his highest ever round in the event—as Bill Rogers was the only competitor to break par. Four years later, in 1985, Nicklaus missed the cut and Sandy Lyle won with a finishing score of two over par. However, eight years later, in 1983, a rain-softened St. George's yielded a little and Greg Norman produced one of the finest displays of shotmaking ever seen in an Open Championship when he posted a

PRO-FILE
GREG NORMAN

It's all about confidence

Jack Nicklaus once described Greg Norman as a better shotmaker than Seve Ballesteros. The pair first played together in the Australian Open in 1976, where the 21-year-old Australian topped his opening drive and shot an 80. However, a pep talk from Nicklaus afterward convinced Norman that he had what it takes. After all, it was only five years earlier, at the relatively old age of 16, that Norman had first struck a golf ball. Norman has been a great player over four different decades and confidence has always been his trump card. Totally convinced of his ability, as soon as he started to play he had a burning ambition to be the best golfer in the world, an ambition he was never afraid to state publicly.

Norman's first Open Championship victory came at Turnberry in 1986, where his second-round 63 in gale-force wind and rain was described by Tom Watson as "the greatest round ever played in a tournament in which I was a competitor". Norman's piercing iron play was the foundation of his victory, as it was in the 1993 Open Championship at Royal St. George's, where a stunning 64 set him on his way to his second major title.

record-breaking total of 267, 13 under par.

Heading into the final round, Nick Faldo was at the top of the leader board, a shot clear of Norman. Also within striking distance were many of the game's greatest players at the time, including Bernhard Langer, Nick Price, Ernie Els, Fred Couples and Payne Stewart. However, Norman blitzed the course with a closing round of 64 to finish two strokes ahead of Faldo and three ahead of Langer. Norman's final round of 64 will be remembered, alongside his second-round 63 at Turnberry in 1986, as his best ever in the major championships.

The 18th at Royal St. George's is one of the toughest finishing holes in major championship golf. Out-of-bounds runs all the way down the right and a bunker dominates the middle to left side of the fairway. The perfect drive is down the left, but most golfers will still face at least a 200-yard approach shot into a green protected on the right by bunkers and on the left by a sharp downslope.

7

Trouble Shots

Although most golfers would gladly play every shot from a perfect lie
in the center of the fairway, such is the nature of the game that it is
inevitable that from time to time—or perhaps even more frequently—
you will find your ball in a rather difficult situation. Fairways are
rarely dead flat and your ball has only to miss its intended landing
area by a few yards to find a tangled lie in the rough or be blocked
out by the trees. Even hitting the fairway is no guarantee of a perfect
lie. Old divots or nasty side slopes can cause problems for golfers.
However, a substantial part of the appeal of golf is working out ways
of playing recovery shots. Renowned specialists such as Seve
Ballesteros and Tiger Woods relish the challenge of a shot that is a
little out of the ordinary and get a real thrill out of evaluating the lie,
visualizing the shot, and then pulling it off successfully.

Scramble a good score

The ability to extricate yourself successfully from troublesome situations on the golf course is a hallmark of a good player. There are plenty of golfers who can post low scores on the days when they hit plenty of fairways and greens in regulation, but struggle when they are not quite so consistent. Tiger Woods is constantly top of the "scrambling" stats on the PGA Tour, which means that he is an expert at damage limitation.

MAKE A STEEP SWING IN THE ROUGH

"A most important fundamental of shots from rough is to contact the ball before hitting the turf," Gary Player recommends in *Gary Player's Golf Secrets*. "You should meet the ball with a sharply descending clubhead. An upright backswing, with the wrists breaking early, will help achieve this downward hit."

EXTEND DOWN SLOPE TO AVOID FAT AND THINS

If you are prone to catching the ball fat or thin, David Leadbetter recommends that you hit some practice shots off a downhill lie with a short iron and play the ball back in your stance. The downslope will encourage you to extend your follow-through low to the ground and also to transfer your weight correctly across to the left foot in the downswing.

TAKE A PITCHING WEDGE TO PLAY A WATER SHOT

"Two factors must come into play before I will attempt to hit a ball from the water," writes Seve Ballesteros in *Golf Tips from the Stars*. "First, at least half the ball must be visible above the water; second, I must be able to achieve a reasonably firm footing, when taking my stance. Then, to play the shot, I invariably choose a pitching wedge, because this club not

only has loft to lift the ball out of the water as swiftly as possible, but also because it has a sharp, leading edge which will obviously cut through the water better than a sand wedge. I position the ball well back in my stance, my hands significantly ahead, and then make a short, steep backswing before pulling the club down hard into a spot right behind the ball. Remember to put on those waterproofs, though!'

MOVE BALL BACK IN STANCE FOR ANY BAD LIE

Tiger Woods believes that if you are in any doubt as to your ability to hit a shot from a poor lie, you should play the ball further back in your stance.

CHOKE DOWN THE GRIP FROM SLOPING LIES

When playing from any kind of uneven lie, Julie Inkster tries to swing with the contour of the

---

Strategy
Don't swing until you're ready **25**
Keep the ball low **102**
Miss breaking putts on the "pro" side **128**

Swing theory
Rotate right forearm in takeaway **35**
Timing beats brawn **40**

Club selection
Never swing flat out with irons **68**
Clean strike key to fairway bunker success **81**

ground and allow the ball to curve naturally. She also chokes down on the club for control and abbreviates the length of her backswing to strike the ball more crisply.

🔘 AVOID WEDGES WHEN PLAYING FROM HARDPAN LIES
Tommy Horton recommends that, when playing from hardpan or a bare lie, you should avoid using a club with a wide or heavily flanged sole, such as a pitching or sand wedge, and instead use a club with a straighter-faced leading edge and thinner sole.

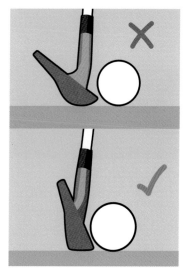

🔘 FADE THE BALL FROM A FLYER LIE
"Weather and wet ground conditions invariably produce "flyers"—shots that travel

farther but bite less quickly than normal, due to reduced backspin caused by moisture on the ball and clubface," notes Jack Nicklaus in *Jack Nicklaus' Lesson Tee*. "One obvious way to counteract this is to take less club, but a more sophisticated and reliable way is to fade the ball into the green. The extra height and spin resulting from a straight out-to-in cutting action will generally counterbalance the effects of a wet ball and clubface."

🔘 STAND TALL WHEN BALL IS ABOVE YOUR FEET
Because the ball is actually a little closer to your upper body when you are playing a shot with the ball above your feet, you must adapt your posture a little to compensate. Tiger Woods says that a really great tip he uses is to think of himself as standing tall throughout the swing. This is crucial in helping you keep your balance through the shot. Tiger also aims right of the target to allow for the fact that the ball will move from right to left from an uphill lie.

🔘 AIM RIGHT WHEN BALL IS ABOVE YOUR FEET
With a sidehill lie where the ball is above the level of your feet, you should always aim a little

right of the target, because the combination of the slope and the closed clubface at impact will cause the ball to fly to the left in the air.

🔘 IMPROVE FAIRWAY BUNKER PLAY IN STAGES
Tommy Horton recommends that you should improve your fairway bunker play in stages, starting with hitting the more forgiving lofted clubs out of the sand before progressing to the straighter-faced clubs.

🔘 STOP AT A 4-IRON FROM FAIRWAY BUNKERS
From a fairway bunker, Tiger Woods advises amateurs against using anything longer than a 4-iron unless the ball is lying perfectly on the sand and sitting up nicely.

◉ OPEN CLUBFACE SLIGHTLY FROM THE ROUGH

The grass will wrap itself around the clubhead and close the blade of the club when you are playing from the rough. Compensate for this effect by opening the clubface slightly at address.

◉ WIND ACCENTUATES THE SPIN

Julius Boros says in *Swing Easy, Hit Hard*: "Hitting against a wind accentuates the spinning action on the ball in all directions. Slices and hooks curve more and faster. By this same reasoning a hard ball hit with a crisp backspin will sometimes climb higher in the air than usual and may drop short of the target. When hitting any shot against the wind I use a longer club, shorten up on my grip a little, hit a little easier and let the wind stop the ball. The desire to hit harder against the wind should be suppressed. Swing normally."

◉ ALLOW FOR SIDESPIN ON A MUD BALL

A ball with a lump of mud stuck to it will not fly the same as a ball without! Working out what will happen to the ball's flight-path is critical to choosing the right club and the correct shot. Generally, the ball will fly left if the mud is on the right, and vice versa. This movement will be exaggerated if you put any spin on the ball. And then you have to work out how far the ball will fly! To help cope with this, Tiger Woods suggests you take more club than you would ordinarily take for the shot, and concentrate on making a softer swing to reduce the chance of putting unwanted spin on the ball.

◉ HIT GROUND SAME TIME AS BALL FROM HARDPAN

"From hardpan it is usually smarter to use a club without a definitely flanged sole—one that will cut under the ball instead of bouncing," says Doug Ford in *The Wedge Book*. "It is vital to hit the ball before, or at the same instant as, contacting the ground."

◉ TEE IT LOW DOWNWIND

Some time-honored advice comes from Ted Ray, writing in *The American Golfer Magazine* in 1924: "When the wind is with you, try a low tee. You will then find that a greater command is obtained over the ball. It will also rise high enough to add additional length, which might be expected with the wind's assistance."

WIND

◉ TAKE MORE LOFT OUT OF THE ROUGH

It is very difficult to generate backspin out of the rough because blades of grass get trapped between the ball and the clubface at impact. Because of this, it is advisable to use a more lofted club than you would normally use from a normal lie in the fairway.

Swing theory
Don't keep your head down **60**
Practice your putting rhythm **153**
Fingernails point at sky to cure a hook **178**

Accuracy & distance
Choke down on irons for ultimate control **66**
Calculate your pitching carry yardages **87**
Aim for the top of the flagstick **110**

Setup
Adjust stance in first practice swings **95**
Take a firm wide stance in the wind **168**

80

THREE STEPS TO PLAYING UNDER TREES

In *Jack Nicklaus' Playing Lessons*, the man himself gives us this piece of advice: "Playing from under tree limbs and other swing restrictors isn't as difficult as it might seem, given three conditions: First, acclimatize yourself to the feel of the restricted action by properly "measuring" it with plenty of practice swings. Second, forget the obstacle and concentrate on swinging as slowly and smoothly as possible. Third, prevent the anxious peeking that always wrecks these shots by really looking hard at the ball until it vanishes from sight. Also, don't give up in these situations too quickly even when there is no room to make any kind of normal backswing. I've saved many a stroke over the years simply by bumping the ball clear with my putter."

USE KNEES AS SHOCK ABSORBERS

When the ball is below your feet, Nick Faldo says that you should try to use your knees as shock absorbers to create a solid setup and also to ensure that your shoulders can turn back and through comfortably.

TAKE A SAFE DROP

This tip comes in a local rule of the Nyanza Club in British East Africa, quoted in *A Good Walk Spoiled*, by George Eberl: "If a ball comes to rest in dangerous proximity to a hippopotamus or crocodile, another ball may be dropped. At a safe distance, no nearer the hole, without penalty."

ADD WIND TO YOUR YARDAGES

"A headwind should be regarded as part of the golf course—just so many yards added to the hole," says Bobby Jones in *Bobby Jones on Golf*.

KEEP YOUR BALANCE ON THE SLOPES

Greg Norman tells us in *Greg Norman's 100 Instant Golf Lessons*: "You hear all sorts of advice about playing from hilly lies, but what it all comes down to is this: keep your balance. Do whatever you have to do to avoid falling forward, back, away from, and into the ball."

CLUB UP WHEN THE BALL IS BELOW YOUR FEET

"I use a lower-number club on a sidehill lie when the ball is below my feet in an effort to make up for the distance I'll lose because of the lie," writes Julie Inkster in *LPGA's Guide To Every Shot*.

USE YOUR IRONS OUT THE ROUGH

Chi Chi Rodriguez says that the sharper leading edge of your irons will cut through the thick grass in the rough far more easily than the more rounded fairway woods and trouble woods.

CLEAN STRIKE KEY TO FAIRWAY BUNKER SUCCESS

From a fairway bunker, Tiger Woods plays the ball further back in his stance and takes at least one more club than usual. He also chokes down on the club for extra control and makes sure that he has a solid footing. This helps him achieve a cleaner contact with the ball at impact.

Valderrama Spain

17TH HOLE, PAR-5, 536 YARDS

THE DO-OR-DIE APPROACH

Situated on the outskirts of the Sotogrande resort on Spain's Costa del Sol, Valderrama was the venue for the 1997 Ryder Cup and, until recently, hosted the lucrative season-ending Volvo Masters on the PGA European Tour. The owner, the Bolivian billionaire tin magnate Jaime Ortiz Patino, has spared no expense in transforming this former cork-tree plantation into one of the most immaculately maintained and challenging golf courses in the world.

Daunting dogleg tee shots, sloping fairways and lightning-fast, undulating greens combine to test a golfer's strategy, course management, technical skills, and temperament on almost every single hole at Valderrama. The course has been likened to Augusta National and, as with its more illustrious American counterpart, players cannot afford to take their foot off the mental pedal for a moment because even the slightest lapse in concentration can lead to disaster. In fact, many players have been critical of the extreme difficulty of the course, but such comments merely add to the appeal of what is easily the toughest layout in Europe.

The most infamous hole on the course is undoubtedly the par-5 17th, which was controversially redesigned by Seve Ballesteros prior to the Ryder Cup to make it more challenging and dramatic. For years, the hole played to an elevated green, but Ballesteros shortened the length slightly and added a pond in front of the green as well as a sharply shaved slope, which resembles the 15th hole at Augusta.

Length off the tee is obviously a prerequisite when you're attempting to get home in two on

PRO-FILE
SEVE BALLESTEROS

Imagination and inspiration can work miracles

Seve Ballesteros's introduction to golf was a 3-iron that his brother Manuel had given him as a present. With this club, he invented a huge variety of shots that bestowed enormous versatility on his game. Even today, it is still remarkable to watch the Spaniard give clinics, in which he conjures up all kinds of magical recovery shots. A child prodigy in a similar vein to Tiger Woods, Seve posted a score of 51 for 9 holes in his first caddies' tournament at age 10. Even more impressive, however, was the fact that he managed this despite taking a 10 at the first hole—a par-3. The following year, he came second with 42 and, at the age of 12, he won the 18-hole tournament with a 79.

Seve burst onto the world scene as a flamboyant 19-year-old, in 1976 , when he finished joint second with Jack Nicklaus to Johnny Miller in the British Open at Royal Birkdale. Seve led the tournament for three days and surprised everybody with a delicate chip between two bunkers to three feet of the pin, giving him a birdie on the last hole. Ben Crenshaw summed up Seve's genius perfectly when he said: "Seve plays shots that I don't even dream about."

a par-5, but the real challenge on the 17th begins with the second shot. The main problem is that the green is not deep enough to accept a long-iron or fairway-wood approach shot easily, and will leave a player facing a downhill chip or bunker shot that could easily roll right across the green and into the pond, while laying up to leave a full-wedge or 9-iron shot into the green leaves the golfer in danger of spinning the ball back into the water. In the 2000 American Express Championship, Tiger Woods struck two shots into the water on that particular hole after playing what he believed to be two perfect approach shots. Other players had similar problems. "I didn't know what to do. I didn't have that shot in my repertoire," said Nick Price. David Frost took a 10 after three balls wound up in the water.

Thomas Bjorn made a nine. In all, 11 out of 61 players made double bogey or worse. "You know it's bad when there are two ball marks on the green—and they're both yours," said Justin Leonard, whose approach spun back into the water.

Even the Europeans don't like the hole, particularly Colin Montgomerie: "I hate that hole. It still is, and will always be, a very controversial hole."

8

The
Scoring Zone

From anywhere within 100 yards of the flag, most of the world's
finest pros will be looking to land the ball within 10 feet of the
target. At the other end of the scale, many amateur golfers struggle
to retain a smooth rhythm when they have to make less than a full
swing and consequently their rhythm and timing suffer and affect
the quality of their ball striking. The key to consistent pitching is
maintaining a smooth tempo regardless of the length of the swing
required for any given distance.

Pitching perfection

Pitching is an area of the game where amateurs can improve dramatically and the benefits to your game are obvious when you consider that somewhere in the region of 70 percent of the shots in the average round of golf are played from within 80 yards of the green. Most golfers would knock plenty of shots off their handicaps if they could simply hit the green and then two-putt each time—a target that is within most players' capabilities.

KEEP THE GROOVES ON YOUR WEDGES CLEAN

Although the grooves on the clubface don't greatly affect the amount of spin you can generate from a tight, dry lie in the fairway, the club designer Roger Cleveland says that they will help you gain more control out of the rough and longer grass, which is why you should keep the grooves clear of mud, grass, and dirt.

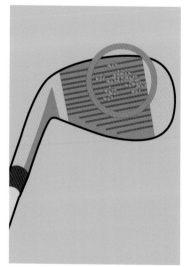

IMPROVE PLAY FROM 120 YARDS FROM HOLE

Dr. Bob Rotella tells us in *Golf is Not a Game of Perfect*: "Low scores depend on how well a golfer plays once the ball is within 120 yards of the hole … Everything that happens from the tee to that 120-yard range is almost insignificant compared with what happens thereafter. In fact, I'll occasionally tell a player that I don't care what he does with his long game— whether he focuses on a target and follows a routine or not—as long as he tries what I suggest about wedging, chipping, and putting."

AVOID EXCESSIVE BACKSPIN ON PITCH SHOTS

Like many top modern professionals, LPGA Tour pro, Hollis Stacy, says that she tries to avoid imparting too much backspin on the ball with her pitch shots because that makes it difficult to control distance accurately. She says that she likes her basic pitch shot to hop two or three times on the green and then stop quickly.

STEEPER BACKSWING LEADS TO BACKSPIN

"To assure backspin, keep your weight on the left foot and allow the forefinger and thumb of the right hand to play an active part in the swinging of the club," counsels Byron Nelson in *Winning Golf*. "This leads to the little additional wrist action, which tends to bring the clubhead up at a sharper angle on the backswing. The desired descending blow follows, producing the backspin."

SWING STEEP ON PITCH SHOTS

Henry Cotton says that once golfers learn to hit down and through the ball, the pitch shot no longer becomes a problem.

Accuracy & distance
Consider receptiveness of the green **69**
Vary length, not speed, or stroke **125**
Yardages are important **161**

Swing theory
Keep belt level for a better turn **41**
Give your swing a trigger **44**
The easier the swing, the better the strike **177**

Equipment
Clubs must suit the player **13**
Cover top of bag before putting umbrella up **214**

◉ LAND THE BALL ON TOP OF THE FLAG

"Most amateur golfers are over-cautious with pitch shots and leave the ball well short of the hole," says Paul Curry, PGA European Tour professional. "To counteract this problem, think about landing the ball on top of the flagstick rather than on the green. This simple piece of imagery will help you become more authoritative in your swing and enable you to land the ball closer to the target."

◉ WEDGES ARE EXTENSIONS OF YOUR OTHER IRONS

In *The Killer Swing*, John Daly advises: "Play your wedge pitches from the fairway just like you would your other short-iron shots. Just because these clubs aren't numbered, like your other irons, doesn't mean you need to play them any differently. Really, they are just extensions of your set of irons—they could just as easily be called a "ten-," "eleven-," and "twelve-iron," respectively. Thinking about them in this way might help you remember to make a full, normal swing when you are at or near your full distance to the hole with these clubs."

◉ CALCULATE YOUR PITCHING-CARRY YARDAGES

To find your pitching yardages hit five balls and monitor where they land. It's a good idea to hit into a practice green so that you can see the pitch marks. Your yardage is where the balls actually land, not finish. Tom Kite, who is probably the greatest wedge player ever, practices like this.

◉ GET AGGRESSIVE WITH WEDGES

"A long swing will encourage you to hit a more aggressive wedge shot and land the ball closer to the target," says John Daly in *The Killer Swing*.

◉ CONSISTENCY IS BETTER THAN SPIN

"One of the first lessons you learn as a pro," says Nick Dougherty, a PGA European Tour professional, "is to avoid backspin because it's difficult to control. I used to play the ball well back in my stance and make a short sharp swing hoping that the extra speed through impact would impart some spin. After watching Seve and Nick Faldo, I now play the ball further forward in the center of my stance and make a longer, more rhythmical swing—back and through. The improved tempo creates a better strike and I know that the ball will land on the green and then release toward the hole in exactly the same way each time."

◉ MASTER YOUR WEDGE SHOT

The short-game maestro Tommy Horton believes that the pitching wedge is the greatest asset to low scoring and, because of this, all golfers should learn to use the club correctly and practice with it until they feel totally confident with it standing over the ball.

SWING SHORT AND STEEP WITH SCORING CLUBS

According to Sandy Lyle, to make the most of your "scoring clubs," you need to make a shorter and more compact swing and concentrate on hitting down through the ball to generate the required loft on the shot from between 90 and 130 yards from the green.

MORE WRISTS FOR HEIGHT AND BACKSPIN

In order to create extra height and still carry the ball a reasonable distance on a full-length pitch shot, Jack Nicklaus breaks his wrists early on the backswing and then throws the club underneath the ball to increase the loft at impact. Properly executed, this flips the ball high with good backswing.

BETTER WEDGE PLAY IN JUST FIVE MINUTES

The PGA European Tour Professional, Chris Hanell, advises: "Once you have a reliable technique, you can enhance your distance control in just five minutes. I carry three wedges—a pitching wedge, sand wedge, and lob wedge. That gives me three 'basic' yardages. In addition, I have three lengths of backswing—hips, chest, and shoulder height—and three different grip positions too—low, middle, and high. If you do the math, you'll calculate that I have 27 different yardages, allowing me to attack the pin from anywhere between 62 and 106 yards. Although there's an occasional overlap between clubs, that still allows me to hit the same distance with a different trajectory."

PITCH OVER WATER—FOCUS ON BACK FRINGE

"On many of the new American-style courses, you'll often face an awkward pitch over water to reach the green on a par-5," remarks Gavin Ryan, a PGA professional in England. "In this situation, it's easy to let your nerves get the better of you. Here's how to overcome your anxieties:

• Select a club that will enable you to comfortably clear the water.
• Focus on the back of the green as your landing area.
• Now ignore the water completely and think only of your target.
• Grip the club more lightly than normal.
• Keep your backswing and follow-through the same length and pace.
• Commit to the shot."

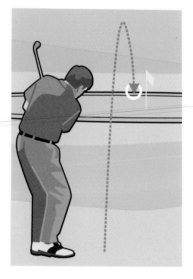

NARROW YOUR STANCE FOR A SLOWER SWING

Tom Kite, a senior PGA Tour professional, says: "Just as I'm a big proponent of having a wide stance to support a fast swing on full shots, I am a big believer that you don't want a wide stance when you're trying to hit

Strategy
Develop a host of short shots **103**
Keep regular stats and performance analysis **188**
Attack the course straightaway **205**

Setup
Rest tee peg on base of spine **27**
Chase the clubhead down the slope **96**

Swing theory
Remember the clubhead strikes the ball **35**
Rehearse hitting zone for better striking **186**

the ball a short distance with a slow, controlled arm swing. So, I encourage you to get your feet very close together. I also will open up my stance, which gets the right leg and right hip in the way of the backswing a bit, which limits my ability to take a long backswing."

FIND YOUR BEST YARDAGE WITH YOUR WEDGES

"The key is to find pitching clubs that you like the look of and then discover your "best lengths" with each one," writes Nick Faldo in *A Swing for Life*.

FIND MAXIMUM ACCURATE WEDGE DISTANCE

One of the first things you should do when learning to master your wedges is find out the maximum distance you can

hit your pitching wedge, sand wedge, and lob wedge accurately. Most golfers overestimate how far they hit these clubs.

AVOID HITTING FULL WEDGE SHOTS IN THE WIND

Wherever possible, avoid hitting pitching-wedge and sand-wedge shots in windy conditions. Playing a punch shot with your 8-iron and 9-iron will give you greater penetration into the wind while hitting the ball a similar distance to the full-out shot.

CHIP OR PITCH?

Harvey Penick offers advice on when to chip and when to pitch in *Harvey Penick's Little Red Golf Book*: "Always chip the ball if:
1. The lie is poor.
2. The green is hard.
3. You have a downhill lie.
4. The wind has an influence on the shot.
5. You are under stress.
Pitch the ball if:
1. The lie is good.
2. You have an uphill lie.
3. The green is very soft.
4. An obstacle is in the way."

CLOSE THE GAP IN YOUR WEDGES

Jim McLean has some advice on the question of wedge selection. He points out that there's a

critical gap between the distance you will get with your pitching wedge and your sand wedge, and if you don't have a suitable gap wedge in your bag you're going to find yourself sooner or later lining up a pitch or chip without the right club in your bag. Gap wedges come in a range of lofts and can help give you a greater choice of shots around the green.

THINK "STOMACH AND BUTTONS" FOR PITCHING

Nick Faldo likes to control his pitch shots with his upper body. Using a three-quarter length swing, he concentrates on turning his stomach away from the ball and then rotating his shoulders in the downswing so that he finishes with the buttons on his shirt facing the target.

SPLIT THE GREEN INTO QUARTERS

"From within 100 yards of the green, you should be looking for a good deal of accuracy with your approach shots," says Beverly Huke, a PGA professional. "To narrow your margin for error and to focus your mind more effectively, I recommend that you split the green into quarters and then aim to play to a specific quarter— usually, but not always, the one that contains the pin."

Pinehurst No. 2 North Carolina

16TH HOLE, PAR-5, 531 YARDS

PURSUE PITCHING PERFECTION

Pinehurst No. 2 in North Carolina is revered by purists as one of the world's finest and most traditional golf courses. It's softer on the eye than the more extravagantly designed modern courses, and lavish spectator mounds, man-made water features, and sprawling bunkers are replaced by towering avenues of pine trees and their rustic needles adorning the edges of the fairways, sweeping undulations, and upturned, gently contoured greens.

As with many of those who experience St. Andrews for the first time, it is often said that the first-time visitor to Pinehurst No. 2 often wonders what on earth all the fuss is about. The course is by no means visually spectacular and lacks many of the modern trimmings, such as island greens, huge undulating putting surfaces, and man-made water hazards. However, like St. Andrews, Pinehurst is living proof that a great course doesn't necessarily need glitz and glamor to make it great. Indeed, it is difficult to find a player who does not include the course in his or her list of personal top five favorites.

Ranked only behind Pebble Beach as the best golf course in the United States, Pinehurst is a test of the short game. The fairways are generally wide and generous and fairway bunkering sparse. However, when it comes to being on and around the greens, the course really bares its teeth. The small, crowned putting surfaces do not easily yield birdie putts and, if you are not skilled enough to land your ball within a five- or six-yard radius of the pin, you are highly likely to see it ferried away into either a bunker or a steep collection area.

PRO-FILE

TOM KITE

Shorten swing to strike more effectively

Tom Kite has never been a particularly long hitter, but he is renowned for the quality of his wedge play and is regarded as one of the world's best within 100 yards of the green. His proficiency in this area of the game contributed to his many PGA Tour victories and his success in the 1992 US Open at Pebble Beach. During the 1980s and the early 1990s, Kite was consistently in the top five on the Money List. He was a pupil of the great teacher Harvey Penick, who continually stressed the importance of developing and maintaining a sharp short game.

One of Kite's key pitching philosophies is to accelerate the clubhead through impact. In order to do that, the backswing must be slow, and short enough to strike the ball authoritatively without causing it to travel too far. Kite also focuses on ensuring that his follow-through is a little longer than his backswing. "Again, we want to swing the club with a slow enough pace that we can accelerate through the shot. I really like the idea of having the follow-through being longer than the backswing. If you have speed going through the ball, then you'll have a longer finish."

The most recent major championship staged at Pinehurst No. 2 was the 1999 US Open, which was won in dramatic style on the final green by the late Payne Stewart. Unlike many traditional US Open layouts, where a thick collar of rough circumnavigates each green, Pinehurst has its fringes shaved, allowing the players to contemplate the option of playing either a bump-and-run chip or a putt from the edges of the apron.

In dry, still conditions, the par-5 16th is easily reachable for many of the game's longer hitters, but for most amateurs it remains a three-shotter. The landing area for the second shot narrows considerably near the green and the smart play is to lay up between the one bunker on the left and the start of the cluster of greenside bunkers on the right to leave a full pitch into a long but narrow green. The green also has a ridge that effectively creates two separate targets. The slope rises gently on the front portion of the green and tilts to the rear at the back.

9

Around
the Green

There's a common misconception among most golfers that the
world's top players are so accurate that they hit every single fairway
and green. In fact, the most accomplished Tour professionals will,
on average, hit only around 13 or 14 greens in regulation. This
means that even the straightest hitters, such as Colin Montgomerie
and David Duval, will have to chip and putt to save their par at least
four or five times each round. So, if the world's top players often
have to rely on the quality of their short game to keep their score
going, imagine how important this is for the club golfer. The ability
to scramble around the greens will rapidly reduce your handicap
and take the pressure off your long game.

Touch, feel, and technique

A good short game is dependent on three factors—good technique, good feel for distance, and a good imagination. The world's best chippers, such as Seve Ballesteros, Jose Maria Olazabal, and Tiger Woods, not only possess exemplary technique, they also have the ability to conjure up a shot in their imagination and execute it successfully. If you can develop all three aspects, you're well on the way to mastering the short game.

LEARN THE SHORT GAME BEFORE THE LONG GAME

Many of the world's best exponents of the short game, such as Seve Ballesteros and Jose Maria Olazabal, learned to chip and putt before attempting the full swing. Bobby Jones spent many hours chipping and pitching shots to the 13th green at the Atlanta Athletic Club, then sinking the putts. "I don't remember any glimmering thought of form or any consciousness of a method in playing a shot," Jones wrote later. "I seemed merely to hit the ball, which is possibly the best way of playing golf."

PRACTICE SWINGS DEVELOP FEEL FOR SHOT

To improve your distance control and judgment of pace from off the green, make several practice swings while looking at the hole to develop your hand-eye coordination. This allows your brain to react instinctively to what your eyes see. Jose Maria Olazabal makes at least four or five rehearsals in his preshot preparation. Now recreate the same length and pace of your last practice stroke when playing the shot for real.

CHOOSE A CLUB WITH ENOUGH LOFT

Although many players advocate that you can chip with virtually every club in the bag, Ben Hogan advised that you should not go lower than a 4-iron as the long irons don't have enough loft. Hogan very rarely played any kind of chip shot with anything stronger than a 6-iron.

STRAIGHT LINE FROM LEFT SHOULDER TO BALL

The secret to successful chipping, according to Johnny Miller, is to create a straight line with your left arm and the club shaft at address and maintain that relationship throughout the shot. He believes this prevents you from creating unnecessary wrist action.

POSTURE IS IMPORTANT FOR CHIPPING, TOO

"Posture is rarely mentioned in connection with chipping or pitching," says Gary Smith, a PGA professional, "but it is vital for the short game as it allows you to strike the ball consistently each time, which is the key to improving your touch and feel around the greens. To lower yourself to the ball, create a nice angle in your lower back, and tilt yourself forward from your waist in exactly the same way that you would for a full shot."

Club selection
Hit the driver off the deck **71**
Hit a 3-wood downwind **168**

Swing theory
Head controls balance **36**
Straight left arm can cause problems **42**

Setup
Flare both feet slightly for extra control **34**
Build yourself a practice station **185**

⬤ SET HANDS 3 INCHES
AHEAD OF BALL
In *Play Better Golf with John
Jacobs*, the eponymous author
counsels: "There are two
essential points to work on
when preparing to chip, beyond
the standard preparations for
a golf shot. The first is to place
your weight predominantly on
your left side—"leaning" on
your left leg would aptly
describe it. The second is to
ensure that your hands are
leading the club—that they are
about three inches ahead of the
ball when you are in your final
address position."

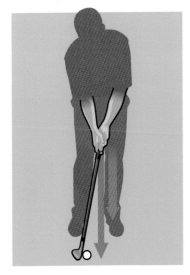

⬤ DEVELOP TECHNIQUE FIRST,
THEN TOUCH
Touch and feel are crucial
elements of a consistent short
game, yet you can achieve a

good feel for distance and an
accomplished touch only if you
first of all have a solid technique
to rely on. Only when you are
confident of how the ball will
react once it leaves the clubface
can you begin to develop your
judgment of pace and control.

⬤ USE A ONE-LEVER SWING
FROM SHORT RANGE
"From approximately 20 yards
and in, use a one-lever swing—
that is no wrists," Michele Conte
advised in *Golf for Women* in
December 2001. "The less
movement, the less room for
error. Think 'wristy is risky'."

⬤ ADJUST STANCE IN FIRST
PRACTICE SWINGS
Because of the variety of
different lies and distances that
you can expect to face around
the greens, you will encounter
plenty of shots that require an
adjustment to the grip, stance,
and ball position. Dr. Bob
Rotella recommends that you
familiarize yourself with the
changes in address position by
making several practice swings
before playing the shot.

⬤ CHIP CLOSE ENOUGH TO
ONE PUTT
"Chip and pitch shots are more
important for the weekend golfer,
who misses more greens than

does the touring pro," Gary
Player advises in *Gary Player's
Golf Secrets*. "I can think of no
quicker way to lower one's
handicap than the ability
consistently to chip close enough
for one putt instead of two."

⬤ PRACTICE LANDING ON
THE SPOT
After starting by visualizing
where he wants to land the ball,
Gary Player makes several
practice strokes next to the ball
to gradually enhance his feel for
the shot. With each of his
practice swings, he visualizes
the landing area and adjusts the
length of his swing to produce
the correct shot. Once he has
prepared fully for the shot, he
holds the image of the landing
area in his mind while playing
the chip for real.

TRY TO HOLE YOUR CHIPS
A simple change in attitude can improve your chipping dramatically. Rather than simply looking to get the ball close to the hole, think about holing the shot instead. This improves your focus and concentration and narrows your margin for error. Simply trying to get the ball fairly close can lead to sloppy execution of the shot.

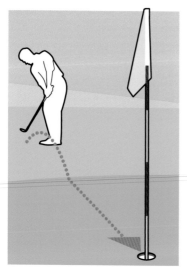

CHASE THE CLUBHEAD DOWN THE SLOPE
To avoid mishitting the ball off a downhill lie, set up with most of your weight on your front foot. Keep your weight there throughout the swing and make sure that the clubface remains as close as possible to the ground in the downswing and into the follow-through.

DON'T LET THE GOLF CART RUIN THE ART OF CHIPPING
Lee Trevino believes that golf carts have helped ruin the art of chipping and pitching because golfers often park a considerable distance away from the green and take a selection of clubs to the green. If they are the wrong choice, instead of walking all the way back to the cart to replace them, the golfer will play the shot with the wrong club. Given the choice of walking or riding, take the walking option, as Trevino's philosophy applies to the long game, too.

HOW TO CHOKE DOWN ON CLUB CORRECTLY
Luther Blacklock, a PGA professional in England, advises on how to maintain your body position: "A common error is allowing your posture to become slumped when you choke down on the grip for extra control over a chip. To maintain good posture, slide the clubhead toward your feet so that the shaft angle becomes more upright. Now you can grip further down the handle of the club without losing your body angles."

ALLOW WRISTS TO "GIVE"
Although it is advisable to keep your wrists out of the chip shot, there is nothing wrong with allowing them to soften a little in response to the momentum of the clubhead. The Irishman Darren Clarke believes that a slight hinge of the wrists on the backswing can inject feel and rhythm into the shot, as long as your hands then go on to lead the club through impact.

GET INTIMATE WITH A WEDGE
From just off the edge of the green, most of the world's top players will be looking to hole the shot. John Daly believes that the secret to holing your share of chips is to get intimate with one particular club and practice with it until you feel confident that you could even get the ball close to the pin blindfolded or with your eyes shut.

Accuracy & distance
Pace off your long putts **132**
Practice long-range putts before first tee **154**
Make it your goal to putt past the hole **213**

Strategy
Study your partners' putts **131**
Control your own game **142**

Swing theory
Swing within yourself **36**
Bad putters move their heads and bodies **176**

WOMEN SHOULD BE MORE LIKE MEN ON GREENS

In *Gary Player's Golf Secrets*, Player says: "Women seem to have a physical advantage over men when it comes to the short game. They have a much more sensitive touch—if properly developed—around the green. It's a shame that so often they waste this talent by trying to be ladylike."

USE PUTT-CHIP FOR ULTIMATE CONSISTENCY

"Nowadays, any time I'm within 15 yards of the green with a decent lie and a clear path to the pin, I'll chip using my putting technique," says Zimbabwean-born Tony Johnstone in *Master Your Short Game*. "By that I mean I hold the club with my reverse overlap putting grip, adopt my normal putting stance and place my hands a fraction ahead of the ball, just as I would if I was addressing a putt on the green."

HIT SHORT SHOTS HARD

"Acceleration through impact is as vital to the short game as it is with your longer irons and woods," opines Greg Norman in *Greg Norman's 100 Instant Golf Lessons*. "It is the only way to put proper backspin on these shots, for maximum control. So be crisp and aggressive on even your shortest shot, leading the clubhead with your hands as you make a descending hit on the ball."

PUTT WITH A LONG IRON FROM THE FRINGE

From just off the green, in most instances, it is easier and safer to putt the ball to the hole, using a putter or one of your straight-faced irons. The reduced loft on the clubface will get the ball running to the hole.

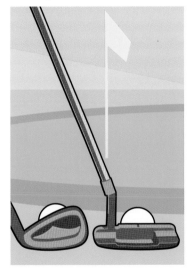

GOOD SHORT SHOTS BETTER THAN GOOD LONG ONES

Good short shots are extremely beneficial to your game. On an average length par-4, you can hit a good drive, followed by a good approach shot and still struggle to make par. If you make a mistake with any of the next shots you can still make a bogey or worse. On the other hand, you can hit a drive into the rough and a sloppy approach and still save your par with an excellent chip or pitch that stops next to the hole.

PUSH HANDS FURTHER FORWARD FROM A BARE LIE

From a scrappy or bare lie on hard ground it is vital that your hands remain ahead of the ball through impact. To ensure that this happens, push your hands slightly further forward toward the target at address than normal. As you play the shot, make sure that your hands return to the same position at impact as they occupied at address.

POSITION SHIRT BUTTONS AHEAD OF BALL

"One of the secrets to playing the chip shot well consistently is the ball position," says Jonathan Yarwood, a PGA professional who teaches at the David Leadbetter Golf Academy in Florida. "If you are in any doubt as to whether you have the ball far enough back in your stance, hang a club from the buttons on your polo shirt. If the shaft is ahead of the ball, you're in perfect position."

KEEP HANDS OUT OF CHIP SHOT FOR CONSISTENCY

Most badly struck chip shots are caused by excess hand and wrist action during the stroke. Don't allow your wrists to break when you hit a chip shot. Control the swing with your arms and shoulders and keep your hands and wrists out of the shot.

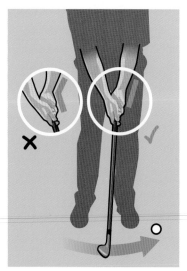

CHIP AND ONE-PUTT FOR SUCCESS

"The answer is a strong short game," maintains Gay Brewer in his book *Score Better Than You Swing*. "I know that if I didn't have one I wouldn't have won the Masters in 1967. I hit the ball pretty well most of the time, but I won because on the last day I chipped and one-putted 10 times during my 67—and won by one shot."

KNOW YOUR CARRY/ROLL RATIOS

In order to become an accomplished chipper you will need to know how each club in your bag performs. Assuming that you make the same length of swing with each club, your sand wedge will spend 90 percent of the time in the air and only 10 percent on the ground, while your 4-iron will spend 10 percent of the time in the air and 90 percent on the ground. Your 7-iron will carry about 50 percent of the way and then roll along the ground for the remaining 50 percent of the distance.

USE THE LEAST LOFTED CLUB POSSIBLE

While Ben Hogan avoided using the straighter-faced clubs for chipping, Lee Trevino believes you should use the least lofted club possible. He maintains that the extra roll on a mid-to-long iron enables you to reduce the length of your swing and thereby reduce your chances of mishitting the ball. According to Trevino, a short and compact chipping action with a 4-iron is a far more effective way to cover 40 or 50 feet on the green than making a longer and wristier swing with a pitching wedge or sand wedge.

DEVELOP A HOST OF SHORT SHOTS

Contrary to what you may think, the world's top players spend more time working on their short game than their full swing. Nick Faldo uses this time to experiment and develop a whole assortment of short-range scoring shots for every eventuality.

TOSS BALLS TO IMPROVE YOUR FEEL

Greg Norman was a talented enough player to become one of the world's top golfers, despite the fact that his short game never quite matched the quality of his impressive ball-striking. One day he decided to teach himself how to chip by spending a day tossing balls onto a practice green and watching how each one reacted once it hit the ground.

Setup
Get fussy with clubface alignment **104**
Set weight on front foot for long punch **169**

Swing theory
Use your feel to square the blade at impact **36**
Lower body controls shape of the shot **41**

Equipment
Line up putts without ball in rain **210**
Constantly check your spikes **215**

READ YOUR CHIPS LIKE PUTTS

The PGA Tour professional Frank Nobilo tells us that all the top golfers of the world read their chip shots just as they do their putts, adding: "Once the ball lands on the green and begins to roll it behaves exactly like a putt, so you should allow for any contours and break around the hole if you want to get the ball close consistently. It's easy to think that you are playing the ball back in your stance for a chip shot when in actual fact you could be doing the opposite. When your feet are open to the target, it is easy to think that the ball is further back than it actually is. To check if you are setting up correctly, take your normal chipping stance and then without moving your heels swivel your toes so that they point straight out in front of you. The ball should be played opposite your right heel."

STICK TO YOUR CHIPPING METHOD

The majority of top players judge their chip shots by looking at the overall distance from the ball to the target. However, a few prefer to pick out a landing area just a few feet onto the green, focus their attention purely on that spot, and think of it as their target. According to the golf psychologist Dr Bob Rotella, the first method is preferable, but, if you are going to spot-chip, make sure that you commit to that method every time for consistency.

KEEP CHIPPING SIMPLE

One key principle that all of the top players adhere to in the short game is never to play a complicated shot when a simple one will do the job. Just as a top striker in football will never attempt an elaborate maneuver when a simple tap-in is all that's needed, good players will take the opportunity to play a straightforward chip rather than a fancy lob shot wherever possible.

PUNCH, DON'T SCOOP

The most common and destructive chipping fault of them all is trying to scoop the ball up into the air with your hands through impact. To prevent this from happening, set up with most of your weight on your front foot and with your hands ahead of the ball. As you make your swing, simply think about recreating your address position at impact. This will ensure that you punch the ball forward.

HANDS REMAIN LEVEL OR AHEAD OF CLUBFACE

According to Harvey Penick, the most important chipping fundamental is to keep your hands ahead of, or level with, the clubhead through impact and into the follow-through.

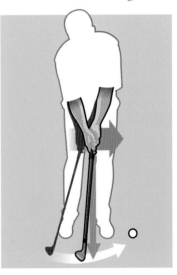

INCREASE NUMBER OF PRACTICE SHOTS NEAR HOLE

The number of practice swings or strokes that you make prior to playing a shot should increase the nearer you get to the hole. You may need to make only one practice swing before hitting an approach shot from the fairway, for example, but you should spend more time on practice swings as you move into the key scoring zone from within 70 yards of the green as this will enhance your feel.

⬤ LEAVE THE FLAG IN WHEN CHIPPING

The decision whether to have the flag left in or taken out when chipping from just off the edge of the green presents a huge dilemma for many golfers. Fred Couples is of the opinion that it is better to leave the flag in because it can stop the ball from running too far past the hole or even allow it to drop in the cup. If you leave the flag out, the speed has to be perfect for the ball to drop in.

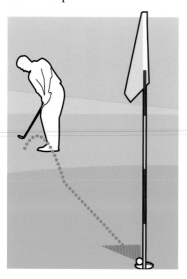

⬤ PUTT-CHIP FOR MORE CONTROL

"For greater short-range control or when faced with a shot onto a green that slopes sharply downhill, many top players will play a putt-chip, which is basically a putt using an iron,"

says Simon Holmes. "To play this shot correctly, take your putting stance and posture, hold the club with your putting grip and then raise your hands at address to recreate the more upright lie of the putter. To really "soften" the strike, address the ball out of the toe of the clubface. Now when you make your putting stroke, you will strike the ball out of the 'dead' part of the clubface and you will take the pace out of the shot."

⬤ A FORWARD DEFENCE STROKE FOR SOLID CONTACT

"A good swing image to hold in your mind when playing a chip shot is of a forward defensive stroke in cricket, where your weight moves forward and your hands remain ahead of the bat as you strike the ball," counsels Damien Tudor, a PGA professional. "The same principle applies to a chip shot. Your weight should be on your front foot at the point of impact and your hands ahead of the ball."

⬤ STRIKE BALL ON DOWNSWING FROM A BAD LIE

"Generally speaking," says Lee Trevino in *Swing My Way,* "the worse your lie, the more important it is to contact the ball on your downswing rather than

at the very bottom of your swing arc. If the ball sits down in heavy grass or rests on relatively bare ground, the worst thing you can do is hit the ground behind it. Therefore you must "trap" the ball with your clubhead on your downswing before it has a chance to dig into the grass or cut into the ground."

⬤ WHEN TO CHIP OR PITCH?

Differentiating between a chip shot and a pitch shot can be confusing for many golfers. It's almost impossible to base the decision on yardage since you can play pitch shots from 20 yards out and chip shots from 40 yards away from the green—and, of course, vice versa. A chip becomes a pitch shot when your wrists start to hinge and your hands pass waist height on the backswing.

Strategy
Putt inside the dustbin lid **133**
Treat long par-4s as par-5s **162**

Swing theory
Coordinate shoulder and chin in the swing **41**
Practice fundamentals **189**

Setup
Widen your stance for stability **113**
Set hips in concrete for a stable stroke **122**

⦿ STEEP ATTACKS LEAD TO CRISP CHIPS
A fairly steep attack into the ball allows you to squeeze the ball between the clubface and the turf at impact for a crisp strike with a little check spin. A good way to groove this steeper attack when practicing is to place an umbrella or a golf shaft three inches behind the ball and hit some shots. If your club catches the umbrella or shaft on the downswing, either your angle of attack is too shallow or you are trying to scoop the ball into the air.

⦿ USE STRAIGHT-FACED CLUB UNDER PRESSURE
Harvey Penick gives this advice in *Harvey Penick's Little Red Golf Book*: "Under pressure around the green, always go to the straightest blade that will do the job. It may require a 3-iron to get the roll you need."

⦿ MAKE A BRISK SWING FROM A BARE LIE
To chip the ball off a bare lie, play the shot in exactly the same way you would a normal chip, but increase the tempo of your swing slightly. This gives you the best possible chance of keeping your hands ahead of the ball through impact and striking the ball crisply.

⦿ USE A FAIRWAY WOOD FROM A HARDPAN LIE
In *Golf for Women* in December 2001, Debbie Doniger wrote: "When your ball settles on hardpan near the green, the key is to hit the ball first so you don't dig your club into the ground. You could choose an iron but you'll probably get a cleaner hit with a fairway wood."

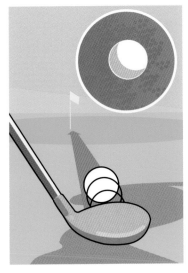

⦿ QUALITY OF SHORT GAME DETERMINES SCORE
Like many top professionals, Nick Faldo is convinced that the quality of his short game from within 125 yards of the green determines how well he plays and scores in a tournament. When he's chipping and putting well, he expects to get up and down in two to save pars and make birdies with sharp pitch shots on par-5 holes. If he is not so good around the greens, the loose shots add up quickly and affect his scoring dramatically.

⦿ IDENTIFY LANDING AREA THEN FORGET HOLE
Once you have visualized how you want to play a chip shot to your satisfaction, and have selected your club, pick out a target area on the green where you want to land the ball, then forget about the hole completely. Make your target landing zone on the green as small as possible for maximum accuracy. As you play the shot, concentrate purely on landing the ball on your chosen spot.

⦿ SHORT GAME MORE IMPORTANT THAN DRIVING
"Pros get together and they talk about one another's putting strokes, what kind of putter this guy is experimenting with, and so forth," Gay Brewer writes in *Score Better Than You Swing*. "They don't talk about who's driving the ball 280 yards all the time. It doesn't make that much difference whether you're hitting it 230 or 280, and if your short game's good enough it doesn't make as much difference as you'd think whether you put your drives smack down the middle of the fairway."

ALWAYS LAND THE BALL ON THE GREEN

When you are planning your chip shot, always have the goal in mind of carrying the ball over the fringe or rough and onto the putting surface. You can never be sure how the ball will react if it lands in the longer grass, but you can predict how it will bounce and roll if it lands on the green. Use the club that will enable you to land the ball about four or five feet onto the green and then roll out to the rest of the way to the hole.

TAKE A LESS LOFTED CLUB ON AN UPSLOPE

The most important thing to remember when chipping from an uphill lie is that the slope will act as a launching pad and add loft to the shot. To hit the ball

the same distance as you would from a flat lie, you will need to take a less lofted club. You should also remember that the ball will still fly high and stop quickly once it lands on the green.

PRACTICE YOUR CHIPPING FOR REAL

The ELPGA Tour professional Marie Laure de Lorenzi says: "Most golfers' idea of practicing their chipping is simply to hit lots of shots around the green. However, unless you hole out after hitting each chip you never find out how good you really are. The best way to practice your chipping is to hole out after every shot. This will give you instant feedback on the quality of your chipping and your short-range putting."

TAKE MORE LOFT IN LOW GRASS

"If your ball has settled low in the grass, but still rests on grass, expect a low-flying shot," warns Arnold Palmer in *The Arnold Palmer Method*. "Chip with a more lofted club to get height and to dig the ball out easily. Conversely, a ball that sits up high in the grass will be a high-flyer, so it's wiser to chip with a less lofted club to cut down the height."

KEEP THE BALL LOW

Always putt if you can putt. Chip if you can't putt. Pitch if you have no other option around the green. The safest shot is always the lowest shot.

TRUST CLUBFACE TO LOFT BALL INTO AIR

Johnny Revolta writes in *Tips From the Top*: "When it comes to chip shots it seems that practically every golfer has an inborn fear he won't give the ball enough loft. He wants to see that ball travel in a high arc, so he sets his weight back on the right leg and makes a jerky swing with his hands back of the clubhead at the moment of impact … To correct these faults, first make sure your left wrist is straight and on a line with the shot."

Equipment
Match your clubs to the course **154**
Avoid touching metal on golf clubs **215**

Strategy
Practice your green-reading skills **193**
Play the course, not the man **205**

LEARN YOUR CHIPPING IMAGINATION

In order to become more creative in your shotmaking around the green, David Leadbetter recommends that you toss some balls underhanded to the hole to learn how the ball reacts from different speeds and trajectories. While you are doing this, make a note of where you need to land the ball in order for it to run out to the hole, and use this data to help you select the correct club and length of swing for real.

KEEP LEFT WRIST FLAT THROUGH THE SHOT

Getting your setup right is crucial to developing a successful chipping technique. Start by setting up with a narrow stance (about 12 inches from heel to heel), and open it slightly by withdrawing your left foot a little from the target line. Open your shoulders a little as well. Place your weight toward your left side and keep your hands in front of the ball to facilitate the downward strike that is necessary to make good contact with the ball. Play the ball well back in your stance, just inside your right foot. As you make the stroke, concentrate on keeping your left wrist as flat as possible, as it would be during your putting stroke.

MASTER VARIABLE FACTORS FOR BETTER CHIPPING

In *Bobby Jones on Golf*, Jones points out that: "A drive is nearly always a drive … But a chip may be anything, and it rarely is the same thing twice. Especially over keen greens, a man must be a good judge of slopes, and the speed of putting surfaces; he must also be keenly appreciative of the effect upon the roll of the ball to be had from the lie of the ball, the loft of the club and the trajectory of its brief flight."

LEAVE YOURSELF AN UPHILL PUTT

You need to plan your chip shots carefully in order to leave a simple putt for your next shot. Ben Hogan showed exemplary course management skills around the green by always trying to leave an uphill putt, where he could then roll the ball in positively up the slope. The last thing he wanted to do was leave a tricky downhiller.

WEAKEN YOUR GRIP FOR SOLID CHIPPING

The PGA professional Stuart Dowsett advises: "Weakening your grip by turning both hands to the left on the club so that just one knuckle is visible on your left hand but at least three can be seen on your right will improve your chipping. The weak grip forces you to cut across the ball at impact, which means it is almost impossible to stub the clubhead in the ground behind the ball and scuff the shot."

KEEP THE BALL LOW AND UNDER CONTROL

Wherever possible, always keep the ball low to the ground around the green. Playing the highflying shot may be more fun and look more impressive, but it is harder to judge, and the longer swing introduces more risk into the shot. A short and compact swing with a straighter-faced club is nearly always the best option when there are no obstacles blocking your route to the hole from off the green.

CHOKE DOWN ON GRIP TO SHORTEN STROKE

Enid Wilson tells us in *A Gallery of Women Golfers*: "It is surprising how few people ever bother to experiment with the simple run-up, but those who do take the trouble rarely regret it. There is nothing complicated about it. The length of the stroke is controlled by the position of the hands on the shaft, for it follows automatically that when the hands are near the bottom of the grip the stroke is restricted. Going down the grip is a detail that escapes many golfers, who try to control distance by checking the force of the downswing as the clubhead nears the ball—this being one of the best ways of guaranteeing a fluff."

SET SHAFT STEEPER AT ADDRESS FROM BAD LIE

When the ball is lying on hard ground with no grass underneath it to cushion the impact, it's a good idea to set the shaft of the club at a steeper angle than normal, so that your hands are higher and the heel the club rises off the ground a little. The reason for doing this is that the steeper shaft angle creates more of a "V"-shaped attack into the ball, enabling you to pinch the ball off the ground.

CHIP WITH ALL YOUR CLUBS

"I'm a great one for trying to keep things simple wherever possible," Tony Johnstone declares in *Master Your Short Game*. "Instead of having to manufacture a variety of shots with just one club to suit specific situations, I can concentrate purely on technique and then simply vary the club and the length of my swing to produce shots of different lengths and trajectories."

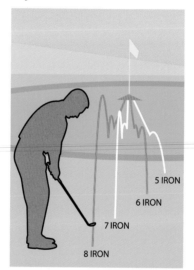

5 IRON
6 IRON
7 IRON
8 IRON

GET FUSSY WITH YOUR CLUBFACE ALIGNMENT

The PGA professional, Nick Bradley, comments: "Good chipping, like putting, starts with a careful alignment of the clubface. If you want to get the ball close to the hole, you need to read a chip shot in almost exactly the same way you would a putt. Look at the whole shot carefully—particularly around the hole where the ball will turn most as it slows down—and then aim the clubface according to the amount of break. Be very precise when you set the club behind the ball. Check and double-check while looking at the target that it's aiming where you want it."

CHIPPING FROM THE ROUGH, PLAY IT LIKE A BUNKER SHOT

Most amateurs dread a delicate chip from the rough, especially if the direction the grass is growing is against the clubface. The best advice is to imagine you are playing a bunker shot. So, open your stance a little, and lay the clubface more open than you would if you were chipping from a good lie. Take a long swing, and aim to make contact with the grass a couple of inches behind the ball. Concentrate on getting the clubhead through the ball.

NEVER STRIKE THE BALL ON THE UPSWING

If the ball is perched nicely on top of the grass, it is a far easier option to sweep it away by striking it at the base of your swing arc than to strike it on the upswing.

Club selection
Use 8- or 9-iron to reach back of green **110**
Adjust clubs according to greens **156**

Swing theory
The easier the swing, the better the strike **177**
Raise right heel for better ball-striking **193**

⬤ SHORTER BACKSWING, LONGER FOLLOW-THROUGH

One of the main causes of an inconsistent short game is decelerating the clubhead through impact. When the clubhead slows down through the hitting area, it is very easy for the hands to compensate by "flicking" at the ball, which will cause you to lose control over the strike and judgment of distance. As a general rule, it is preferable to make a slightly shorter backswing and a longer follow-through than the other way round.

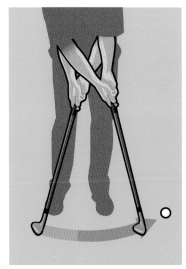

⬤ EXPERIMENT WITH CLUB SELECTION

Some top players prefer to chip with just one "favorite" club, since they believe this enhances their touch and feel, while other players believe you should match the club to the situation. Seve Ballesteros, for example, likes to play the majority of his chip shots with a 9-iron, but Tiger Woods will use anything from a 5-iron to a lob wedge. Try both methods and see which one works better for you.

⬤ MASTER THREE CHIPPING CLUBS

To take full control of your short game, Nick Faldo advises you practice with three key clubs— 6-iron, 8-iron, and wedge—and switch among them at random until you are confident of playing a variety of shots with each.

⬤ INJECT ARMS, WRISTS, AND LEGS INTO CHIPPING

Jim McLean has worked with some of the greatest chippers in the game and he has some interesting observations on how their successful techniques seem to be at odds with what's in the coaching manuals. Contrary to what many golfers will have been taught about keeping hands, wrists, and legs quiet or stiff, McLean says that players like Seve Ballesteros and Phil Mickelson often inject hand, wrist, and even some leg action, sometimes, into the shortest of chips. McLean says that the game's greatest short-game players most definitely do not play with stiff or rigid wrists, but rather will use soft arms and even some hands.

⬤ PRACTICE WITH A FRIEND

One of the best ways to sharpen up around the greens is to practice with a friend. Simply playing for the drinks in the clubhouse afterward will focus your attention, sharpen your concentration, and simulate a real-life, on-course situation.

⬤ LEARN FROM HOGAN

Lee Trevino says in *Swing My Way*: "In his heyday Ben Hogan probably hit more greens than any player in the history of the game. Yet, I'm told, he would practice short shots from off the green for hours on end, day after day. Isn't that interesting— and educational!"

Royal Birkdale England

6TH HOLE, PAR-5, 492 YARDS

DEALING WITH THE DUNES

Unlike the majority of the other golf courses on the Open Championship rota, Royal Birkdale is comparatively flat, with very few fairway undulations, blind-approach or tee shots, swales, slumps, and hollows. At times it does not play like a true links course, but nevertheless it remains a stern challenge with imposing sand dunes, heavy rough, and ditches. Past winners at Royal Birkdale include Arnold Palmer, Lee Trevino, Tom Watson, and Ian Baker-Finch—interestingly, no Europeans among them!

Royal Birkdale, on the northwest coast of England, is one of the most popular Open venues, especially among US golfers. Blind shots are few and far between and you are unlikely to see a straight drive kick sideways into a hidden pot bunker. This cultured links course is a more "what you see is what you get" proposition than the other venues that stage the world's most historic championship.

The course's most defining features are without doubt the giant sand dunes that flank the fairways and greens, creating imposing amphitheatres that separate the golfer from the eyes of the outside world. The stark contrast in color between the dusty dunes and the emerald fairways and greens creates a sharp definition and frame to each hole. The Birkdale greens are also less intimidating than those at other wind-strewn links courses, although they are known to dry out and speed up quickly during the summer. The breaks and borrows are difficult to read for the first-time visitor.

Dunes have been enhanced to provide stadium-style viewing for spectators and many of the holes have been remodeled over the years. Seve Ballesteros and Nick Faldo both made their

PRO-FILE
JOSE MARIA OLAZABAL

Close-range concentration and imagination

Spain's Jose Maria Olazabal is far from being one of the world's most powerful players and, in fact, is renowned for his occasional wildly inaccurate driving, yet he has still won two Masters at Augusta National—a course that traditionally plays into the hands of the longer hitters—and also 18 European Tour events during his career. Olazabal has an exquisite short game that he developed at an early age through pitching and chipping around the greens at the golf club in San Sebastián, in Spain, where his father was the greenkeeper. With only a handful of clubs at his disposal, Olazabal was forced to use his imagination to manufacture shots and it is this invention and versatility that has formed the foundation of his artistry around the greens. Another key aspect of Olazabal's short game, which you can learn from, is the intensity of his attitude and preshot preparation. He stares down the shot with a steely intent and makes several practice swings while looking at the hole to get a feel for the shot and the length of swing required. Unlike many amateurs, who quit on their shots around the green, Olazabal accelerates the clubhead through the ball to generate spin and control on his pitch shots.

professional debuts here. In 1976, Seve led the Open Championship by three shots on the final day, courtesy of some inspirational chipping and putting and may very well have won had Johnny Miller not stormed through the field with a closing 66 to win.

But Birkdale's finest moment was the climax to the Ryder Cup in 1969. With the sides tied at 15 points each, Jack Nicklaus and Tony Jacklin stood on the 18th tee knowing their match would decide the outcome of the competition. Both reached the green in two shots, but Nicklaus raced his first putt four feet past the hole, while Jacklin rolled his ball to within a couple of feet. Nicklaus knocked his putt in before conceding Jacklin his putt for a half.

The 6th hole epitomizes the challenge of Royal Birkdale. It is a demanding dogleg par-5, and there is a heavy premium on accuracy from the tee, as trouble lurks in ditches, slopes, heavy rough, and an elevated green surrounded by mounding and gorse, and protected at the front by two imposing bunkers.

10

In the Bunker

It is probably fair to say that most professionals regard the regular greenside bunker shot as one of the most straightforward in the game. The reason for this is quite simple: it's the only shot in golf where you don't have to strike the ball and where you actually have a club—in the form of a sand wedge—that is specially designed to make the job much easier. What's more, there is more of a margin for error when playing from the sand than in any other short shot around the green. However, the fact remains that, while the world's top pros would much rather face an explosion shot out of a bunker, the average amateur golfer would rather see his ball finish almost anywhere other than the sand.

Beat your bunkerphobia

Bunker shots strike fear into the hearts of many amateurs, but there really is no need for such a widespread panic. By and large, the matter is a problem of confidence. Whereas professional golfers walk into a bunker and expect to hit a good recovery shot, most amateurs step in with fear and trepidation and, not surprisingly, this is reflected in a nervy and hesitant swing. Overcome your fear and you'll improve your bunker play immediately.

● TAKE ADVANTAGE OF MARGIN FOR ERROR

According to Tony Johnstone in *Master Your Short Game*: "There's more margin for error with a bunker shot than there is with any other shot in golf. Whether you hit one, two, or three inches behind the ball, as long as you accelerate the clubhead confidently through the sand, you'll get the ball out of the bunker every time."

● FORCE YOURSELF TO PLAY GOOD BUNKER SHOTS

You have to convince yourself that bunker shots are not difficult and that you have the ability to play them successfully before you can step into a bunker with complete confidence.

● USE 8- OR 9-IRON TO REACH BACK OF GREEN

The PGA Tour professional, Per-Ulrik Johansson, advises: "When the pin is on the upper tier at the back of the green, playing the shot with your sand wedge is difficult since you need to carry the ball all the way and judge the distance perfectly. This is when you can use your 8-iron or 9-iron instead. Choke down on the grip, open the clubface slightly and make your normal swing. Because of the reduced loft on the clubface, the ball will fly lower than normal and run more on landing."

● LIGHTEN GRIP TO HIT THE BALL FURTHER

When Tiger Woods wants to hit a longer bunker shot he relaxes his grip pressure to hold the club lightly. This creates more clubhead speed, which is key to successful shots out of the sand.

● SPEND TWO HOURS IN THE SAND

Greg Norman believes that the quickest way to knock several shots off your handicap is to spend a couple of hours in a practice bunker. This will go a long way to eliminating the fear that most golfers have of sand and improve your confidence playing these shots.

● AIM FOR THE TOP OF THE FLAGSTICK

PGA European Tour Professional Nick Dougherty says that most amateur golfers leave the ball well short of the hole from bunkers. He advocates that you

Club selection
Take extra club into the wind **168**
Leave your favorite clubs at home **185**
Use your wedge from against the collar **212**

Setup
Eyes over ball gives best view of the line **122**
Open clubface when playing from gorse **171**
Play ball forward in stance on wet greens **213**

Swing theory
Punch it low for control and spin **170**
Keep leading leg still during the stroke **193**

should aim to land the ball either on top of the flagstick or beyond the hole in order to generate sufficient clubhead speed through the point of impact.

BALANCE A GLASS ON THE CLUBFACE

Johnny Miller has some interesting advice in *Pure Golf*: "In the bunker, try to keep the clubhead open through the hitting area. A good mental

image to help accomplish this is picturing a glass balanced on the face. If the clubface closed the glass would fall off."

VARY LENGTH OF SWING NOT SAND TAKEN

The legendary bunker player, Gary Player, has always recommended that you try to hit about two inches behind the ball on most sand shots. He believes that this should remain constant as you control the distance of the shot by varying the length of the backswing and the force of the downswing.

KEEP YOUR KNEES FLEXED IN THE SAND

Just as they do in the full swing, the knees stabilize the upper body as you make your swing. According to the top coach David Leadbetter, once you have flexed your knees at address, you must maintain the flex right up until impact in order to keep your height and control how much sand you take before the ball.

SQUAT LOWER IN THE SAND

"The sand shot is different from your normal swing," says JoAnne Carner in *LPGA's Guide To Every Shot*, "in that you have to squat a little more and drop your hands. I play my hands way down by my knees because it allows me to quickly break my wrists on the backswing … A taller posture will limit the type of shots you can play."

TRUST THE PHYSICS FOR A PLUGGED LIE

If the ball is fully plugged, Nick Faldo advocates that you should experiment by closing the clubface slightly. He also recommends that you consider using a pitching wedge instead of a sand iron, which will eliminate the bounce on the club and thereby get the clubface under the ball. Faldo says that, as long as the clubhead goes down, the ball will pop up out of the bunker and run once it hits the green.

DRAW LINES IN SAND TO GROOVE CORRECT STANCE

When you practice your bunker play, it is a good idea to draw two lines in the sand—one along the ball-to-target line and the other along the line of your feet, aiming 20 to 30 degrees left of the target. This will help you get used to the concept of swinging to the left of the target.

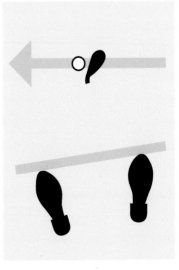

● ALWAYS TEST THE SAND

The first thing that Chi Chi Rodriguez does when entering a bunker is to test the depth and texture of the sand. Once he has done this, he plants his feet firmly and shuffles them into the sand until he has a good solid footing.

● KEEP BACKSWING SAME LENGTH FOR EVERY SHOT

David Leadbetter says that you should make a fairly full backswing for most sand shots to create a consistent rhythm, and then vary the distance you hit the ball by changing the length of your follow-through. The key mistake that he says you must avoid, however, is making a short backswing and then stubbing the clubhead into the sand.

● PUTT OFF THE "TOE" FROM THE SAND

Although generally regarded as a high-risk shot, Jack Nicklaus says that putting from a bunker can be a high-percentage shot if the ball is lying on firm, dry, and level sand, and if the trap is shallow with a minimal lip. When playing this shot, Nicklaus uses his normal putting stroke but addresses the ball off the toe of the club to reduce backspin and give the ball a chance to roll out toward the hole. He strikes the ball a little harder to compensate for the off-center strike.

● WEIGHT FORWARD WHEN CHIPPING FROM BUNKERS

If you are going to chip from the sand, Gary Player advises that you should keep your weight on your front foot throughout the swing and concentrate on striking the ball before hitting the sand.

● SLICE THE LEGS OFF THE BALL

"A useful way to think of this shot is to imagine that the ball has grown some legs maybe two inches long, and that you're trying to slice them off without touching the ball," writes Gay Brewer in *Score Better Than You Swing*.

● TAKE MORE SAND FROM A DRY LIE

On a short-range shot from sand that is dry or fluffy, many pros aim to take a couple of inches of sand before the ball, but if the sand is wet or coarse, they will attempt to hit much closer to the ball.

DRY

● TRY A LOB WEDGE FOR EASIER SPLASH SHOTS

The European Tour professional, Colin Montgomerie, says that, while a sand wedge offers the ultimate control from a bunker, a more lofted lob wedge is a much better choice of club in this situation for most amateur golfers. The extra loft on the clubface means that you can play the shot from a square stance and with the clubface in a square position.

Strategy
Leave flag in on long putts **126**
Elbows follow the rail **133**
Try less hard on the course **143**

Swing theory
Keep head and body dead still **124**
Don't make long swing if short one will do **163**

Equipment
Close the gap in your wedges **89**
Thin layers beat the cold **171**

TAKE LESS SAND ON AN UPHILL LIE

Gary Player has said that, when he finds himself with an uphill lie in the sand, he knows that the ball will fly very high and inevitably finish short of the target unless he strikes the sand very close to the ball. Whereas he would normally aim to take two inches of sand on every bunker shot, in this instance he will aim to strike just one inch behind the ball.

WIDEN YOUR STANCE FOR STABILITY

The 1999 US Ryder Cup captain, Ben Crenshaw, says that you should take a slightly wider stance in a bunker than for playing a normal short pitch. You will find that this helps you anchor your swing and enables you to control the shot with your wrists, arms, and shoulders to create a shallow attack into the ball.

VARY AMOUNT OF SAND TO VARY SPIN

When judging the amount of sand to take with the shot, Tiger Woods works out how much spin he wants to put on the ball. If he wants the ball to run out and roll once it lands on the green, he aims to make contact with the sand about three inches behind the ball so that it comes out with very little backspin on a nice cushion of sand. If he wants a higher trajectory and more spin, he'll hit closer to the ball, about an inch behind it.

SPANK THE SAND

On his website, Ben Crenshaw advises: "Lay the face of the wedge off a bit. As this shot needs to be spanked off the sand, there is no need for digging! The reason for this is the leading-edge of the club will enter the sand and get out quickly. SPANK the sand, SPLASH the sand, SKIM the sand behind the ball, but don't HOE it. Hoeing need only be applied if the ball is buried."

SHARPER EDGE HELPS UNPLUG A BURIED LIE

Jack Nicklaus believes that a thinner-flanged sharper-edged club than the sand wedge, such as a pitching wedge or a 9-iron, will do a better job of removing the ball from a buried lie.

MAKE A FULL FOLLOW-THROUGH

"There is greater tolerance in playing out of a sand trap than for any other shot in the game," says Byron Nelson in *Winning Golf*. "It is possible to hit one, two or even three inches behind the ball as it rests in the sand, and still get it out onto the green. The most prevalent mistake by the average golfer is in taking too short a swing, and failing to hit all the way through. Remember, this shot is always played with a full swing. It is fatal to hit into the sand and not follow through."

BUY YOURSELF A GOOD BUNKER GAME

"The one shot in golf that you can buy is a good shot out of a bunker onto a green," advises Tommy Armour in *Tommy Armour's ABC's of Golf*. "When the sand wedge with its inclined flange came into the game there no longer remained a fine art in getting out of a trap."

PULL DOWN WITH FINGERS OF LEFT HAND

In *The Killer Swing,* John Daly has this advice: "Pull down pretty firmly with the last three fingers of your left hand, then try to follow an image of slicing a cut of sand out from under the ball. This will help keep the clubface open at impact, so that you get greater loft and cut spin on the shot."

JUDO-CHOP THE BALL FROM A PLUGGED LIE

"When I find my ball buried in the sand," writes Lee Trevino in *Swing My Way,* "I play a shot that I've never seen anyone else try. Most golfers play the buried lie by cutting into the sand with the clubhead square or closed to the left, to make sure that its leading edge will dig well downward and under the buried ball. Personally, I don't care for this technique because the ball comes out too low and too hot. I want a softer shot with more backspin that will settle quickly on even a small area of green. So what I do is play the ball back about in the center of my stance, with most of my weight on my left foot. Then I swing the club practically straight up and down. I almost, you might say, give the back of the ball a downward judo chop with the clubface—just stick the clubhead in the sand with no follow-through. The ball rides up the clubface, taking on tremendous backspin, then flies up the sand in front of it nice and high and floats onto the green like a feather dropping on a pond."

DOUBLE THE LENGTH OF SWING FROM SAND

When faced with a greenside bunker shot, Jack Nicklaus would swing twice as hard as for a pitch shot of the same distance to overcome the resistance of the sand.

SQUARE THE CLUBFACE FROM WET SAND

Whereas most bunker shots from dry sand are played with the clubface in an open position to take advantage of the bounce on the sole of the sand wedge, this is not recommended when the sand is hard or wet. In this situation, it is advisable to square up the clubface at address and perhaps even use a pitching wedge or a 9-iron to play the shot instead, since they have a sharper leading edge and less bounce angle on the sole.

WET

MATCH YOUR SAND WEDGE TO THE SAND

Lee Trevino says you should select a sand wedge that suits the sand at your home club. If you play in soft, fine-grained sand, purchase a sand wedge with plenty of bounce on the sole to prevent the clubface from digging in too deeply. If you play from coarse or thick sand, you'll be better off using a sand wedge with less bounce and a lower and sharper leading edge for more penetration.

Accuracy & distance
The perfect putting pace **126**
Look beyond the target **147**
Lay up to your favorite yardage **162**

Swing theory
Don't eliminate hands and wrists from stroke **124**
Lengthen putting stroke in the wind **171**

SWING SMOOTHLY AND EVENLY THROUGH THE SAND

In *How To Think and Swing Like a Golf Champion*, Dick Mayer advises: "The most important single feature of a sand shot is that the clubhead must go through the sand smoothly and evenly. Too many players do everything right, except that they 'quit' when the clubhead hits the sand. There is only one remedy for this common ailment. You should keep your hands firmer on the grip than normally. I don't mean to keep them rigid— but be sure they are firm enough to withstand the shock of hitting the sand."

OPEN FACE AND HIT HARDER UNDER PRESSURE

"One sand shot technique is to hit bunker shots as hard as you want," says JoAnne Carner in *LPGA's Guide To Every Shot*. "The more the pressure is on, the more I'll open the blade and hit just a little farther behind the ball and hit it hard. This helps relieve the tension that comes when I'm under pressure."

SWING HARD FROM AN UPSLOPE

Because of the face of the bunker acts as a launching pad, you can be aggressive when playing from an upslope and make a full swing, safe in the knowledge that, because there is more upward than forward momentum on the shot, you will struggle to hit the ball too far.

REMEMBER THE "V" IN THE BUNKER

Chris Hanell, a PGA European Tour professional, says the best tip he has ever received on bunker play is to practice "with a "V" shape drawn in the sand. Your clubface aims down one side of the "V" directly at the hole, while your feet and body are aligned with the other. Play the ball forward in your stance in relation to the line of your feet. From here, all you need to do is swing the club along the line of your body, holding your body angles, and the ball will pop out on a cushion of sand."

HOLD TIGHT WITH LEFT, LOOSE WITH RIGHT

The bunker shot is played mainly with the left hand, according to Tommy Horton. He believes that you should keep the left wrist firm with the back of the hand facing the target through impact to prevent the clubface from closing through impact.

CHASE THE CLUBHEAD DOWN THE SLOPE

In *A Swing for Life*, Nick Faldo imparts this advice: "The downhill lie is possibly the most difficult of all sand shots around the green. Resigned to the fact that the ball will come out low with little or no backspin, your thoughts must be geared toward releasing the clubhead down and along the contour of the slope— "chasing" the ball toward the target."

ACCELERATE CLUBHEAD THROUGH SAND

To ensure that you accelerate the clubhead through the sand on a greenside bunker shot, make sure that your follow-through is at least as long as your backswing. If your follow-through is shorter than your backswing, your swing is too tense and short and you will struggle to control the shot.

Pine Valley New Jersey

10TH HOLE, PAR-3, 145 YARDS

THE ULTIMATE BUNKER CHALLENGE

Set amid the towering pines of a New Jersey wasteland, Pine Valley is hailed as one of the best and most traditional golf courses in the whole of the United States, if not the very best of them all. At only 6,765 yards long, and with tight corridor-like fairways and imposing scrubland, the infrastructure of the course isn't deemed suitable for staging professional events, but it has twice hosted the Walker Cup—in 1936 and 1985.

Designed by George Crump and H. S. Colt in 1912, Pine Valley took seven years to complete and opened for play in 1919. One of its most distinctive features is the lack of rough surrounding the fairways and greens. That probably sounds very appealing to most amateur golfers, but this majestic course is anything but unprotected. Although it is relatively short by modern standards, desert scrubland, pot bunkers, raised greens, and towering pine trees await any errant drive or approach shot. The impeccably lush fairways are the only true sanctuary in what is otherwise a sandy wilderness. Most of the world's top players have visited the course, many of whom have accepted the club members' wagers of shooting below 80 at their first attempt and have subsequently failed.

The notorious desert scrubland, which meanders its way throughout the whole course, is designated as one huge sand trap, while the raised greens, which resemble upturned saucers, resist anything less than the perfectly judged approach shot. Indeed, it has often been said that at Pine Valley you're either safe or in very big trouble!

PRO-FILE
GARY PLAYER

Vary distance with swing speed and length

South Africa's Gary Player is the finest bunker player of all time. He is renowned for his finesse and control out of the sand, and his bunker play formed the foundation of a sharp short game that enabled him to win eight majors. He claims that one of the reasons he won so often was because he could shoot fearlessly at the pins, knowing that, if his ball did find a bunker, he could recover.

However, if you questioned Player on the secret of his success, you would get just a one-word answer: practice. After winning the US Open, Player holed a splash shot from the sand, a feat that prompted a spectator to tell him that he was lucky. Player waited a moment before replying: "You know, it's amazing: the harder I practice, the luckier I get."

According to Player, the most important thing when playing a splash shot is to feel that your club is getting through the sand. He advocates that you should set up with your weight mainly on your left side and with your head directly above the ball. His final piece of advice is to keep the swing smooth and accelerate the clubhead through the sand.

The nature and variety of the sand hazards here demand several different types of recovery shot. While hitting a full shot from the scrubland requires a similar technique to that employed from a fairway bunker or any tight lie, golfers must also be able to play a whole range of regular splash shots and also negotiate deep pot bunkers, where very often the safest and most sensible route is sideways back onto the fairway or even away from the hole altogether.

Without doubt, Pine Valley's most distinctive and hazardous holes are its selection of par-3s, each of which requires the golfer to carry the tee shot over thick scrubland, pot bunkers, or water from tee to green. The par-3 10th hole is the shortest hole on the course, but it totally epitomizes the challenge of Pine Valley, requiring a precise short iron into a sharply raised green surrounded by a combination of regular bunkers, a claustrophobic pot bunker, and a strip of scrubland that runs along the right side of the putting surface.

11

On the Green

Putting is often described as a game within the game and,
to a certain degree, that's true. The skills required to stroke in a
sloping, downhill, four-footer certainly bear very little resemblance
to those utilized when hitting a full shot from the fairway or
crunching a drive off the tee, yet it is on the greens where most of
the tournaments on the professional circuit are won or lost.

At an amateur level, putting is an area where most golfers could
make a dramatic improvement to their scoring. Whereas most top
pros expect to take somewhere in the region of 26 to 28 putts per
round, the average club golfer takes around 35 to 40. However,
there are no physical reasons why you cannot become an
accomplished putter. Unlike the full swing, the putting stroke
doesn't require immense strength or exceptional hand-eye
coordination and athletic ability.

Pursue putting perfection

Probably more tips have been written about putting than any other area of the game. One of the main reasons for this is that there is more room for individuality in putting than in the full swing. The best way to improve your putting quickly is to work on your distance control, since unless you are an extremely accurate iron player, most of your approach putts are likely to be from fairly long range.

SET EYES AND SHOULDERS PARALLEL TO PUTTING LINE

"Once you have the putter face aimed at your target, make sure you set your eyes and shoulders parallel to that line," writes Nick Faldo in *A Swing for Life*. "Only then do you get a true perspective of the path to the hole." Faldo believes that if your eyes are inside or outside the line, you will get an inaccurate view.

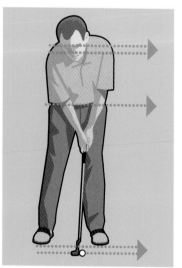

IT'S NOT HOW, BUT HOW MANY ON THE GREENS

European Tour professional Tony Johnstone has this advice in *Master Your Short Game*: "Looks aren't important when it comes to putting. Only the end result matters. I've often said that if standing on my head and holding my putter between my knees would help me hole more putts, I would do it without a second thought."

DON'T SET EYES AHEAD OF BALL, NEARER HOLE

Tiger Woods likes to set his eyes a couple of inches to the right of the ball at address. He believes that this gives him a much more accurate view of the ball-to-target line. The key thing that Tiger is looking to avoid is positioning his eyes too far in advance of the ball at address. In this situation he could easily get a distorted view of the line of the putt.

COMFORT IS THE KEY AT ADDRESS

Comfort is your number-one priority at address. If you are not relaxed standing over the ball, you will always struggle to make a smooth putting stroke. It is far better to be a little unorthodox in your setup yet remain comfortable than to be technically correct yet awkward or uncomfortable, since the unease will almost certainly result in an inhibited stroke.

Equipment
Why matched sets aren't always the best **13**
Keep grips tacky **17**
Forget about your equipment **204**

Strategy
Ask golf club staff for course information **153**
Play a round of golf on the range **188**

Swing theory
Keep your body moving **44**
Feel the clubhead to improve rhythm **47**

GET A FRIEND TO CHECK PUTTING ALIGNMENT

It's advisable to ask a friend or golfing partner to monitor your setup and, in particular, your alignment on a regular basis. John Daly recommends that, after you've checked straight putts, you should work on your blade alignment on breaking putts so that you can consistently align yourself the correct distance, left or right, of the center of the hole.

VISUALIZE BALL RUNNING TWO FEET PAST HOLE

To ensure that you get the ball up to the hole, always visualize the ball running two feet past and remember that the ball will take the break more as it runs out of steam near the hole side.

KEEP GRIP PRESSURE LIGHT FOR BETTER CONTROL

The LPGA Tour professional, Jackie Gallagher-Smith, believes: "One of the key causes of leaving putts well short of the hole is gripping the club too tightly. This reduces your feel and prevents you from feeling the weight of the clubhead in your hands. Grip the club as softly as you can without losing control during the stroke for the ultimate in distance control."

HOVER PUTTER ABOVE GRASS AT ADDRESS

"To avoid snagging the putter in the grass at the beginning of the stroke and losing rhythm and control, hover the putter a fraction of an inch above the ground at address," says the LPGA Tour professional, Jackie Gallagher-Smith. "Now you can glide the putter away from the ball without any risk of losing control of your stroke."

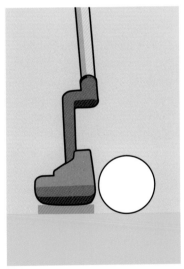

POUR THE WATER TO JUDGE THE BREAK

To gauge both break and grain, Payne Stewart said that he imagined that he was pouring a bucket of water on top of the grass. Then he would picture which way the water ran to highlight the break and the direction of the grain.

USE SAME TYPE OF GOLF BALL

"It is difficult to develop consistency in your judgment of distance if you play with golf balls of different constructions and compressions," believes David Williams, a PGA professional. "A soft three-piece Balata golf ball, for example, will not roll as far as a more durable two-piece distance ball when struck with the same putting stroke. Ideally you should use the same brand, construction, and compression [of] golf ball, but if that's not possible, make sure that you stick to the same type of construction as this will improve your entire short game."

FOCUS ON THE BACK OF THE BALL

Greg Norman says in *100 Instant Golf Lessons*, "When I putt, I don't just look at the whole ball, I look at the back of the ball. By focusing on the back, you help ensure that you'll strike the ball from straight behind it, which in turn will encourage you to make the proper low back-and-through stroke."

PUTT QUICKLY TO ESCAPE NERVES

Chi Chi Rodriguez says that you should putt quickly, otherwise you think too much about your technique and become nervous.

SET HIPS IN CONCRETE FOR A STABLE STROKE

Paul Eales, a PGA European Tour professional, maintains: "It is vital that you keep your lower body still during the stroke since if your legs and hips move too much, it can cause the putter to move off line. A good way to achieve this is to imagine that your legs are in concrete and cannot move. This will help you control the stroke with your arms and shoulders and avoid the lower body movement that can ruin your stroke."

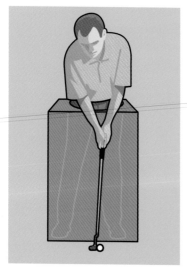

FIRST IMPRESSIONS COUNT

"Your first impression of how a putt will break will be right more often than any other impression you might form," reckons Dr. Bob Rotella in *Putting Out of Your Mind*.

TAKE ONE LOOK AT THE TARGET AND GO!

Per-Ulrik Johansson the Swedish Ryder Cup player and PGA Tour professional, says: "The most important change that I made to my putting routine at the end of the 2001 season was to restore the flair to my stroke. Rather than stand over the ball for ages thinking about the technique and the length of stroke, I decided to speed up the process. Once I've completed my address, I take one last look at the hole, hold the image of the line and distance in my mind, and then instinctively start my stroke, relying purely on the information that my eyes have transmitted to my brain to judge the speed."

GET IN TOUCH WITH YOUR SENSITIVE FINGER

To improve your control of the putting stroke and to guide the putter head back and through consistently, John Daly recommends that you crook the tip of your right index finger under the grip rather than around it, as you would do when hitting a full shot with a normal swing. Although this is slightly unorthodox, Dalys says that because this finger is so sensitive, it greatly helps judge distance on putts.

EYES OVER BALL GIVES BEST VIEW OF THE LINE

Although not an essential factor of good putting, setting up with your eyes directly over the ball at address gives you the best view of the line of a putt and therefore makes it easier to align the putter face correctly. This way you can trace the line of the putt with your eyes from the ball to the hole without having to alter your setup position.

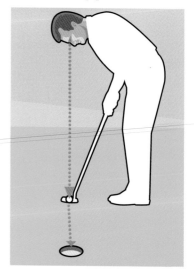

THROW RIGHT PALM TO THE HOLE

According to Tommy Horton, a good way of keeping the putter face square to hole and, in turn, reducing the chances of pushing or pulling your putts, particularly from short range, is to think of throwing your right palm toward the hole in the follow-through.

Setup
Hands cover clubhead at 9 o'clock **35**
Move ball back in stance for any bad lie **78**
Narrow your stance for a slower swing **88**

Accuracy & distance
Take less sand on an uphill lie **113**
Make carry over water comfortable **154**

Swing theory
Extend butt of club away from right hip **37**
Turn hands to the left to stop a hook **178**

FIND YOUR PUTTER'S SWEET SPOT

Striking the ball out of the sweet spot is a key to consistent putting. Fred Couples says you can find the sweet spot of your putter by holding it vertically with your thumb and index finger in front of your eyes. Tap the clubface with the pointed end of a golf tee or the end of a pencil. If the putter head twists at all, you haven't struck the sweet spot. When the putter head rebounds straight back, you have.

POLISH YOUR BUILDING BLOCKS

"Much of the inconsistency of putting is the result of the complexity of the way golfers swing their putters ..." remarks the short-game teaching specialist Dave Pelz in *Dave Pelz's Putting Bible*. "The building blocks of the game are aim, path, touch, rhythm, ritual, feel, face angle, stability, attitude, routine, putter-fitting, power source, impact pattern, flow lines, green reading ... The good news is that most golfers (you included) are usually pretty good at most of these putting skill blocks. The bad news is that few golfers have all fifteen of them formed and polished well enough to make putting a strength of their game."

HOLD HANDS HIGH FOR CONSISTENCY

Excessive hand action during the stroke is a major cause of inconsistent putting. To keep your hands more passive, hold them a little higher at address so that the shaft angle of the putter becomes steeper. The Swedish Ryder Cup golfer, Per-Ulrik Johansson, transformed his putting immediately and managed to retain his PGA Tour Card in 2001 as a result of making this small adjustment to his technique during the last three weeks of the season.

USE THE REVERSE OVERLAP GRIP

Most tournament golfers use a slightly different grip for putting than for normal full shots. The reverse overlap is similar to the normal Vardon grip with the exception that the left index finger extends down the grip and rests on top of the fingers of the right hand. This adjustment allows your hands to work together more as a single unit and reduces the risk of excess wrist action during the stroke.

CARRY THE PUTTER IN YOUR LEFT HAND

"You should make it a habit to carry your putter in your left hand. Or in both hands, if you wish," says Harvey Penick in his *Little Red Golf Book*. "But never carry it in your right hand alone. Your left hand and arm are an extension of the putter shaft. That is the feeling you want to have. I see pros on the Tour place the putter behind the ball with their right hand. Then when they put their left hand on the club, they have automatically changed their aim. Put your putter behind the ball with your left hand, or with both hands."

TIGHTEN YOUR GRIP ON SHORT PUTTS

Several Tour pros use a slightly different technique for holing short putts. Fred Couples, for example, grips the club tighter than for medium or long putts, because he believes that this helps to keep the putter low to the ground and on line.

● STAND A LITTLE OPEN AT ADDRESS

Many top golfers, including John Daly, like to stand a little open to the target when setting up for a putt, since he believes this enables him to swing the putter along the correct path and strike the ball solidly each time.

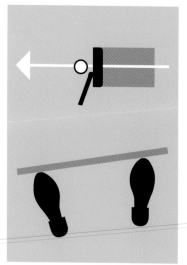

● KEEP HEAD AND BODY DEAD STILL

One of the main reasons why Arnold Palmer addressed all his putts in a knock-kneed fashion was because holding his knees close together gave him the feeling of keeping his upper body steady and solid during the stroke. Palmer believes that the one and only technical secret to putting is holding your head and body motionless as you swing the putter back and through.

● LEFT HAND LEADS THE STROKE

Arnold Palmer says that the key to the putting stroke is preventing the right hand from taking over and closing the putter face at impact. Palmer says that he always ensured that his left hand led the way so that the blade accelerated beyond the point of impact for a firm and decisive stroke.

● ACCELERATE AND STRIKE SOLIDLY

Bob Rosburg gives his two principles in *The Putter Book*, 1963, and they are (1) "Try to always hit the ball with the clubhead accelerating at impact;" and (2) "Try to hit the ball solidly." (If you do the first, it is easy to do the second.)

● SLIGHT FORWARD PRESS IMPROVES STROKE

Tommy Horton believes that a slight forward press before starting the putting stroke makes it easier for the left hand to travel through toward the hole after striking the ball. He believes that this is essential for creating the correct speed.

● PERFECT YOUR PUTTING POSTURE

Good posture is as important for putting as for the long game.

When you create a good spine angle, your arms can hang freely from your shoulders and away from your chest, which then makes it easier to rock the shoulders to control the stroke. If your posture is rounded and slumped, your arms become jammed in against your upper body and they have very little room to swing freely back and through.

● DON'T ELIMINATE HANDS AND WRISTS FROM STROKE

In *A Swing for Life*, Nick Faldo takes issue with one particular piece of advice: "Some people say the hands and wrists should be eliminated from the equation. I don't agree. If you isolate the hands, you end up with a wooden stroke and little or no feel. To create the momentum

Strategy
Straight line from left shoulder to ball **94**
Take hands out of the stroke to beat yips **178**

Club selection
Club up when the ball is below your feet **81**
Take one more club than you need **160**

Swing theory
Dominant hand controls the takeaway **42**
The two reasons for shanking **178**

that gets the ball rolling, your hands and wrists must be alive and free to flex and respond naturally. All the best putters have what I call "lag" in their stroke."

MAKE SEVERAL PRACTICE PUTTS LOOKING AT HOLE

You need as much visual feedback and hand-eye coordination as possible to lag the ball close to the hole from long range consistently. Make several practice putts while looking at the hole to get a feel for the length of stroke that you need and let yourself respond naturally to what you see.

PUTTING FLAWS MIRROR SWING FLAWS

"A putting stroke is a miniature golf swing," Johnny Miller tells us in *Pure Golf*. "If you watch any player, a good player or a hacker, I guarantee you'll see the exact same physical characteristics in both the full swing and the putting stroke."

PUTT LIKE A PENDULUM

Many of the world's top golfers control the putting stroke with their shoulders, because they believe that the larger muscles in the upper body are more reliable and consistent than the hands and wrists. They rock

their shoulders up and down in a pendulum-style movement to swing the putter back and through.

TAKE ONE LOOK AT THE HOLE AND GO

Davis Love III relies on instinct when it comes to long-range putting. After reading the break and aligning himself carefully, he concludes his pre-putt routine by taking one last look at the hole, returning his eyes to the ball and instantly starting his stroke. There's no time to think about mechanics or pace required. Pure instinct controls the length and power of the stroke.

LOOK TO HOLE EVERY PUTT

Many pros say that you should attempt to lag long putts into a small, imaginary circle around the hole, but the golf psychologist, Bob Rotella, says that you should attempt to hole every putt, regardless of its length, since this will reduce your margin for error.

STRIKE PUTTS SO THAT THEY DIE AT THE HOLE

That old adage, "never up, never in", was not a favorite of Harvey Penick's. "It's true that a ball that never reaches the cup never goes in, but neither does a ball that goes past it," says Penick in

his *Little Red Golf Book*. Instead he favors putts that die at the hole because at least there is a possibility they will topple in. Hit a putt too hard and more often than not it will hit the hole and spin away.

VARY LENGTH, NOT SPEED, OF STROKE

Good distance control on the greens stems from a rhythmical putting stroke. To maintain good rhythm, keep your backswing and follow-through approximately the same length. On short putts, your backswing and follow-through will both be fairly short, while on longer putts the length of the stroke will increase either side of the ball. Never consciously try to hit the ball harder to hit it further.

POINT LEFT ELBOW TOWARD HOLE AT ADDRESS

One of Bobby Jones's putting keys was to bend his left arm so that his elbow pointed directly at the hole. This gave him a greater freedom of movement and also kept his left hand and wrist under control during the stroke.

THE PERFECT PUTTING PACE

In the course of his famous putting and short-game experiments, Dave Pelz discovered that the optimum speed of a putt will take the ball 17 inches past the hole if it misses on any green. Pelz claims that this ideal pace enables the ball to hug the surface of the green for a consistent roll and with enough topspin for it to hold its line.

USE WHOLE OF PUTTER FACE TO STRIKE BALL

When the putter rises too far off the ground during the stroke it becomes difficult to strike the ball cleanly, and very often the putter face becomes delofted at impact. Keep the sole of the putter as low to the ground as possible to maximize the loft and to ensure that as much of the clubface as possible makes contact with the ball.

HOLD THE HOLD FOR CONSTANT GRIP PRESSURE

While many players, including top professionals, loosen their grip on the putter, and then regrip it after making a practice stroke, Greg Norman claims that your hands should not move on the club from the moment you form your grip to make a practice stroke until you strike the putt for real. Norman says that Tom Watson and Raymond Floyd approach their putting in a similar way.

LISTEN OUT FOR A GOOD PUTT

Ben Crenshaw says that you can hear and feel a solid strike. Avoid complex technical thoughts and simply try to stroke the ball solidly with an even tempo in your backstroke and through-stroke.

WEIGHT ON FRONT FOOT FOR BETTER BALANCE

Chi Chi Rodriguez's main putting thought is to keep his weight on his front foot, so that he retains his balance and keeps his eye on the back of the ball during the stroke.

LEAVE FLAG IN ON LONG PUTTS

On most long-range putts, Jack Nicklaus likes to leave the flagstick in the hole, because he finds that this improves his depth perception and judgment of distance, particularly if the hole is in shadow.

FAST GREENS EARLY, SLOW GREENS LATE

Generally speaking greens get slower through the day because grass grows very quickly,

Accuracy & distance
Don't overestimate your wedge distance **71**
Know yardages with every club in bag **158**

Swing theory
Push left arm down in takeaway **45**
Clear your hips and swing your arms **179**

126

especially in some climates. A putt taken first thing in the morning can be a lot slower if taken at the end of the day. This is true nine times out of 10, but there are occasions where the reverse can be the case. For example, a damp, slow green first thing in the morning can become lightning fast by the afternoon if a hot wind gets to dry it out.

◉ IF IN DOUBT, AIM STRAIGHT

The PGA European Tour professional Colin Montgomerie adopts a simplistic approach to reading the lines on some putts: "If in doubt over the line of the putt, aim at the center of the cup and strike the ball positively."

◉ RAP PUTTS TO HOLE, DON'T STROKE THEM

"One of the main causes of hesitant putting is focusing too much on making an even-paced rhythmical stroke," believes Gary Smith, a PGA professional. "If you watch Tiger Woods, you'll notice that he releases the putter with an authoritative "pop" into the back of he ball. When the ball leaves the clubface faster, it rolls straighter and more positively, holds its line better and is less susceptible to the inconsistencies in the putting surface that can knock a slow-rolling ball off line."

◉ CHECK DISTANCE FROM THE SIDE

"Simply looking at the putt from behind the line often has a foreshortening effect, leading you to believe that the putt is shorter than you think," says David Williams, a PGA professional. "If you want proof, hold one of your arms directly out in front of you at shoulder height. Now hold the same arm out sideways. From this angle, your arm looks much longer." Swedish LPGA Tour pro, Marlen Hedblom, always views putts from the side to determine the gradient and distance.

◉ PUTTS BREAK AWAY FROM HIGHEST MOUNTAINS

If he's playing on a mountain course, Tiger Woods will look for the highest peak as he reads his putt because he knows that the ball is likely to break away from it, even if the putt looks fairly straight.

◉ KEEP YOUR STROKE SIMPLE

One of the main reasons for Ben Crenshaw's continued putting success over the years is that he has adhered to a simple method. Crenshaw avoids complex and technical thoughts and makes a point of staying loose and relaxed, while thinking only of the pace and direction of the putt in question.

◉ NEVER SECOND-GUESS YOURSELF ON THE LINE

Once you've read the green carefully and selected your line, commit to your decision. Conclude your putting routine with one last glance at the hole before starting your stroke. Don't stand over the ball thinking about technique. Keep your putting as instinctive as possible.

◉ GREENS RUN FASTER IN THE AFTERNOON

The greens will be faster in the afternoon because the sun and wind will dry them out and golfers will have walked all over and flattened the putting surface. John Daly recommends that you should make allowances for this extra speed by making a slower stroke.

● TUNNEL-VISION APPROACH TO READING GREENS

The reason why many top tour players, including Tiger Woods and Fred Couples, cup their hands around their eyes when reading a putt is to block out all the unwanted distractions so that they can focus purely on the line and improve concentration.

● MISS BREAKING PUTTS ON THE "PRO" SIDE

Top professionals always allow a little extra break on putts with lots of break because the ball then has a chance of falling into the hole at the front, from the top side or even at the back edge of the cup. Once your ball falls below the perfect line, it will always be moving away from the hole and will never have a chance of dropping in.

● VOLUNTEER TO REMOVE FLAGSTICK FROM HOLE

The PGA professional Mark Arnold is quite shrewd with this piece of advice: "When you walk onto the green, offer to remove the flagstick. This allows you to walk from your ball to the hole and enables you to look at the line and the slope without holding up play. Once you have removed the flagstick, take the opportunity to return to your ball by walking back on the other side of the line so that you glean as much information as possible."

● START READING GREENS AFTER APPROACH SHOT

Don't wait until you have reached the green to start to read putts. It is often far easier to get a clear idea of how the green slopes and the general lie of the land from further away than it is when you are standing right on top of the putting surface. Pay attention to your putt as soon as you have struck your approach shot.

● SPLIT YOUR HANDS TO BEAT THE YIPS

"Most players like [Bernhard] Langer who have successfully beaten the "yips" have done so by separating their hands on the club," says Tony Johnstone in *Master Your Short Game*.

● PATH OF PUTTER MUST MATCH THE LINE

Although striking the ball out of the center of the sweet spot is a foundation of consistent putting, Lee Trevino says that you still have to strike the ball with the putter head moving down the intended line of the putt with the face square to that line.

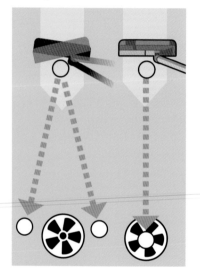

● LEARN FROM WATCHING PLAYING PARTNERS' PUTTS

Good powers of observation can pay dividends on the green. If you are the last person to putt, watch very carefully to see how your playing partners' putts roll, especially as they slow down around the hole. This will help you judge the pace and break of your own putt, particularly if another player is on a very similar line.

Club selection
Take a pitching wedge to play water shot **78**
Use straight-face club under pressure **101**

Setup
Lie of the club influences the setup **25**
Turn left foot to right to beat a hook **176**

IDENTIFY WEAR AND TEAR AROUND THE HOLE

Gary Player counsels in *Gary Player's Golf Secrets*: "If there is more damage to the grass on one edge than on the other, chances are good that putts will roll to that side. Such damage is caused when balls bang against the low side of the hole. Naturally, on a slanted green, putts will bounce against the low side of the hole with more force and frequency than against any other side."

VISUALIZE THE WHOLE LINE

Johnny Miller writes in *Pure Golf*: "I'm not a believer in spot putting, picking a spot between the ball and the hole over which the ball should travel. I prefer visualizing the total line to the hole."

TREAT EVERY PUTT AS STRAIGHT

"Once you have read a green and calculated how much the putt will break," says Sarah McLennan, a PGA professional, "forget about the hole and simply concentrate on aiming the putter face and your body squarely to your intended line. Every putt is straight because you start the ball rolling toward the apex of the putt and simply allow gravity and the contours to ferry the ball down to the hole."

PLAY BALL OFF TOE OF FACE ON DOWNHILL PUTTS

When you are confronted with a slick, downhill putt, Tom Watson recommends that you address the ball and strike it with the toe of the putter, as this will naturally deaden the strike at impact and enable you to control the pace of the putt.

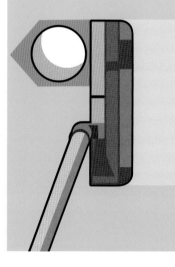

ADOPT TRAFFIC-LIGHT APPROACH TO PUTTING

"Knowing when to go for your putts and when to play safe will help you become a more consistent performer on the greens, advises Nick Bradley, PGA professional. "I have a traffic light system for evaluating putts. Red means danger. Normally that means a medium-length, sharp downhiller. Amber is for putts where you need to be a little cautious, such as those where there is a lot of break. Green is for putts where there is very little danger in making a positive stroke. A straight, slightly uphill putt is the ultimate "green light" putt as you can afford to be aggressive safe in the knowledge that the ball won't fly too far past the hole."

LOOK AT BREAK FROM LOW SIDE OF PUTT

The PGA Tour professional, Chuck Winstead, says: "After you've looked at your putt from behind the ball to see which way it will break, always take a look at a long putt from the side, halfway between the ball and the hole on the low side. This gives you a better perspective of the true distance and the gradient, while you get a more accurate view of the slope when you look from an angle where the putt will break toward you."

FIRST THOUGHTS ARE THE BEST

After reading the green, you must determine the line of your shot. Chi Chi Rodriguez says that you should go with your initial instinct and also survey the putt from behind the hole if you are having trouble deciding on the line.

⬤ MAINTAIN THE "Y"
THROUGHOUT YOUR STROKE
For maximum putting
consistency, you should strive to
maintain the "Y" shape formed
between your arms and the shaft
of the putter at address
throughout the whole of the
stroke. This will ensure that your
putting motion is controled by
your shoulders and arms without
too much hand action.

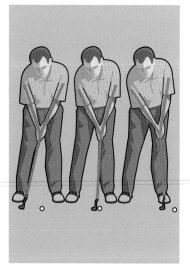

⬤ AIM AT THE APEX OF
A BREAKING PUTT
When you face a breaking putt,
try to visualize the entire line to
the hole and focus on the apex of
the putt, where you believe the
ball will first begin to break
toward the hole. If you make that
point your target, all you then
have to worry about is judging
the pace correctly.

⬤ PUTT TO A TEE PEG TO
INCREASE CONFIDENCE
Many top golfers work on their
short putting by aiming at a tee
peg instead of a hole because
missing short putts—even in
practice—can damage your
confidence and lead to hesitancy
out on the course. The smaller
target forces you to take more
care with your alignment and the
quality of your stroke, while the
biggest benefit of all is that the
hole will look absolutely
enormous afterward.

⬤ HIT THE SWEET SPOT
EVERY TIME
"Consistent putting starts with
striking the ball on the putter's
"sweet spot" every time,"
maintains Lee Trevino in *Swing
My Way*. "Missing the sweet spot
makes any given putt finish
shorter than it normally would."

⬤ INSPECT THE AREA
AROUND THE HOLE
A putt will always break most as
it slows down and runs out of
pace near the hole and thus
becomes far more susceptible to
the contours of the green. Check
to see how the green slopes
during the last couple of feet of
the putt around the hole, and
then use this information to
help you decide on your line
and the speed.

⬤ KEEP PUTTER HEAD LOW
ON FOLLOW-THROUGH
Although it is very important to
keep the putter head low to the
ground on the backswing,
Gary Player maintains that it is
even more important to keep it
low to the ground on the follow-
through, since this will prevent
you from lifting your head too
early before the putter strikes
the ball.

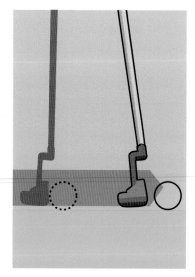

⬤ CENTER OF HOLE CHANGES
ON CURLING PUTTS
In *A Swing for Life*, Nick Faldo
maintains: "A point that is often
overlooked is the fact that on a
curling putt, the center of the
hole actually changes. Think
about it. If you study the line of a
hardbreaking left-to-right putt, in
your mind's eye you would see
the ball enter the hole from the

Swing theory
Strength is a match for beauty **37**
Check your grip after every shot **46**

Strategy
Leave the flag in when chipping **100**
Stay alert and observant **143**

left edge as you look at it. If the middle of the hole is normally represented by 6 o'clock, that severe left-to-right slope could make the effective center nearer to 9 o'clock. It's important that you bear this in mind."

USE BUILDINGS TO SPOT SLOPES

If you struggle to spot slopes on the green, check in the distance for any buildings. The human eye is very good at spotting any deviance from the perpendicular, so a vertical wall or a horizontal roof will help you notice even the tiniest break on the green. The PGA European Tour professional, Tony Johnstone, consistently struggled to read the lines on putts and he has used this method to help him throughout his career.

STUDY YOUR PARTNERS' PUTTS

Use the time while the other golfers in your group are preparing to putt to study the green and read your own putt in detail. Chi Chi Rodriguez says that you should pay close attention to the way in which your playing partners' putts break, particularly around the hole, so that you can determine the correct speed and break of your own shot.

REMOVE GLOVE FOR PUTTING FEEL

Many players, including Gary Player and Arnold Palmer, remove their glove before putting as they believe this gives them more feel over the stroke and distance.

LESS BREAK ON UPHILL PUTTS

Because of the extra speed required to get the ball up to the hole, the ball will break less on an uphill putt. This effect is magnified if the grass is wet and the ball will travel even straighter since extra power will be required to reach the hole. The ball will always break more on a downhill putt because less speed is required to get it to the hole. If the greens are very dry, the ball will break even more, because there is less resistance.

PLUM-BOB TO SPOT SUBTLE BREAKS

Subtle breaks on the green are often difficult to see, but an effective way to spot minor undulations is to hold your putter vertically in front of you so that it bisects the middle of the hole. This is known as plum-bobbing and many top putters, including Ben Crenshaw and Loren Roberts, use it as an integral part of their putting

routine. By acting as a perpendicular reference point, on a breaking putt one side of the hole will look higher than the other and enable you to spot the correct line.

STAND WELL BACK FOR BETTER VIEW OF BREAK

Nick Bradley, a PGA professional, says: "When reading a putt, avoid standing too close to the ball, and instead move several feet further away from the hole. This view gives you a wider perspective of the overall lie of the land, which often reveals several clues as to the way in which the ball will break. When you stand right next to the ball you can get a tunnel-vision view of the line of the putt and, therefore, less information."

KEEP THE PUTTER LOW

A common denominator among good putters is keeping the putter head low—no more than an inch or two off the ground— throughout the whole putting stroke. Golfers who tend to raise the putter head too much in the air greatly increase their probability of misstriking the ball.

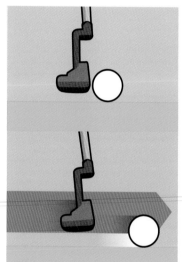

LIGHT GRIP PRESSURE IMPROVES TOUCH AND FEEL

Tiger Woods identifies grip pressure as a likely cause for many common putting problems amateurs suffer from. Tiger likes to take a light grip on his putting strokes as it helps him with everything from judging lagged putts, to gauging speed on short, breaking putts, to overall putting stroke confidence.

SQUEEZE THE TOOTHPASTE FOR BETTER FEEL

A common feature with a lot of amateurs is that they increase their grip pressure when they face a long-range putt. On the contrary, Greg Norman believes that, the longer the putt, the looser you should hold the putter. Norman says he feels as though he were gently squeezing a new tube of toothpaste when he holds the putter.

DON'T CARRY BEFORE YOU PLAY

Henry Cotton recommends that you should avoid carrying any heavy items, such as a suitcase or a heavy golf bag, just before you go out to play, as he believes that this can ruin your touch and feel for putting.

PACE OFF YOUR LONG PUTTS

The PGA professional Stuart Dowsett believes that a good way to learn what length of stroke is required to get the ball to the hole on long putts is to pace off your putts as you walk from your ball to the hole during a round. Measure the distance of each putt in paces and then remember the length of stroke required to reach the hole. This information will help you judge putts of all lengths more accurately.

PRACTICE WHEREVER AND WHENEVER YOU CAN

"I've spent a few nights rolling putts across a motel room rug, I'll tell you," reveals Gay Brewer in *Score Better Than You Swing*.

FOCUS ON THE TARGET, NOT THE PACE

"The last thing you want to do if you're trying to make putts is worry about speed," asserts Dr. Bob Rotella in *Putting Out of Your Mind*.

MATCH LENGTH OF STROKE TO LENGTH OF PUTT

The LPGA Tour professional, Catrin Nilsmark, gives us this advice: "Watch the top players and you'll see that the rhythm or tempo of their stroke remains the same regardless of whether they are standing over a two-footer or

Accuracy & distance
Straighten left leg for 20 more yards **58**
Always carry ball to green with chip shots **214**

Club selection
Take one club more than you think you need **68**
Analyze your home greens **159**

a 42-footer. All that changes is the length of the backswing and follow-through as they match the length of their stroke to the putt in question."

PUTT INSIDE THE DUSTBIN LID

Gary Player's famous piece of advice regarding long-range putting is still relevant today. Player recommends that you should visualize a circle around the hole about the same size as a dustbin lid into which you should attempt to roll the ball. He believes that this is a far more easily achievable goal than trying to judge the distance perfectly.

HIT TO THE ZONE FROM LONG RANGE

To avoid leaving putts consistently short of the hole visualize a two-foot zone behind the hole into which you should roll the ball. You can practice this by placing a club on the ground behind the hole and making it your goal to hit each putt with enough strength to roll past the hole but not touch the shaft.

KEEP GRIP PRESSURE LIGHT ON LONG PUTTS

In *Total Shotmaking*, Fred Couples tells us: "I believe in maintaining a relatively light

grip pressure for all shots, including putts. The tighter you grip the handle, the less feel for the putter head you'll have during the stroke. And I think you need to retain all the feel you can, particularly on long putts."

LOOK AHEAD OF THE BALL AT ADDRESS

When Payne Stewart won the US Open in 1991, he hit all his putts while looking two inches ahead of the ball. This prevented him from lifting his head too early prior to impact and decelerating the putter through the ball. The senior Tour professional, Brian Barnes, goes as far as looking at the hole while making his stroke for exactly the same reason, and also to improve his feel.

VISUALIZE YOUR PUTTS MISSING

"Knowing how the ball will miss the hole will help you select the right line," says the PGA professional, Nick Bradley. "Find a putt of about 10 feet and imagine yourself hitting the ball straight at the hole without allowing for any break. Visualize the way the ball will miss the hole in your mind. With the image of the ball missing the hole fresh in your mind, ask yourself: 'If the ball has missed the hole three inches to the left, then what is the starting line?' A second "movie" should start to run in your mind working off the bad image to reveal the correct line. See the movie once again and watch the ball start on its new line and fall into the cup."

ELBOWS FOLLOW THE RAIL

Controling his putting stroke primarily with his shoulders, Faldo likes to think of his elbows working back and through along a rail for maximum consistency.

HEAR YOUR PUTTS DROP

Chi Chi Rodriguez says that you should listen out to hear if your putt has dropped rather than look for it. Looking up too early is one of the main causes of missed putts.

● VISUALIZE BALL ROLLING BACK TO YOU FROM HOLE

Many top golfers refuse to strike a putt until they can clearly visualize the ball rolling successfully into the hole. An effective method of visualization is to imagine the ball rolling back from the cup toward you along the perfect line. The European Tour professional Nick Dougherty does this before every single putt. By tracing the ball back from the hole to its original start position he then knows what line to start the ball on and can therefore align his body and the putter more accurately.

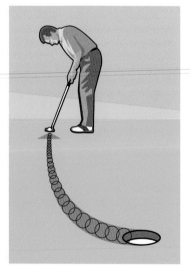

● DISTANCE IS MORE IMPORTANT THAN LINE

Distance is far more important than line on long putts. The evidence of this is that you rarely miss a putt by four or five feet either side of the hole, but many amateurs consistently leave the ball several feet short from long range. If you take care of the distance, the line will look after itself.

● RELAX OVER SHORT PUTTS

Walter Hagen once commented that many amateurs can nonchalantly hole putts from six feet with one hand when they are out of a hole because they are relaxed. When golfers begin to miss short putts it is usually because they are gripping the club too tightly, which is the sign of too much tension. It can be difficult to adopt the same carefree attitude for real, but staying relaxed will improve your success rate.

● FOREFINGER AND THUMB CONTROL PUTTING FEEL

"The feel of the putterhead comes from the forefinger and thumb of the right hand," says Byron Nelson in *Winning Golf*. "My reason for pinching the end of the thumb of the right hand in to the top of the shaft is that I have found it much easier in this manner to keep the face of the club square to the hole. It eliminates the turning, open or closed, of the face of the putter."

● PUTT TO THE FRINGE FOR DISTANCE CONTROL

Catrin Nilsmark has this advice: "A good way to improve your distance control from longer range is to place a ball or a tee peg about three feet from the fringe of a practice green and then try to roll another ball into that gap. Once you've done that, then try to roll the next ball into the gap between your first practice ball and the fringe and so on until there is no room left. This is an exercise that I often perform before and during tournaments to sharpen up my touch."

● HOLE TEN FIVE-FOOTERS BEFORE YOU PLAY

Mark Calcavecchia believes that amateurs should hit at least ten five-foot putts with different

Setup
Move ball closer at address **71**
Lay club on ground parallel to target **185**

Swing theory
Functional is better than pretty **38**
Minimize weight transfer to turn correctly **47**

134

breaks and speeds before they go out to play. He believes that becoming proficient from this distance is the key to drastically reducing your handicap.

WRONG LENGTH PRACTICE STROKES ENHANCE FEEL

The PGA professional, Nick Bradley, advises: "Judging distance from long-range on the greens is the key to avoiding three-putts for bogeys as well as making unexpected birdies. A quick way to improve immediately is to line up your putt, then while looking at the hole make a practice stroke that is obviously too long for the length of the putt. Then make a practice stroke that is obviously too short. If your real stroke is halfway between the two extremes, you won't be too far out with your distance control."

THERE'S NO BORROW ON SHORT PUTTS

"When you don't know that borrow exists, you will tap the ball boldly to the center of the cup and it will fall into the hole." warns Tommy Armour in *Tommy Armour's ABC's of Golf*. "Complete knowledge, born of observation, experience, and thinking, teaches you that very, very rarely is there such a thing as borrow on a really short putt."

MAKE PRACTICE SWINGS PARALLEL TO PUTT LINE

Tom Watson has a practice routine that helps minimize the adjustments he makes between his practice putt and the actual putt. A few inches to the side of the ball, Watson lines up his feet, hips, and shoulders parallel to the line of the actual putt he's going to make. He also lines up the clubface down the same line. Keeping this overall alignment, he then moves into position for the actual putt.

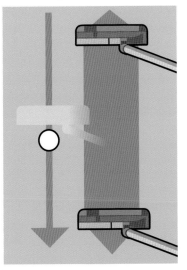

LET YOUR BODY REACT TO THE TARGET

Too many golfers become so preoccupied with the mechanics of their putting stroke that they forget about the target. If you've practiced enough, all you need to think about once you've

addressed the ball correctly is your target. Allow your body and eyes to react to the image of the target in your mind.

LEAVE A DEAD SAFE SECOND PUTT

There will be times when you will be more concerned with leaving a safe second putt than holing the first. If you are faced with a harshly breaking putt, think about where you want to leave your ball should you miss.

PLAY BALL JUST AHEAD OF CHEST BONE

There are no set rules when it comes to putting. You see lots of different styles, but one fundamental that most top players adhere to is playing the ball just ahead of the sternum at address. This enables the putter to strike the ball slightly on the upswing for a more positive roll and better contact.

PLACE THE PUTTER WITH LEFT HAND, NOT YOUR RIGHT

Harvey Penick warns against placing your putter behind the ball with your right hand and then adding your left hand because he fears this alters your aim. Penick favors placing the club either with your left hand, or with both hands on the club.

PRACTICE BREAKING PUTTS YOU DON'T LIKE

"Most golfers have a preference for a particular type of putt," says Catrin Nilsmark, LPGA Tour professional. "Right-handers generally prefer putts that break from right-to-left, while most left-handers prefer a left-to-right borrow. If you lack confidence trying to hole a particular breaking putt, practice the ones that you don't like more often so that you get used to seeing the ball fall into the cup from the opposite route."

MAKE JUNIORS HOLE EVERY PUTT

Harvey Penick recommends that youngsters should be encouraged to hole every short putt so that they become aware that this is a fundamental part of the game

and so that they become accustomed to the pressure of holing short putts to win when they are older.

HOLE OUT STRAIGHT

Curtis Strange says that you should never aim outside of the hole on short putts because you will have to stroke the ball more softly to allow for the break and could easily miss the putt. Aiming inside the width of the hole allows you to make a positive stroke and strike the ball firmly, knowing that the ball won't break too much.

LIMIT YOUR BACKSTROKE ON SHORT PUTTS

The LPGA Tour professional, Nancy Lopez, says that you should reduce the length of your backswing to just three or four inches and then accelerate the putter toward the hole, keeping the blade square to your intended target.

DON'T FORGET YOUR TIMING

Tommy Horton believes that the importance of good timing in the putting stroke is underestimated. Although the putting stroke is much shorter than a full swing, Horton believes it requires the same sense of timing as full shots.

IF IN DOUBT, AIM STRAIGHT AT THE HOLE

Avoid falling into the trap of looking for breaks that don't exist on the greens. If you cannot see a clear break, chances are the slope is negligible, in which case, a well-struck putt is unlikely to break significantly.

HOW TO BEAT THE YIPS

Bobby Jones once said that all golfers—pros and amateurs—hole a lot of 10-foot putts because they won't feel bad if they miss from that distance and therefore make a more positive and relaxed stroke. Many amateur golfers miss short putts because they are afraid of missing them. The best approach is to prepare as solidly as you can, then adopt a "don't care if I miss" attitude on every putt.

Strategy
Trick yourself into feeling confident **53**
How to plan your round **157**

Accuracy & distance
Commit, don't steer **73**
Keep your drive in play **160**

136

FOCUS ON A BLADE OF GRASS BEHIND BALL

Many missed short putts are caused when golfers look up too early too see if they have holed the putt or not. If your head and shoulders move too early in the downswing, the putter can be dragged off line. To counteract this problem focus on a blade of grass behind the ball and stare at it until you have struck the putt. Nick Faldo is particularly disciplined at this. On putts of less than six feet, he keeps his head down and stares at the grass behind the ball until he hears the ball fall into the hole.

THE PUTTING STROKE

Many thousands of words in instruction books, videos, and magazine articles have been devoted to what is, in principle, a fairly simple and straight-forward movement. As with the full swing, your goal in putting is to return the clubface squarely to the line of the target at the point of impact.

PRACTICE WITHOUT AIMING AT A HOLE

The hole is a major distraction when you are working on your putting, since, if you miss a practice putt, you automatically assume you've made a poor

stroke—which isn't necessarily the case. In his book, *Bobby Jones on Golf*, the legendary golfer recommended that you should simply stroke balls back and forth across the practice green without aiming at anything in particular. This will enable you to focus purely on your technique, touch, and rhythm.

SHORT PUTTING

There are several reasons why golfers miss short putts, the most common of which are complacency, poor alignment, anxiety, or a hesitant stroke. The best holers out, such as Tiger Woods and Ernie Els, like to take the break out of play where possible from short range by rolling the ball positively into the hole. This means that all they need to get right is the line.

AIM THE LOGO AT HOLE ON SHORT PUTTS

Selecting the correct line and then aiming the putter face accurately is the secret to holing out successfully from short range. Point the logo on your golf ball at your intended line and then use it to align your putter face squarely. Once you are confident that you are aligned correctly you can make a more positive stroke.

SPOT PUTTING CAN HELP HOLE SHORT PUTTS

"If you're missing the short ones, select a specific spot two or three inches in front of the hole and try to make the ball run over it," advises Jack Nicklaus in *Golf My Way*. "I think such a tiny target is more specific than the four and a quarter inch hole itself and thus it forces you to line up and stroke more precisely."

PUTT TO THE BACK OF THE HOLE

To ensure that he makes a positive stroke, Christy O'Connor Jr. always aims for the back of the hole rather than trying to let the ball drop in at the front of the cup. He advocates that you should hit the ball with enough pace for it to finish two feet past the hole if it misses.

Augusta National Georgia

"GOLDEN BELL," 12TH HOLE, PAR-3, 155 YARDS

THE PUTTING CHALLENGE

Augusta National Golf Club, Georgia, is the permanent home of the first major championship of the season—the Masters—which is played during April. The challenging and beautiful course is testimony to the vision of the legendary Bobby Jones, who asked the British golf-course architect Dr. Alister MacKenzie to help him create his dream course. Always in immaculate condition, the course is famous for its lightning-fast greens.

Augusta National is probably most renowned for the speed and severity of its greens. The slick and undulating putting surfaces are so quick that they have been likened to putting on linoleum, a pane of glass, or in a bath tub. Ian Woosnam famously prepared for one tournament by practicing his putting while standing on a snooker table.

On the stimpmeter, there is nothing to suggest that the greens at Augusta are going to be any quicker than a regular PGA Tour event or any of the other major championships, but it is the severity of the undulations, which often go unseen on television, that cause the players the most problems. In many instances, a 40-foot uphill putt is far preferable to a three-foot putt down the slope, and all competitors know that the secret to shooting a low score is accurately controlling their approach shots so that they finish below the hole. Very often you will see players aiming well away from the hole and almost putting in the opposite direction, knowing that the break will ferry the ball toward the hole. Not surprisingly, even the top players can become intimidated by the greens.

PRO-FILE
BEN CRENSHAW

Keep it simple and consistent

Ben Crenshaw has been one of the world's best putters for several decades. One of the reasons for his consistency is the familiarity of his stroke and his equipment. Crenshaw uses a similar style of blade putter to the one he used at the beginning of his career, and his technique is essentially the same, too. Crenshaw's emphasis is on getting comfortable at address and concentrating on maintaining a smooth rhythm and striking the ball solidly. When reading a green, he thinks about the pace and then visualizes how far to the right or left the ball should travel around the hole. As far as Crenshaw is concerned, the skill is getting as close to the hole as possible every time and if the ball drops it is a bonus.

Crenshaw's putting has earned him two Masters victories—in 1984 and 1995. One of the keys to his first win was holing a seemingly impossible 60-foot putt on the 10th hole, which shook his opponents Larry Nelson and Tom Kite. In 1995, he holed a four-foot birdie putt at the 16th and a 10-footer at the 17th before nursing a 10-foot downhiller to within two feet of the hole at the last to win by one stroke from Davis Love III.

The most famous stretch of holes on the course is undoubtedly the 11th, 12th, and 13th, collectively known as Amen Corner. The apex of the three holes—the par-3 12th—has often been labeled the most treacherous short hole in the world. Its difficulty is certainly not its length. Playing at just over 150 yards long, the green is encircled by towering pine trees that cause the wind to swirl around and make it difficult for the players to select the correct club for the tee shot. The difficulty is intensified by the fact that the landing area on the green is very narrow and on the last day the flag is usually tucked behind a bunker that lies in front of the green, just beyond Rae's Creek, which also collects its fair share of balls. Any tee shot that overshoots the green is likely to end up in either a deep swale or the bunker and facing a green that slopes sharply away toward the water. The most sensible play, adopted by most of the pros, is to aim the tee shot to the widest part of the green.

12
The Mental Game

There is no greater asset for a golfer than confidence. When you are playing well, you feel that there is nothing you cannot achieve—no shot you cannot hit, no putt you cannot make, no chip you cannot get stone dead to the hole. You feel almost invincible. At the other end of the scale, most golfers will have experienced days when nothing seems to go right no matter how hard they try, and their confidence quickly drains away to be replaced by negative thoughts and images. At the top level of the game, mental strength and resolve are just as important assets to a top player as a silky-smooth swing and a sensitive putting touch. Most top players have a psychologist to help them deal with the pressure of competing at the highest level and to maintain their self-belief.

Create a winning attitude

It is often said that golf is 90 percent mental and, all things considered, that is a fairly accurate statement. Even the most mentally resilient golfer can experience the pangs of self-doubt that inevitably follow a run of bad holes or shots. However, overcoming your fear, nerves, and anxiety on the golf course is part and parcel of becoming a good golfer. The correct mental approach is as important as your fundamentals or the quality of your swing.

PUTTING IS A BAROMETER OF YOUR GAME

Chi Chi Rodriguez believes that putting is a good barometer of the entire game and he claims that, if you are putting well, it is highly likely that the rest of your game is good, too.

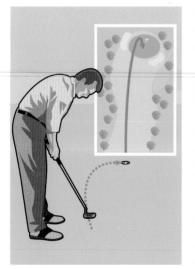

ROUTINES MUST BE SECOND NATURE

"A routine is not a routine if you have to think about it," says Davis Love.

GET SCARED LOOSE INSTEAD OF STIFF

"The late Bernard Darwin, the eminent British golf writer, made a beautiful report of how poised and nerveless I was as I stroked my last putt of the 1931 British Open—which I won by a stroke from Jose Jurado," writes Tommy Armour in *Tommy Armour's ABC's of Golf*. "The undramatic fact is that I was virtually unconscious, and the putt must have been holed by good habit and instinct. The lesson, if any, I got out of that and similar situations is to try to train yourself to get scared loose instead of stiff."

BELIEVE IN YOURSELF

"The right mental approach can be just as important as a golfer's swing," writes Gay Brewer in *Score Better Than You Swing*. "I discovered this during the five lean years I spent on Tour immediately after turning pro. Of all the lessons I learned in that time, I think the biggest was

about confidence. As I see life nowadays, the first thing anybody has to do to be any good at anything is to believe in himself. In golf, once you can play a little, this is the key."

ELIMINATE THE DOUBT

In *Every Shot I Take*, Davis Love III says: "If you can get rid of the doubt, you significantly increase your chances of not missing the shot. So how do you get rid of doubt? Practice, for one thing. If you've played the shot in practice, then you can play it on the course."

TAKE CONTROL OF YOUR OWN GAME

According to Tiger Woods, the only way to get used to the pressure that comes with being in contention to win is constantly to put yourself in that position. That way you will have a better chance of dealing with the feelings and pressure that accompany the heat of battle.

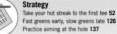

Strategy
Take your hot streak to the first tee **52**
Fast greens early, slow greens late **126**
Practice aiming at the hole **137**

Swing theory
Control your rhythm **37**
Become a good swing copier **41**
Make your real swing in front of the pro **186**

Equipment
Grease the thread of your spikes **17**
Keep head, hands, and feet warm at all costs **211**

⬤ STAY ALERT AND OBSERVANT

The best golfers are very observant. From monitoring the strength of the wind, to checking out the potential danger areas on the hole, you need to be alert to score well. Always learn from your playing partners' shots so that you have as much information at your disposal before you play your own ball.

⬤ LEARN FROM YOUR EXPERIENCES

All of the world's top players learn from their experiences—good and bad—on the golf course. Tiger Woods says you should use the mind's immense memory capacity to store these experiences away ready for the day when you can put them to good use.

⬤ A HOT STREAK IS YOUR TRUE POTENTIAL

Try to avoid thinking of a hot streak as a lucky run of play, but instead as your true potential as a player. If you make a note of how you behave, make decisions, and approach your shots while in the zone, you can learn how to get into this productive state more often.

⬤ MAKE A NOTE OF YOUR MISTAKES

Many top players, including Nick Faldo, will sit down after a game and reflect on any significant shots or poor decisions they may have made. Ben Hogan was the first top professional to visit the practice range after a competitive round as well as before, and it is always a good idea to spend some time on the practice range to address your key problems while they are fresh in your mind.

⬤ TRY LESS HARD ON THE COURSE

One of the key pieces of advice that Davis Love III's father gave to him was to try less hard on the golf course than you do in practice. The range is the place to experiment and work, while the golf course is the place to relax and let things go.

⬤ BUILD A TARGET PICTURE

In *Be the Target*, Byron Huff identifies: "The six components of the target picture. The first five components—the target, the terrain around the target, the wind, the lie, and the slope of the stance—determine the sixth component—the ball flight path."

⬤ LEARN TO GRIND OUT A SCORE

The top professionals constantly turn potentially mediocre rounds into subpar scores simply by remaining composed and waiting for the right opportunity. Whatever your level, the ability to turn a 96 into a 90 or an 85 into an 80 or 81 is invaluable. Simply thinking sensibly will save you many strokes throughout the year.

DON'T RISK WASTING SEVERAL SHOTS TO SAVE ONE

Self-discipline is one of your greatest allies on the golf course. Many golfers waste countless numbers of strokes during every round by attempting to play adventurous recovery shots that deep down they know they have very little chance of executing successfully. Don't put three or four shots on the line by trying to save one.

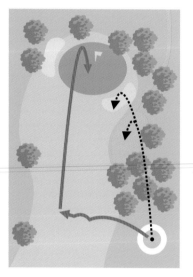

VISUALIZE TO REALIZE

Sandy Lyle admits that it took him many years to appreciate that the action of hitting a golf ball required as much mental energy as physical. Lyle claims that picturing the successful outcome of a shot in your mind programs the brain to complete the task.

PUT THE BAD SHOTS BEHIND YOU

Gay Brewer counsels in *Score Better Than You Swing*: "You have to forget the bad shot and go on to the next one. If you don't you'll just hit a whole mess of poor shots."

ELIMINATE NEGATIVE SELF-TALK

Rather than talk about what they do well, most amateurs focus on the negative aspects of their game. Stop that negative self-talk straightaway. It subconsciously eats away at your confidence, places doubts in your mind, impedes your progress, and ruins your enjoyment of the game. Focus on what you do well and don't waste time or energy thinking about bad shots.

THINK OF YOURSELF AS A GOOD PLAYER NOW

There's a famous saying in psychology: "As you think, you become." Follow this piece of advice and start thinking of yourself as a good golfer right now. Imagine what it would be like, how you would think on the course, how you would approach the game, and how confident you would be if you were a low handicapper or a professional. Then act that way yourself.

FOCUS BEFORE YOU REACH THE BALL

While spending several hours on the golf course it is almost impossible to remain fully focused for every single second. Between shots, Greg Norman allows his mind to wander away from his round and drift to all sorts of subjects, from family to business, but he clicks back into full concentration well before he reaches his ball.

PUT A BAD HOLE OUT OF YOUR MIND

To help him cope with the anger and frustration that inevitably follows a bad hole, Nick Faldo tries to pretend that a week has elapsed since he made the mistake to lessen the risk that his emotions will affect his next shot.

Accuracy & distance
Never rely on best shot to clear a hazard **158**
Structure your putting practice **190**
Close your eyes for better distance control **192**

Club selection
The three yardages you need to know **70**
Check position of tee markers **160**
Get pin-high at approach shots **161**

144

THE BRAIN DOESN'T UNDERSTAND "DON'T"

"The main problem with the brain is that it cannot differentiate between the commands do and don't," says David Norman, the golf psychologist. "So if you tell yourself: "Don't hit the ball into the pond," your brain thinks that is what you want it to do. In such a situation always think about what you want to achieve, not what you want to avoid."

FOCUS ON TARGET AND FEEL IN PRACTICE SWING

Dr. Bob Rotella likes his pupils to make their practice swings thinking only of the target and feeling the correct swing without even thinking about mechanics. However, if you have to focus on technical thoughts, Rotella recommends that you make two practice swings. In the first swing, think about your mechanics; in the second swing, you concentrate purely on target and feel.

OVERCOME YOUR FEAR OF FAILURE

The key factor that prevents amateurs from playing to their full potential is the fear of failure. Why is it that you can hit the ball confidently on the range, then stand on the first tee in a club competition the following day so nervous that you can barely take the club back? Is it because you have turned into a bad player overnight or because your swing has suddenly developed a destructive flaw? No. The difference is that on the range you can't lose your ball, you can't make double or triple bogeys and there are no harsh consequences, such as penalty shots, for wayward shots.

PICK THE SMALLEST TARGET

"Before playing any shot— from a drive to a three-foot putt—you must pick out the smallest possible target to minimize your margin for error," advises Scott Canfield, a PGA professional.

AVOID SETTING LIMITS

How many times have you been playing solidly for most of the round only to fall apart over the closing holes after you looked at the scorecard and realized that you had a great chance of beating your best score? Avoid setting yourself scoring limitations and instead go for the best score possible.

NEVER ATTEMPT TO STEER YOUR SHOTS

Committing 100 percent to each shot will help you keep the ball in play more easily than trying to steer the ball down the fairway. You will also feel much better in yourself knowing that you are playing the way you want to rather than spending four hours on the course worrying about the consequences of poor shots.

ALWAYS COMMIT TO MAKING A POSITIVE SWING

Your ultimate goal is to take a fearless approach to the golf course and your first step is to make a pact with yourself to swing positively every time and play each shot how you want to play it. Try it out for nine holes by yourself when you don't have the added pressure of worrying about how your new mental approach will work in front of your peers.

○ SNAP YOURSELF BACK TO REALITY

"If you suffer from a lack of focus at the right time, struggle to be specific with your target, allow negative images to creep into your mind, or let your mind race ahead or dwell on past mistakes, pop an elastic band around your wrist before you head to the first tee," advises Nick Bradley, a PGA pro in England. "Painful as it sounds, pulling on the elastic band and letting it go onto your wrist as you approach your ball will jolt you and remind you to avoid the bad habits. This generates a state of awareness and alertness that allows you to see your habit for what it is, thus allowing you to act positively."

○ CHARM YOUR GOLF BALL

Sam Snead has some charming advice in *The Education of a Golfer*: " 'This isn't going to hurt a bit,' I tell the ball under my breath. 'Sambo is just going to give you a nice little ride.' Or I might say, 'Hello, dimples, I see you're sitting up fat and ready; let us have some fun …' By acting as if the ball is human, I distract myself—leaving no time for thoughts of this and that. Sometimes the ball looks back at me and seems to say, 'Okay, Sam, but treat me gently!' That's

a ball that's friendly, the kind that will go for you … Get charming with your golf ball if you want pars and birdies."

○ DON'T OVERREACT TO BAD SHOTS

Many amateur golfers fall into the trap of believing that the quality of their golf mirrors their self-worth as a person. You must understand that any shot, regardless of whether it is good or bad, is not a representation of your character, ability, or luck.

○ SELECT SMALL TARGETS TO AIM AT

A target gives your brain a task to focus on. Simply aiming somewhere down the fairway or on the green is not specific enough and will lead to sloppy play. Pick out a small target,

such as a marker post, a tree in the distance or a particular quarter of the green. This makes you more task-oriented, improves your concentration, and reduces your margin for error. Golf isn't just about the quality of your good shots. It's the quality of your bad shots that determines how well you score.

○ PICTURE PERFECT CONTACT

Picture yourself making the perfect swing and perfect contact with the ball. Picture the flight and trajectory of the shot you want to hit and the ball landing close to your intended target. Hold the image in your mind as you play the shot and make the picture as vivid as possible so that it is more realistic.

○ BELIEVE YOU HAVE THE RIGHT CLUB FOR THE SHOT

Harvey Penick has some advice for the indecisive golfer. He says that when you pick the club for the shot you must believe that you have picked the right club, and hit the shot with confidence. If you hit it well and it turns out you were a club too much or too little, you're not going to be far from your target. However, if you pick a club as a compromise because you're not sure which club to take, and you address the ball wondering whether you

Setup
Better long than short **59**
Distance you hit varies from day to day **70**
Wrong length practice strokes enhance feel **135**

Swing theory
Steep attacks lead to crisp chips **101**
Maintain the "Y" throughout your stroke **130**
Find your natural rhythm **186**

should really have clubbed up or down, then you're guaranteed to be heading for trouble.

LOOK BEYOND THE TARGET
In his book, *Be the Target*, Byron Huff says that because most amateur golfers concentrate only on the ground between their ball and the target, this is where most of their shots land and this is a main reason why they underclub and fail to reach the putting surface.

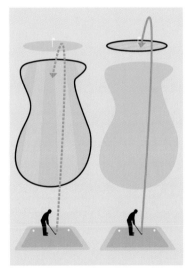

BUILD A LIBRARY OF GOOD MEMORIES
It is very difficult not to become annoyed after a bad hole, but, instead of focusing on your bad shots, think instead about the good ones. We all like to sit down at the end of the round with our playing partners and reminisce over what might have been if, say, we hadn't three-putted the last three holes, fluffed that chip on the last green, or driven out of bounds at the opening hole. Rather than pay attention to what you did poorly, focus on what you did well. Replay the good shots in your mind and build a library of positive memories.

TOTAL CONCENTRATION
Concentration doesn't necessarily mean that you become so wrapped up in your own thoughts that you don't speak during the round. It simply means that you should be focused when preparing for and playing each and every shot. When it comes to playing an important shot, you will struggle to play it well if you are chatting away while going through your preshot routine or talking to your playing partners as you prepare to hit the shot.

COMPETE AGAINST YOURSELF
In *Every Shot I Take*, Davis Love III tells us: "In golf, the only thing that really matters ... is what you do against yourself. Have you played to the best of your capabilities? Did you enjoy yourself on the course? How did you do against par?"

ANYONE CAN BE A GOOD PUTTER
John Daly informs us in *The Killer Swing*: "You have to get it through your head that you are not cursed with some kind of voodoo spell that condemns you to putting poorly forever. There's no lid on the hole for anyone."

DON'T LOSE SIGHT OF THE TASK AT HAND
Every so often Nick Faldo walks off the 18th green in a tournament and has absolutely no idea of how many shots he has played. He believes that this is the ideal mental state for golf and that most amateur golfers would improve if they stopped trying to calculate how many strokes they need to take over the closing holes to beat their best score.

Southern Hills Oklahoma

18TH HOLE, PAR-4, 420 YARDS

GOOD OLD-FASHIONED SOUTHERN HOSPITALITY

Set in the rolling tree-lined hills in Tulsa, Oklahoma, Southern Hills Country Club is one of those rare golf courses that manage to exist in the middle of a city. However, the club's urban proximity hasn't dented its appeal as it regularly features in lists of the country's top-20 courses, which is a huge tribute to the designer Perry Maxwell, who made best possible use of the available land to create a compact yet highly individual golf course.

The Southern Hills Country Club is one of America's finest and most traditional Championship golf courses, having staged 13 Major Championships in its 67-year history.

The land on which the course is built was donated by wealthy oil magnate, Waite Phillips, after the stock market crash in the early 1930s. He was approached by local businessmen to finance a new family-orientated country club that would feature a swimming pool, stable, horseback trails, polo field, skeet range, tennis courts, clubhouse, and golf course.

Phillips agreed to donate the land if the businessmen could prove that there was a sufficient number of people interested in such a project. They were given two weeks to garner pledges from at least 150 Tulsans for $1,000 each. The money was raised and the clubhouse was constructed in 1936. Perry Maxwell, who redesigned the Augusta National, was hired to design the golf course.

The course is long, narrow, and very, very tough. The fairways are narrow and dramatic, placing heavy emphasis on accurate driving. The par-3s are all long and challenging, as are the par-5s.

PRO-FILE
RETIEF GOOSEN

Confront your mental demons

Despite winning several tournaments worldwide and becoming one of the most highly respected golfers on the European Tour in the late 1990s, South Africa's Retief Goosen admitted that he lacked the self-belief and confidence to win Major Championships. Aware that this was holding him back and preventing him from achieving his potential, Goosen consulted Belgian golf psychologist, Joss Vanstiphout, and the pair worked closely on improving all aspects of the mental side of his game. Visualization, positive imagery and body language, and established preshot routines, all play a crucial role in remaining focused at the highest level of the game. The greatest test of Goosen's preparatory work came in the 2001 US Open at Southern Hills where he led the field on all four days, but three-putted the last hole from fairly short range to allow Mark Brooks to force a playoff the following day. Many golfers have crumbled at the thought of missing a two-foot putt to win a Major, but Goosen regrouped successfully and went out the following day to beat Brooks and win his first Major Championship.

The 18th hole at Southern Hills is one of the truly great finishing holes in Major Championship golf. It is a dogleg right, which requires a long and accurate drive to a plateau on the left side of the fairway 200 yards out from the elevated green, which slopes sharply from back to front. Because of this, a long-iron or fairway-wood approach shot must carry to the green, otherwise the ball is likely to roll some 20 or 30 yards back down the apron toward you. Retief Goosen experienced the treacherous nature of the hole in the 2001 US Open Championship when he three-putted from close range to miss the opportunity to win the event on the Sunday evening.

His playing partner, Stewart Cink, also three-putted the last and missed out on the 18-hole playoff between Mark Brooks and Goosen the following day. Although Goosen once again bogeyed the 18th hole in the playoff, this time he had the cushion of a healthy lead and he notched up his first Major victory.

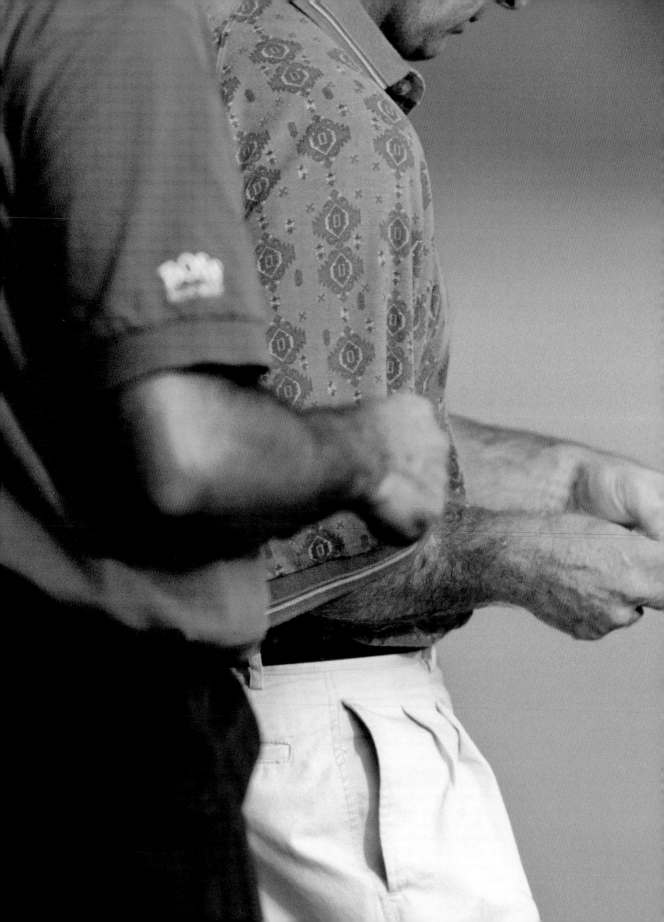

◐ ORGANIZE THE CONTENTS OF YOUR GOLF BAG

Make sure that you have everything you need to play the opening hole ready before you walk to the first tee. You will need a golf ball, tees, scorecard, pencil, glove, and pitch-mark repairer, so have these items readily to hand. You don't need to waste time and nervous energy rummaging around in your bag when you should be focusing on the tee shot.

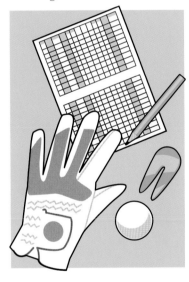

◐ DEVELOP A PREROUND ROUTINE

To maximize the effectiveness of your time before you tee off, develop a preround routine, whereby you check in, get changed, and then go through the same warm-up and practice routine each time. The consistency in preparation will increase your confidence.

◐ ASK GOLF CLUB STAFF FOR COURSE INFORMATION

If you are playing at a course you have never previously visited, you can glean some vital information from staff at the club on the difficulty of the course. The assistant pros will generally be more than happy to tell you, for example, some of the key characteristics of the course and even advise you on how to best play some of the holes.

◐ PRACTICE YOUR PUTTING RHYTHM

Just as the time on the range is not for rebuilding your swing, the time on the practice putting green isn't for working on the mechanics of your stroke. Prior to your round, focus on your rhythm, rolling the ball smoothly and striking the ball solidly. Leave the technical work until after your round.

◐ PRACTICE SHORT SHOTS BEFORE YOU PLAY

"If you are a recreational player, warming up is also important to get your mind and body ready for the game," advises Annika Sorenstam in *LPGA's Guide To Every Shot*. "Start with short irons, finish with full swings, and always take some putts to get a feel for the green and to finish your practice with confidence. Remember 63 percent of your score is from approach shots to the green (pitching, chipping, and putting) so make sure to practice short shots before you play."

◐ USE RANGE TIME TO LOOSEN YOUR MUSCLES

Avoid working on your swing technique on the practice range before you go out to play. Use your time to loosen your muscles gently and to work on your rhythm and tempo. Resist the temptation to make technical changes before you tee off because you will inevitably end up feeling confused and trapped in myriad conflicting swing thoughts.

● PRACTICE LONG-RANGE PUTTS BEFORE FIRST TEE

The PGA professional, Mickey Walker, counsels: "On the first few holes of a round, it's highly likely that your first few putts will be from fairly long-range. Prepare for this by hitting at least half a dozen 30- to 40-foot putts on the practice putting green. This will enable you to get a feel for the pace of the greens and also an idea of the length of stroke you will need on the longer putts."

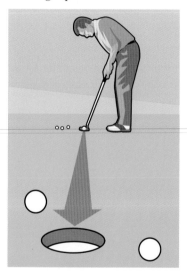

● DON'T WASTE TIME OVER THE BALL

In *LPGA's Guide To Every Shot*, Annika Sorenstam tells us: "In general I'm a fast player, and I don't like slow play. I think a lot of golfers tend to take too much time reading putts, figuring out the wind, and calculating the yardage. I personally think that once you calculate the yardage, there are not that many shots to choose from. Try to make it simple. Try to hit a good shot and always try to curve it less—the less time you have to think about what kind of shot to hit, the better your shot will most likely be."

● MAKE CARRY OVER WATER COMFORTABLE

"When you are hitting a drive to carry a hazard, allow yourself a good 20 yards extra safety margin," says Christy O'Connor Jr. in *Golf Masterclass*. "The ball should then run on into a safe area. If you can't safely carry the hazard, then lay up short of it."

● MATCH YOUR CLUBS TO THE COURSE

Golf courses vary considerably in length, style, and difficulty. You can tailor your set of clubs to each course you are playing. You may decide, if you are playing a short course, for example, that several long irons are not necessary, and that you would be better off adding an extra fairway wood or a wedge in favor of a long iron if there are a lot of long carries into the greens.

● SEE WHERE ARCHITECT DOESN'T WANT YOU TO HIT

Phil Mickelson has a useful routine when he first steps on the tee. He notes where the architect intends him to hit the ball, and he looks at where the architect doesn't want him to hit.

● SET SIMPLE GOALS FOR THE ROUND

Helen Alfredsson urges in *Golf for Women*: "Set goals for yourself before each round and keep them simple. Pick one or two aspects to try to improve on—say you won't have any three-putts, or you'll hit ten fairways instead of eight in your round. Or, if you shoot a 45 on the front, go for a 44 on the back. Little goals add up to big achievements—like lower scores."

	Strategy		**Swing theory**		**Club selection**
	Know and control your bad shots **40**		Good balance makes good swings **37**		Learn to play with just one club **69**
	Stick to what has already worked **198**		Swing from left toe to right heel **45**		Take at least one extra club in cold weather **215**

● EAT RAISINS DURING YOUR ROUND

"Your body is like a motor car engine," the legendary Gary Player tells us in *Gary Player's Golf Secrets*. "You have to put fuel in or it runs out of gas. Therefore, I always carry some raisins in my bag and eat them during the round. They are full of energy and easy to digest."

● USE FAVORITE CLUB IN PRESSURE SITUATIONS

During every round of golf, there will be times when you have to play a pressure tee shot when you need to find the fairway. In these kinds of situations, boost your confidence by using your favorite club to play the shot. Rather than a driver, a midiron may be a better choice of club. It's far better to be 150 yards or so straight down the middle of the fairway than 180 yards in the trees.

● PLAY THE SHOT YOU KNOW YOU CAN HIT

English PGA professional, Nick Bradley, says "Experienced tour players never fight against the shape of shot they have taken to the range on the day of a tournament. Under pressure, the seasoned pro will hit the shot he knows he can hit rather than the one he would like to."

● HOLE SHORT PUTTS TO INCREASE CONFIDENCE

Many of the top golfers conclude their preround warm-up by holing several two-foot putts. This gives them the confidence of seeing the ball drop into the hole before they head to the first tee, and puts them in the correct frame of mind when they face their first short putt of the day on the course.

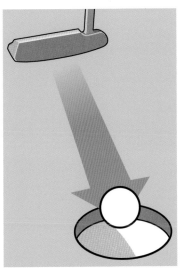

● LOOK TO SEE WHERE HOLE IS GOING TO BITE YOU

The PGA professional, Keith Wood, maintains that the purpose of a golf hole is "to test your technique and your strategy. Prepare yourself for the challenge by looking at course planners and/or the yardage boards on the tees to find out where the hazards are and your most sensible route into the green. Look to see where the hole is most likely to catch you out and increase your margin for error with your shot selection so that you stack the odds in your favor."

● KNOW WHERE NOT TO HIT THE BALL

Tiger Woods says that he likes to eliminate one side of the fairway on his tee shots so that he avoids the main hazards and the trouble areas. He claims that knowing where not to hit the ball is just as important as where to hit it. Analyze the hole to find out where the majority of the trouble is located and then play away from it.

● AVOID DISASTERS ON THE OPENING HOLES

The opening few holes in a round of golf set the tone for the entire day. If you start badly, you immediately put pressure on yourself to make up for the dropped shots and invariably you start to play more aggressively. Use the first few holes to settle into your round. If you can avoid dropping more than one shot at any hole in the first half an hour, you will be able to build on your early confidence and improve as the round continues.

ALWAYS PLAN AT LEAST ONE SHOT AHEAD

To work out the best way to play a hole, Annika Sorenstam looks at the hole backward from green to tee. By working out the best angle into the green, she knows where she will need to place her tee shot. She always plans at least one shot ahead.

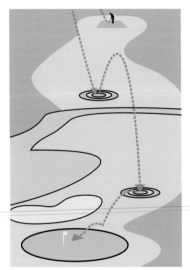

USE ALL OF THE TEE BOX

Many amateur golfers always tee the ball directly in the center of the tee markers. However, you should remember that the teeing area stretches back two full club lengths behind the markers, so you have many different positions to choose from. Teeing up on either side of the area, for example, allows you to aim more easily at specific sides of the fairway.

ADJUST CLUBS ACCORDING TO GREENS

Per-Ulrik Johansson prefers to take as many significant factors as possible into account on each and every shot made. On an approach shot, for example, the condition of the greens will influence your club selection. If they are wet and receptive, the ball will stop quickly on landing. If they are hard and fast, you may need to use a more lofted club to achieve the same distance, since the ball will bounce forward and run 10 to 20 yards on landing.

SPLIT EACH ROUND INTO SIX MINI-ROUNDS

To maintain your concentration, split each round into six sets of three holes and then aim to play each set in a specific number of strokes. The Swedish Ryder Cup player, Per-Ulrik Johansson, uses this tactic. His target is to play each set of three holes in 1-under-par. If he plays one set poorly, he has a new task to focus on for the next set. Likewise, if he birdies the first three holes, rather than think that his good play must soon end, he can focus on a new target. Set a realistic target for your own level of play and continually set yourself a new challenge.

USE THE TEE BOX TO CUT OFF DOGLEGS

"Very few golfers use the full width and depth of the teeing area," Per-Ulrik Johansson, the PGA Tour professional, asserts. "On a dogleg hole you can improve your chances of cutting off the corner by teeing the ball at either the left or right edge of the tee box. On a dogleg right, tee off from the left edge and aim to the right. On a dogleg left, setting up on the right and aiming down the left will provide a better angle."

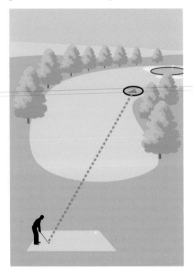

DON'T ATTEMPT TO CURVE BALL ROUND DOGLEGS

In *Pure Golf*, Johnny Miller has this advice: "You'll be working against the odds by trying to play the ball close to the corner of a dogleg. If you aim straight

Swing theory
Improve quality of your mistimed shots **37**
Build up to your ideal rhythm **40**
Match length of stroke to length of putt **132**

Strategy
Putts break towards highest mountains **127**
Plan in advance like a pool player **203**

Accuracy & distance
Let right shoulder lag behind in downswing **37**
If you can't see a break, don't play for it **136**

156

down the middle you can draw, hook, hit the ball straight, or fade it and not get into trouble. You have more options. About the only time I would recommend trying to work the ball around a dogleg is, first, if you have the shot in your bag, and second, there is a good reason for attempting the shot."

PLAY YOUR OWN GAME

One of the key lessons that Nick Faldo taught Colin Montgomerie during their Ryder Cup matches was the need to play to your own strengths. Focus on what you do well and avoid dwelling on the areas of the game where you don't excel.

HOW TO PLAN YOUR ROUND

If you play most of your golf at the same course, you have the perfect opportunity to devise a good game plan. Start this process by thinking about how you normally play each hole and ask yourself if there is a better or more sensible way to negotiate it. If one particular hole or holes consistently cause you problems, analyze whether it is poor strategy that is to blame for your poor run of scoring or simply bad luck. Chances are it is the former. If so, adopt a totally different strategy the next time you play.

MAKE A BOGEY WORST SCORE ON ANY HOLE

Colin Montgomerie often says that pars and bogeys add up slowly on the scorecard while double and triple bogeys add up very quickly indeed. This strategy doesn't mean you should accept that you are going to drop a shot any time you find yourself in trouble on the course, but that you should not compound an error by making another one.

BE AWARE OF HAZARDS BUT DON'T FOCUS ON THEM

You need to know the positioning of the key hazards when planning your strategy for the hole, but it is important that you do not focus on them. Tiger Woods says that he looks to see where the hazards are on the hole and then uses that

information to help him select the correct club and determine his strategy. Once he has done that he focuses on the shot in hand and forgets about the hazards completely.

KNOW WHEN TO TAKE YOUR MEDICINE

Every golfer hits the ball into the trees every so often. However, while professionals will generally accept that the most sensible course of action is simply to chip the ball out sideways and back onto the fairway, many amateurs believe they can pull off miraculous recovery shots, even when the odds are stacked against them. If the downside of taking on a shot is leaving yourself in an even worse position afterward, always play the percentages and take the safe route back to the fairway.

START AND FINISH WARM-UP WITH WEDGES

To warm up your muscles before a round of golf, start with your sand wedge to give yourself confidence and hit a few balls with each club in the bag, working your way up to the driver. Finish your warm-up with a few wedges to restore your rhythm before heading to the first tee.

◯ KNOW YARDAGES WITH EVERY CLUB IN BAG

Knowing how far you hit the ball with each club in the bag is vital information that will determine your strategy on every shot. Without that knowledge at your disposal, your club selection on any shot is nothing more than guesswork. To record your accurate yardages, take 10 balls onto the practice field. After hitting all 10 balls, ignore your two best and two worst shots, measure the remaining six balls and take an average of the total. Like it or not, that's your yardage with that club.

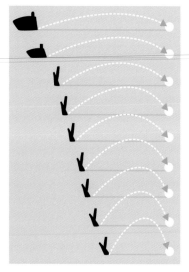

◯ WORK THE BALL INTO THE PINS

Johnny Miller believes that either drawing or fading the ball into the flag is the ideal way to reach pins that are either tucked behind hazards or set in the back corners of the greens, because you are combining the percentage play of aiming at the center of the green with the attacking strategy of curving the ball in toward the target.

◯ NEVER RELY ON BEST SHOT TO CLEAR A HAZARD

If you decide to hit a long shot over the water, it's critical to know how far it is to reach the water and, also, how far it is to clear the hazard. Never make that decision without knowing either yardage. If you're going to lay up, make sure that you don't leave the ball right at the water's edge, since that will place even more pressure on your shoulders. If you go for the carry, don't rely on your best shot to make it. Always make it a comfortable shot, not one that's right at the limit of the club in your hand.

◯ MEMORIZE YARDAGES ON YOUR HOME COURSE

Club golfers often play the same course week in, week out, but how many take the trouble to mark down key yardages? Pros will use a practice round to build up a yardage book before a tournament, so that they know precisely where the trouble is off the tee and around the green.

◯ VISUALIZE YOURSELF BACK ON THE RANGE

To reduce the pressure on a tee shot, pretend that you are back on the driving range and hitting the ball into a wide field. This will remove some of the tension from your muscles and help you make a more relaxed and free-flowing swing.

◯ RESPECT TROUBLE AND LOOK BEFORE YOU LEAP

Tiger Woods always aims for a specific part of the green, but, before doing so, he takes into account the putt he wants to leave himself and the penalty that may await him if he doesn't execute the shot perfectly. Woods believes that good iron play is an equal combination of smart strategy and a good technique.

Equipment
Match your putter to your stroke **17**
Use same type of golf ball **121**
Carry lots of small towels in your bag **213**

Swing theory
Think "Sam Snead" to improve driving **60**
Keep putter head low on follow through **130**

KEEP BALL LOW AROUND GREENS WHERE POSSIBLE

Never attempt to play a fancy shot when a straightforward shot is easier and will get the job done just as well. Nowhere is this more important than when you are chipping from around the green. If there are no obstacles, such as rough, long grass, or any kind of ditch or uneven ground between your ball and the hole, there is no point trying to loft the ball into the air. The basic equation to remember is: "less loft = less wrists = more margin for error."

DON'T GET TEMPTED BY SUCKER PINS

Greenkeepers will often position the pins directly behind bunkers or water hazards, where they are accessible only to a perfectly struck shot. These are known as "sucker pins" because, since there is very little margin for error, only suckers aim at them. In most instances, the most sensible strategy is to identify and then play to the largest area of the green.

BRAINS ARE BETTER THAN BRAWN IN THE ROUGH

Sandy Lyle has some cautionary advice for those golfers who think that the best way to get out of the rough is to try and muscle it out. Lyle prefers to use his brains, and first makes sure that he has selected the correct club for the shot he's facing. Then he likes to focus on keeping things simple and accept that sometimes it's best to play the percentage shot that will guarantee to get him back on to the fairway and still leave him the possibility of getting up and down in two shots.

DISCOVER STOCK SHOT AND KNOW WEAKNESSES

A key to consistent golf is developing a stock shot that you can rely on under pressure. At the same time, it's a very good idea to be aware of your swing flaws. Even the best golfers have certain idiosyncrasies that constantly haunt them. Acquaint yourself with your own Achilles' heel so that you will know what to look out for and how it will affect your game. The ability to diagnose the cause of your bad shots is invaluable.

ANALYZE YOUR HOME GREENS

Greg Norman provides this advice in his *100 Instant Golf Lessons*: "Take note of the big greens on your course and jot down the clubs you usually play into those holes. You'll find that some will be two-club greens and others will be three-clubbers, and in these cases you should make note of the clubs for pin positions in the front, middle, and back of the green."

FOCUS ON HOLING OUT

A lot of things go through your mind after you've played a poor approach putt that leaves you three or four feet from the hole. You may be embarrassed; you could be angry or even try to rush so you don't hold up play. You can eliminate a lot of missed short putts simply by restoring a positive mental state and concentrating on your normal pre-putt routine. Always take a good look at the putt and give it the care and attention it deserves.

VISUALIZE A CIRCLE ROUND HOLE ON LONG PUTTS

Most golfers three-putt far too often because they under- or overhit the first approach putt. You can remove a lot of the pressure by visualizing a circular zone 18 inches around the hole into which you should roll the ball. It doesn't really matter whether your putt finishes 18 inches short, long, left, or right of the hole, because that's basically a tap-in.

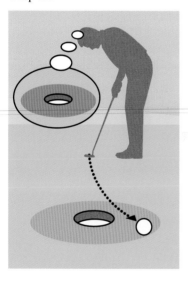

CHECK POSITION OF TEE MARKERS

The Ryder Cup player Irish Christy O'Connor Jr. says that you should always double-check to see if the tee marker yardages correspond with the details on the scorecard. Although the distance on the card may say 180 yards, the tee markers may have been moved considerably forward or backward. You could be playing from anywhere between 150 and 200 yards, which is effectively five clubs' difference.

CAPITALIZE ON THE SHORT HOLES TO BUILD A SCORE

Capitalizing on the par-3 holes is one of the keys to keeping a good score ticking over. If you can make a par at each of the short holes during a round, which is well within most golfers' capabilities, you can cancel out dropped shots at other holes and set yourself up for a decent score.

TAKE ONE MORE CLUB THAN YOU NEED

Many short holes cause problems for golfers because they place a heavy premium on accuracy from the tee. Think carefully about the strength and direction of the wind and look to see where most of the trouble is located. In most cases, hazards are positioned in front of the green, so it is often a good idea to hit extra club off the tee so that even a mistimed or badly struck shot still has a chance of making it to the green.

PLAY THE SAFEST SHOT EVERY TIME

"The next time you compete, try playing the safest shot every time," urges Gary Player in *Gary Player's Golf Secrets*. "There may be an occasion when the gamble might pay off, but on the whole you will score lower because you will have eliminated the double and triple bogies."

NOTHING WRONG AT HITTING A WOOD ON A PAR-3

"There's nothing wrong with hitting a wood on a par-3," says Christy O'Connor Jr., reassuringly, in his book *Golf Masterclass*. "Indeed, a little 5-wood could be the best club possible on a par-3 of … 180–220 yards, and there are plenty of par-3s of that length these days."

Club selection
Hazards in front of the green—selection **72**
Know your carry/roll ratios **98**

Strategy
Greens run faster in the afternoon **127**
Learn from your experiences **143**

WHY SHORT PAR-4S ARE OFTEN FAR FROM EASY

Many coaches advocate playing for accuracy off the tee on short par-4s because holes in the 260–320-yard region are often designed to punish those who attempt to drive as close as possible to the green. The fairway is generally very tight and the landing area often narrows as it approaches the green, making it difficult for you to keep the ball in play off the tee, while the putting surface itself is likely to be very small and well guarded by bunkers and other hazards.

YARDAGES ARE IMPORTANT

"The better you can estimate the distances of your second and third shots, or pinpoint a trap or a tree on a tight driving hole, the more positive your shotmaking becomes and the better your score is likely to be," maintains Gay Brewer in *Score Better Than You Swing*.

GET PIN-HIGH AT APPROACH SHOTS

Per-Ulrik Johansson, PGA Tour professional, assures us: "It is important to get your approach shots pin high on the green because this improves the quality of your misses. A shot that is 10 yards off line

will only be 30 feet away from the hole leaving you a decent chance to hole the putt. If your approach shot is 10 yards off line and also 10 yards short, it's very likely that your ball will be off the green and you will be faced with an awkward chip or pitch to save your par."

KEEP YOUR DRIVE IN PLAY

The last thing you want to be thinking about when standing on the tee of a long and tough par-4 is trying to crush your drive as far as possible. If you think the hole is tough before you hit your drive, it'll be even more difficult when you have to chip the ball sideways back onto the fairway and then still have 280 yards to go to reach the green.

DON'T ASSUME YOU'LL MAKE PAR AT SHORT HOLE

Never assume that you are going to make a par simply because the hole is short. Complacency is the main cause of dropped shots on par-3s. The greens on these holes are often tiny and well guarded by hazards. Spend more time thinking about your club selection and strategy on these holes than on the seemingly more difficult par-4s and par-5s.

KNOW YOUR ATTACKING SHOT

Nick Faldo's favorite attacking shot is the 105-yard wedge and he will attempt to leave himself this shot as often as he can during a round of golf. On a short par-4, he will calculate which club off the tee will leave him 105 yards to the flag, while on par-5s that are out of reach in two shots he will often lay up to his favorite yardage.

SITUATIONS THAT REQUIRE MORE CLUB

Unfortunately, amateurs are often guilty of underclubbing. Always remember to use more club than you would normally expect to take when playing in damp conditions, hitting to an elevated green, or, of course, playing into a headwind.

ALWAYS USE A TEE ON A PAR-3

Using a tee will reduce the risk of a mishit shot. On a par-3, you should always tee the ball up. Jack Nicklaus certainly did and says, "I found out a long time ago that air offers less resistance than dirt."

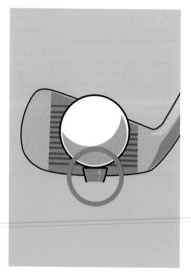

IF LENGTH IS YOUR STRENGTH GO FOR THE GREEN

If length and accuracy off the tee are your best assets, taking out the driver and getting the ball close to the green on a short par-4 can help take the pressure off your short game and gives you the opportunity to take three more shots to get down and still make a par. And, of course, you have the outside chance of making a birdie with a deft chip or pitch.

AVOID GOING FOR GREEN IF SHORT DRIVER

If you are a short or inaccurate driver, the gamble of trying to drive as close as possible to the green on a short par-4 isn't worth taking because you will have to swing harder and faster to achieve the required distance— an approach that often ends in trouble. A much smarter option for the less powerful or less consistent golfer is to hit a smooth long iron or fairway wood into the widest part of the fairway and leave a full shot into the green.

LAY UP TO YOUR FAVORITE YARDAGE

If you can't reach the green on a par-5 with an approach shot, lay up to your favorite yardage. Many of the world's top players will intentionally leave a full shot with a pitching wedge or 9-iron into the green, because they know that they can land the ball close with this club. Very often when you go for the green with your second shot on a par-5 you mishit the shot and leave yourself an awkward pitch over bunkers or water, where you'll need exquisite touch to get the ball close to the hole. From further out, you can comfortably make a confident full swing with your favorite club.

STICK TO YOUR STOCK SHOT

In 34 years as a highly successful Tour pro, Lee Trevino still plays with the fade he started out with all those years ago. Always play to your natural shape unless you are prepared to restructure your swing to straighten it up.

TREAT LONG PAR-4S AS PAR-5S

For most golfers, many long par-4 holes are out of reach in two shots. If that's the case, a sensible strategy is to play the hole as a par-5 by taking a more lofted club off the tee and taking three full shots to reach the putting surface. Using this approach, you should do no worse than bogey the hole and you could even sneak a par. If you try to overpower the hole

Accuracy & distance
Finish with belt buckle facing the target **47**
Treat every putt as straight **129**

Setup
Open clubface slightly from the rough **80**
Set hands 3 inches ahead of ball **95**

162

you could easily lose a ball, mishit your shots and run up a big score on the hole.

DON'T MAKE LONG SWING IF SHORT ONE WILL DO

Keep things simple around the greens where possible. Top pros never play a fancy shot when a straightforward simple play will get the job done just as well. Around the greens, keep your swing as short and compact as possible so that there's less chance for things to go wrong. Most of the time, from just off the edge of the green, all that's required is a slightly extended version of your putting stroke to lift the ball over the fringe and get it rolling toward the hole.

USE YOUR STROKES EFFECTIVELY ON PAR-5S

The par-5s are usually low-stroke-index holes on the scorecard, which is good news for many amateurs because it effectively means you have four shots to reach the green. According to Nick Dougherty, most holes are actually a lot easier if you hit a 3-wood off the tee. You take many of the fairway hazards out of play and, if you can hit two average fairway wood shots, you'll leave only a fairly short-iron approach shot into the flag.

LOOK FOR BAIL-OUT AREAS

Some long par-3s are often out of reach. However, course designers usually make provisions for the higher handicapper or shorter hitter by incorporating a bail-out area— an area of land short of the hole where you can safely play to off the tee. A controlled shot into the bail-out area followed by a deft chip will leave you with a good chance of making your par or a bogey at worst. A wild lunge with a straight-face club could land you in big trouble.

DETERMINING A TEE-SHOT STRATEGY

If you are a long hitter and/or the par-5 hole is fairly short and straightforward, taking a driver off the tee is a calculated risk, since you may be able to reach

the green with your second shot. If, however, the hole is very long and requires three full shots to reach the green, a 3-wood or long iron off the tee may be more sensible. You are more likely to find the fairway and, since you can't reach the green in two shots anyway, the extra distance off the tee isn't that important. You can make that yardage up with your next two shots instead.

TAKING CONTROL OF LONG HOLES

Very often a par-5 will be out of reach in two shots. Therefore your third shot is likely to be from between 40 to 80 yards out. The quality of your pitching holds the key to unlocking the par-5s. If you can get every pitch shot on the putting surface, two-putt and then walk to the next tee, you'll notice a dramatic difference in your scores.

CHOOSE ACCURACY OVER POWER ON LONG HOLES

Statistically, long par-4s are the holes that cause most damage, so, accuracy off the tee is your priority. For the longer hitters, a smoother swing will lead to better contact with the ball and good distance, while the shorter drivers will benefit from keeping the ball in play off the tee.

The Old Course St. Andrews, Scotland

"THE ROAD HOLE," 17TH HOLE, PAR-4, 472 YARDS

THE ULTIMATE STRATEGY TEST

The historic seaside town of St. Andrews in Fife on the east coast of Scotland is known globally as the Home of Golf. The Old Course, which dates back to the fourteenth century, is the most famous stretch of golfing turf in the world and regularly hosts the Open Championship as well as many other important national and international events. Unlike many golf courses of similar stature, the Old Course remains a public facility.

The designer of the famous Old Course is unknown, but whoever was responsible produced a veritable masterpiece that remains as challenging today to those wielding titanium-headed and graphite-shafted drivers as it was to players using feathery golf balls and hickory-shafted clubs. The Old Course is relatively short when compared with many modern designs, but its protection appears in more natural guises, such as semiblind tee shots, undulating fairways, huge double greens, thick gorse, winding burns, hidden pot bunkers, cavernous sand traps and, of course, the unpredictable weather.

Many of the top players have fallen in love with the traditions and the quirkiness of St. Andrews Old Course immediately, while others have not so readily taken to its unique challenge and charm. In his first visit for the Open Championship in 1921, Bobby Jones led all amateurs after the first two rounds. But in the third round he took 46 on the front nine. At the par-4 10th, he took a double bogey. Then, on the par-3 11th, he hit his ball into Hell bunker and eventually picked it up without completing the hole. Jones withdrew and forever

PRO-FILE
TIGER WOODS

Take the trouble out of play

Undoubtedly, many readers would have expected to see Tiger featuring in the driving or long-game section of this book. Although Tiger is an immensely powerful ball striker, even more impressive is his ability to manage his game, particularly in the major championships, where the severity of the course layouts is such that the slightest error in judgment or strategy can prove very costly. Taking his lead from the ultimate percentage player Jack Nicklaus, Tiger has adopted the principle of playing conservative and steady golf when in contention and allowing other golfers to make the mistakes. Perhaps the best example of Tiger's supreme course management came in the Open Championship at St. Andrews in 2000, when he successfully avoided the bunkers on all four days of the event. Prior to the championship, Tiger had watched video tapes of Nick Faldo playing the course in 1990, when he set a record-breaking four-round total to win the event. Although Tiger often took a very conservative line off the tee, he decided that a longer approach shot into the greens was preferable to chipping out sideways from a pot bunker and the risk of a bogey or worse.

viewed the event as his "most inglorious failure" in golf. However, he returned in 1927 and declared that the trophy should remain at St. Andrews should he win, which he did.

The key to playing St. Andrews well is selecting the correct lines off the tee. Certain lines offer maximum relief from hazards and provide more favorable angles into the greens. Nowhere is this more evident than on the notorious "Road Hole," the par-4 17th. The tee shot is semiblind and played over the edge of the hotel grounds that border the right side of the fairway. However, the drive is probably the least demanding feature of the hole. The green itself is a thin slither, protected at the front by a deep bunker and beyond by the "road" itself and a stone wall, where the ball must be played as it lies. The severity of the pot bunker at the front edge of the green makes many golfers elect to miss the green to the right, as this angle provides the best opportunity to get up and down with a chip and a putt for a par.

14

Links Golf

Links golf is the purest, most traditional, and natural form of the game. The earliest links courses were built on sandy dunes reclaimed from the ocean, which provide the perfect terrain and turf on which to play the game. There is no greater challenge in golf than pitting your wits against the best that Mother Nature has to offer: traditional seaside bunkers—deep and steep-faced—present severe problems, undulating fairways give uneven lies, and links rough is among the most punishing on earth. Tough and totally uncompromising even before the wind starts to blow, links golf is the ultimate test of a player's technique and temperament.

Beating the elements

Links golf is the purist's dream. Blind tee shots, dry, fast-running fairways, huge undulating greens, and prevailing winds present challenges that simply do not exist on many modern, manicured, tree-lined golf courses. It is no coincidence that many of the finest exponents of links golf, such as Tom Watson, Seve Ballesteros, Nick Faldo, Tiger Woods, and Jack Nicklaus are also supreme shotmakers and ball-strikers.

TAKE EXTRA CLUB INTO THE WIND

Playing into the wind, Gary Player will often take at least two more clubs than he needs and choke down on the grip to hit a lower shot without changing his swing.

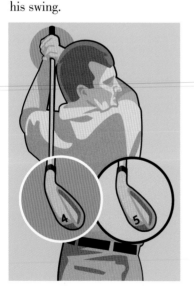

DON'T HIT YOUR WEDGE IN A CROSSWIND

Many Tour pros avoid hitting a full wedge shot in a crosswind because the height on the ball

means it is easily blown off line. Good players prefer to choke down on an 8-iron or 9-iron to create a lower trajectory and more control.

HIT A 3-WOOD DOWNWIND

When he's driving downwind, Tiger Woods will often leave the driver in the bag and use his 3-wood instead. Woods can carry the ball just as far with this club, while the slight increase in loft maximizes his chances of hitting the ball straight.

TAKE A FIRM WIDE STANCE IN THE WIND

"In setting yourself up to hit the ball on a windy day," says Sam Snead in *Natural Golf*, "make sure that you have a firm stance capable of resisting a sudden gust of wind. When hitting the ball into a strong wind, the body moves a little faster coming into the hitting area, and the hands are permitted to follow the ball a bit farther than they would be

under normal conditions. This prevents the ball from taking on its normal loft and keeps it low enough during its flight so that it is not entirely at the mercy of the winds. The stance, of course, is widened and the ball played toward the right foot."

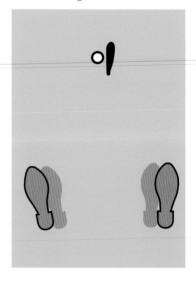

WHEN THE LEFT HAND TAKES CHARGE

One of the unique challenges links courses present, and which often causes amateur players a

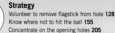

Strategy
Volunteer to remove flagstick from hole **128**
Know where not to hit the ball **155**
Concentrate on the opening holes **205**

Swing theory
Kick left knee to target to start downswing **39**
Take a pause at the top in practice **46**
Let momentum kickstart your coil **60**

Club selection
Avoid wedges when playing from hardpan lies **79**
Putt-chip for more control **100**

lot of trouble, is a delicate chip or pitch out of sandy rough. A typical shot could be a tricky pitch over an obstacle, such as an embankment or dune to the green. Many amateur golfers suffer a crisis of confidence and just hit and hope. But what you need is really no more than just a variation on the sand bunker explosion shot. Take a wedge, and adopt a narrow stance with your hands forward of the ball. Take the club back a little on an out-to-in path, and with a firm left hand. Aim to hit the sand about an inch behind the ball, keeping your hands firm through the point of contact so that your left hand keeps pointing skyward into your follow-through.

RESTRICT YOUR PIVOT IN WET WEATHER
When the ground is soft, wet, and slippery, there is a danger that you can lose your balance if you don't modify your swing. The safest course of action is to limit the amount of shoulder turn.

SET WEIGHT ON FRONT FOOT FOR LONG PUNCH
"I think of it as a long punch shot," says Greg Norman in his *100 Instant Golf Lessons*. "The key is to push the ball outward on a low trajectory rather than lofting it into the air. You can

preprogram this effect at address by setting up with the ball a bit back, just in back of your left heel. The majority of your weight should be on your left side, but you should not put so much weight there that you fall ahead of the ball as you get to impact."

LEARN TO READ THE WIND
In *Be the Target*, Byron Huff has this advice: "Go for a long walk, say five miles on a semiwinding trail, with a friend, spouse, or fellow golfer, in an area where the wind blows. Just obey this one rule: always keep your partner between you and the direction the wind is coming

from. This exercise requires your total attention—if you carry on a conversation you will not benefit from it. You must stay aware of the wind the whole time. If you do, you will be amazed. Not only will you begin to develop an instinct for the speed and direction of the wind: you will also begin to feel that you can anticipate changes in the wind. You'll notice that the wind truly has a life of its own."

ACCEPT THE BAD BOUNCES
In *My Game and Yours*, Arnold Palmer bounces in with this advice: "Troon is so full of ridges and humps that there was absolutely no telling, with the ground as hard as it was, where any shot would end up. One day, on the fifteenth, I hit what I think was probably the finest drive of my life, long and absolutely square, right down the center of the fairway on the exact line I had planned as the maximum protection against trouble. Yet when I got to the ball I found that it had bounced all the way off the fairway and into a thick tangle of downhill rough—as nasty a lie as anybody ever suffered for a roundhouse slice or horrible hook. Things like this can bother you, all right, but you don't have to let them get you really down."

TAKE YOUR PUTTER FROM THE FRINGE

"If there are no hazards between your ball and the hole, and the grass is nice and short—as it is on most links—then putting is almost always the best option," Colin Montgomerie advises in *Golf Monthly*. "The greens on many links courses are also surrounded by sharp undulations. Rolling the ball along the ground over these undulations is far easier than attempting to chip the ball into an upslope or downslope, where it is difficult to judge how the ball will react once it hits the green."

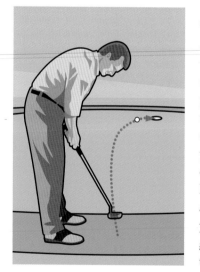

TAKE THE ROUGH WITH THE SMOOTH

When playing a links course you have to accept the odd bad bounce here and there. There will be times when a straight drive takes a sideways kick into the rough or a scrappy lie. Avoid getting frustrated or losing your temper when this happens because that will simply make playing the shot more difficult. Remember that the conditions are the same for everyone.

SAFETY FIRST FROM POT BUNKERS

Your first and only priority when playing out of a deep pot bunker is to simply get out first time. Don't get greedy and attempt to bite off more than you can chew.

OVERESTIMATE THE WIND

Tom Watson thinks many amateurs don't cope with the wind as well as they could. He uses the analogy of a breaking putt to help visualize how to set up and play in a brisk crosswind. With a breaking putt, you aim to the left or right of the cup as necessary to allow for the break. Likewise, with say an approach shot in a crosswind, you must aim left or right of the green to compensate for the way the ball will be moved in the air. Watson also suggests that you shouldn't try and fight the wind, but rather let the wind move the ball having made allowance for the movement in your lining up.

He also suggests that you should overestimate the effect the wind will have on your shot.

PUNCH IT LOW FOR CONTROL AND SPIN

When playing in the wind, the ability to control the ball's trajectory is critical. Nick Faldo is a master of the low punch shot, which flies no more than 20 feet off the ground and stops quickly on the green.

CHECK YOUR EGO WHEN PLAYING OUT OF GORSE

"The first thing you should do when you find your ball lying in thick rough, gorse, or heather," advises Colin Montgomerie in *Golf Monthly*, "is to give yourself an ego check. By that I mean

Accuracy & distance
Focus on aiming clubface squarely **28**
Work your way up to full power **61**
Path of putter must match the line **128**

Setup
Push hands further forward from a bare lie **97**
Remember the "V" in the bunker **115**

Swing theory
Swing the bucket to start the takeaway **37**
Don't move head forward in downswing **42**

forget any fancy thoughts of blasting the ball 200 yards toward the green like you may have seen Ernie Els and Tiger Woods do in the Open Championship."

● LENGTHEN PUTTING STROKE IN THE WIND

The PGA professional, Scott Canfield, counsels: "Many pros advocate that you should shorten your putting stroke in windy weather so that the putter remains on the correct path. However, I believe that this can lead to problems with tempo that will adversely affect the solidity of the strike. I believe it is better to lengthen your stroke slightly in the wind so that the weight and momentum of the putter hold the club on line more effectively."

● OPEN CLUBFACE WHEN PLAYING FROM GORSE

When thick grass or gorse gets trapped around the clubhead at impact it usually twists the face into a closed and delofted position. That's the reason why you see so many shots out of the rough smothered low and to the left. Counteract this effect by opening the face of the club at address.

● THIN LAYERS BEAT THE COLD

You rarely see a top golfer wearing a thick sweater when playing in cold weather. Most players wear several layers of thin clothing since that doesn't restrict their swing and range of movement so much. Wearing several thin items of clothing also insulates the body more effectively and also allows the golfer to peel off layers quickly if the temperature rises.

● GET OUT FIRST TIME FROM A POT BUNKER

When playing from a pot bunker, you may have to contort yourself into a strange position, so you should experiment with two or three ways of forming your stance before you decide on the best way. Make several practice backswings to ensure that you can clear the lip.

● MAINTAIN YOUR BALANCE ON SLOPES

When hitting a shot where the ball is either above or below your feet, balance is your number-one priority, particularly on your backswing and through impact. On particularly steep slopes, you may have trouble keeping your balance in your follow-through, but that is to be expected.

● KEEP A GOOD ATTITUDE IN BAD WEATHER

You are far more likely to drop shots in bad weather because of a poor attitude than by the effects of the wind and the rain. Seve Ballesteros has often said that he used to enjoy playing in the wind and rain on links courses because he felt he had a psychological advantage over players who didn't relish the idea of playing in bad weather.

● USE THE UNDULATIONS TO READ YOUR PUTTS

While the steep undulations that often surround large links greens are usually regarded as hazards in their own right, you can use these slopes to your advantage when reading greens because you can often step back off the green and position your eyes at ground level, thereby giving you a better view of the break.

The Old Course Ballybunion, Ireland

11TH HOLE, PAR-4, 449 YARDS

PITTING YOUR WITS AGAINST NATURE

Tier upon tier of towering sand dunes provide the backdrop and the majority of the hazards at Ballybunion's Old Course in Ireland. Perched on the very edge of the Atlantic Ocean, this imposing yet eminently fair links course has evoked praise from thousands of visitors as well as from many of the world's top golfers, including Tom Watson and Tiger Woods, and is constantly being touted as a future Open Championship venue.

It isn't everywhere that a cemetery forms the prominent hazard on the opening hole of a golf course, yet a sliced tee shot off the first at Ballybunion will find the graveyard situated on the right of the first fairway. As you cast your eyes around the rolling landscape of the Old Course, the vista is conspicuous by its total absence of trees and bushes. Towering, grass-covered sand dunes, babbling brooks, lunar-style hollows, and hidden pot bunkers immediately catch your attention, along with the impressive views out over the Atlantic, the rugged Kerry countryside and the Shannon estuary.

It's a course of sharp contouring, and there is an unkempt look to Ballybunion. Long grass covers the dunes that frame each hole and the whole tract of land looks as though it has been untouched for several centuries. However, if you look carefully, you can see, hidden among the hills, manicured yet still heavily undulating greens that provide such a stark contrast to the barren theme.

The top players consistently state that Ballybunion is a very fair test of golf. There are very few totally blind shots and the fairways are often generous. A

PRO-FILE
TOM WATSON

Love the links

Considering Tom Watson's pedigree in the majors, it is difficult to believe that early in his career he was labeled as a "choker." Prior to arriving at Carnoustie, in Scotland, for the 1975 Open Championship, Watson had led the previous two US Opens only to fall back in the later stages. Carnoustie has a track record for producing champions with established credentials and, although Watson remained handily positioned a few strokes behind the leaders after the first few rounds, nobody took too much notice. However, after three days of sunshine and uncharacteristically low scoring, Carnoustie finally bared its teeth. None of the contenders on the final day broke 70 and Watson found himself in an 18-hole playoff with Australia's Jack Newton, which he won after drilling a 2-iron into the green on the last hole to secure a par.

One of the secrets of Watson's success on links courses was the quality of his ball striking. A crisp and clinical hitter, he produced penetrating iron shots that were ideal for minimizing the effects of the wind. He has always stated publicly that he loves the seaside courses and the variety of shots that you are required to manufacture.

par-71 of 6,542 yards, it is by no means a monster in length and contains five par-3s. In traditional links style, most of the greens will accommodate a low-running approach shot, yet will heavily penalize the misdirected shot.

The contours are the features that bring Ballybunion to life. Rarely will a golfer find a perfectly flat lie in the fairway and more often than not one should expect to be playing from a sidehill lie. "It is all this that causes Ballybunion to offer some of the finest and most demanding shots into the green of any course I've played in the world," said Tom Watson. "Combine this with the winds that are prevalent here and you have a magnificent challenge."

Highlighting a signature hole is a difficult task, yet the par-4 11th hole encompasses everything that characterizes the Old Course. The tee is perched on the edge of a cliff top overlooking the Atlantic and plays to a narrow fairway flanked on the left by imposing dunes and on the right by the ocean.

15

Trouble-shooting

Every player, at some time or other, experiences the frustration of playing poorly yet not knowing how or why the bad shots have suddenly occurred. More often than not, sudden swing or shotmaking problems are caused by a bad habit that, over a period of time, has crept into one's preparation or setup. However, this can be difficult to self-diagnose out on the golf course. It is essential that a golfer be aware of what his or her tendencies are so that they can be rectified as and when they occur during play.

Curing common faults

Such is the fickle nature of golf that all players, including the world's top professionals, develop faults in their game from time to time. Once again, part of the skill of becoming a good player is being aware of your problem shots or swing flaws so that you know how to deal with problems as and when they arise. Drills and practice exercises are particularly effective at grooving good habits and eliminating damaging flaws from your game.

KEEP FEET TOGETHER FOR BETTER BALANCE

Bobby Jones used to practice his footwork and balance by hitting shots with his feet together, starting with gentle mini-swings before progressing to half-swings.

LEARN THE FAULT-FINDING SEQUENCE

In *The Mechanics of Golf*, PGA professional and golf commentator, Alex Hay, tells us:

"To search for a fault without proper regard for the sequence would be futile, for the obvious fault is most certainly created by a mistake at an earlier stage. The sequence is: Grip, Blade, Ball Position, Stance, Posture, Setup, Backswing, Downswing, Through swing, Follow-through."

TURN LEFT FOOT TO RIGHT TO BEAT A HOOK

"I admit my left foot is in a very unusual position because I point it one-half turn to the right," says Chi Chi Rodriguez in his book *The Secrets of Power Golf*. "It appears that I am pigeon-toed when I do this. But understand my reasoning. Because of my very hard downswing, my left foot has to serve as a brace. It keeps me from losing my balance and actually falling. Without the iron left side, there would be nothing to arrest the turning of the hips, and subsequently I would get a hook."

BENT IS BETTER THAN STRAIGHT LEFT ARM

Bob Toski and Jim Flick inform us in *How To Become a Complete Golfer*: "Trying to keep the left arm straight can lead to too much tension in the arms and shoulders. We see players who try to keep the left arm rigid and try to force extension so much on the backswing that the arm reflexively relaxes and breaks down on the forward swing. If you are going to err one way or the other, we would rather see the left arm slightly bent on the backswing."

ACCEPT YOUR LIMITATIONS

Knowing and accepting your limitations and faults is a key to improving your game for golfers of all levels, ages, and abilities.

TAKE HANDS OUT OF THE STROKE TO BEAT YIPS

In *No More Bad Shots*, Hank Haney tells us: "To rid yourself of the yips, keep things as

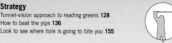

Strategy
Tunnel-vision approach to reading greens **128**
How to beat the yips **136**
Look to see where hole is going to bite you **155**

Swing theory
Hit the second ball for full extension **38**
Check your right arm during the swing **41**
Think "one, two, three" to improve tempo **70**

Club selection
Never rely on best shot to clear water **73**
Take a less lofted club on an upslope **102**

simple as possible. Take your hands out of your stroke. Move only your arms and shoulders. It should almost feel as if you are in a plaster cast."

● TAKE A SQUARE DIVOT FROM THE SAND

Phil Rodgers has this advice in *How to Play Lower Handicap Golf*: "In teaching the basic greenside sand shot, I have my students imagine the back of the ball sitting in the middle of an eight-inch square box. I ask them to clear that whole box out of the bunker. The clubhead enters the sand about four inches behind the ball and exits about two to three inches in front of it. The "divot" is also the width of the box, because the sand explodes out to the sides as well as ahead. It's

basically a square divot. The more rectangular the divot, the worse the shot. It means you've cut the ball out instead of blasting it."

● THE EASIER THE SWING, THE BETTER THE STRIKE

In *A Swing for Life,* Nick Faldo says: "On my travels around the world I don't see too many golfers who swing the club too slowly, but I see plenty who swing it too fast, and it kills them. My advice is to watch players such as Ernie Els and Fred Couples, slow swingers who hit the ball a mile, and learn from their example. The easier you swing the club, the better you'll strike the ball. Plus you will always have that little extra thrust in reserve when you need it."

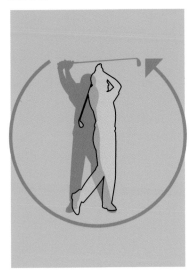

● SPLIT HANDS TO HOLE MORE SHORT PUTTS

"Split-hand putting allows you to stroke the ball solidly in the right direction, even when you feel as if you are about to lose your lunch," explains Paul Runyan in his book *The Short Way To Lower Scoring.* "Split-hand putting is a must for people who become too emotionally involved on short putts. I do not advise the split-hand style for long putts, however. Distance becomes too difficult to control. For most people, eight to 10 feet is the outer limit, except when the greens are lightning-fast or if the putt is extremely downhill."

● SETUP SHOULD HELP YOU WITH YOUR CHIPS

"Almost every poor chipper uses too much wrist and hand action," declares Hank Haney in *No More Bad Shots.* "Do that and you are condemned to scooping the shot. You'll lose the correct angle at the back of your left wrist, hit up on the shot, and hang back on your right side a little. All these actions move the bottom of your swing back, away from the hole. When that happens, you are condemned to hitting the ground behind the ball."

● THE SHANKS CAN DESTROY YOU

"A shank—the shot where the ball goes off the joint of the shaft and the clubhead at any angle except the intended one—is the most terrifying one in golf," says Dai Rees in *Secrets of the Golfing Greats* (edited by Tom Scott). "It strikes without warning, often in the middle of a good round. From the moment a golfer shanks, he becomes a different man. From the easy, happy-go-lucky golfer of a moment before, he becomes a shaking jelly of a man unable to explain why he finds it difficult to hit the ball."

● LEAVE YOUR BACKSEAT DRIVER AT HOME

"Taking loads of mechanical thoughts with you onto the course is like inviting a back-seat driver. It takes the fun out of your game and undermines your swing," say Bob Toski and Davis Love Jr. in *How To Feel a Real Golf Swing*.

● TURN HANDS TO THE LEFT TO STOP A HOOK

"Should your shots begin to curve left," says John Jacobs in *Golf Doctor*, "you obviously will have turned your hands too far to the right and should reposition them less to the right."

● PUT A BALL UNDER RIGHT SHOE TO STOP SWAY

To cure a sway, where your weight shifts laterally in the backswing and downswing, Tony Jacklin recommends that you should place a ball under the outside of your right shoe and then practice making your normal swing. The reason for this, he explains, is that locking your right knee and thigh in position forces your upper body to turn.

● BAD PUTTERS MOVE THEIR HEADS AND BODIES

Hank Haney says that all bad putters move their heads during the stroke and, rather than allow their arms and shoulders to swing the putter, they also move their bodies and have too much lateral movement.

● FINGERNAILS POINT AT SKY TO CURE A HOOK

David Leadbetter says that if you hook the ball you should feel that the fingernails on your right hand point toward the sky through impact in order to reduce the excessive rotation of your right forearm.

● THE TWO REASONS FOR SHANKING

"For a shot to be shanked," Paul Runyan tells us in *The Short Way To Lower Scoring*, "one or both of two things must happen. Less commonly, the clubface might be so open at contact, facing so far to the right, that the hosel leads the rest of the clubhead into the ball by a wide margin. More frequently, the clubhead will be shoved outward from far inside the target line, leaving only the hosel for contact. In that instance we usually have a combination of the two—the clubhead moving out beyond the ball with the face open as well."

● LEARN TO PREPARE BETTER

"The reason most players score badly is that they prepare badly, both for executing each shot and in planning their rounds," reckon Bob Toski and Jim Flick in *How To Become a Complete Golfer.*

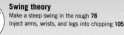

Accuracy & distance
Use a light putter on slick greens **15**
Tee the ball high for distance **61**
Make several practice putts looking at hole **125**

Swing theory
Make a steep swing in the rough **78**
Inject arms, wrists, and legs into chipping **105**

Setup
Hover clubhead off the ground at address **36**
Punch, don't scoop **99**

WAGGLE OR MOVE BEFORE YOU SWING

"Some golfers," says Phil Rodgers in *How To Play Lower Handicap Golf* "are what I call 'dead-stickers', they don't waggle at all. You can play this way, but all the fine players have some motion before starting the swing itself. It's like the conductor of an orchestra, who has a prebeat movement. He swings his arms into the "one," so everyone starts together on "three." The waggle establishes a rhythm and coordination."

DISCOVER YOUR TRUE POTENTIAL

A confidence-boosting way to discover just how good a golfer you could be is to play a practice round using your own version of the Texas scramble.

You can play up to four balls on each hole, each time picking your best shot and then playing each ball again from that position—even on two-foot putts! At the end of the round, your score will give you an indication of just what you could achieve if you played to your maximum ability.

KEEP FEET TOGETHER TO CURE A SLICE

John Jacobs has some "together" advice in *Play Better Golf With John Jacobs*: "If you are a slicer, which 80 percent of golfers are naturally, in simplest terms you never get the clubhead to hit the ball before you are past it with your body—you never hit "early enough" with the club. If you want the fastest cure I know, simply hit shots with your feet together—and I mean together. That way you can only do the job with the clubhead. If you don't you will fall over."

PLAY A PRACTICE ROUND WITHOUT HITTING

Playing a practice round without hitting a driver or any fairway wood off the tee will force you to hit a range of different shots with different clubs and is an excellent way to prepare for a forthcoming round on a much longer course.

CLEAR YOUR HIPS AND SWING YOUR ARMS

"If your shots begin starting out to the right," says John Jacobs in *Golf Doctor*, "or if you begin taking divots behind the ball, combine a conscious clearing of your left hip to the left with the free-swinging of your arms during your downswing."

SHAKE HANDS IN TAKEAWAY AND FOLLOW-THROUGH

A good swing thought to use in the takeaway is of shaking hands with a person standing directly to your right on the backswing and to your left on the follow-through.

FIND RIGHT DISTANCE BETWEEN CHIN AND CHEST

In *How To Feel a Real Golf Swing*, Bob Toski and Davis Love Jr. tell us: "To establish proper head and chin position at address, make a "gun" with your right hand, then point the thumb into your sternum and your index finger under your chin."

The East Course Merion, Pennsylvania

18TH HOLE, PAR-4, 458 YARDS

TRADITIONAL VALUES

The East Course at Merion Golf Club, in Ardmore, Pennsylvania, is on many lists of favorite courses. A traditional layout set in rolling countryside, the design was the brainchild of an amateur architect, named Hugh Wilson, who spent seven months in Scotland and England researching ideas. It has stood the test of time since 1912 and staged more national United States Golf Association championships than any other club.

The members of the Merion Cricket Club, founded in 1865, played a number of sports, including cricket, croquet, tennis, and golf. When the club decided to build a new championship-style golf course in 1911, the committee dispatched a 32-year-old member named Hugh Wilson to the British Isles to study the great links, heathland, and parkland courses. On his return he set about transforming a cramped 126-acre tract of land into a golfing masterpiece. Merion East Course was born and its main characteristics were 120 steep-faced Scottish-style links bunkers—which later became known as "the white faces of Merion"—and distinctive red wicker baskets to mark the holes instead of flags.

The course was immediately put to the test, hosting the 1914 US Amateur championships, where a 14-year-old boy from Atlanta, Georgia, by the name of Bobby Jones led the field after an opening round of 74, which included a putt that ran off the green and into a brook. Speedy greens have been a hallmark of Merion Golf Club ever since. Eight years later, Jones returned to Merion and won the first of his record five US Amateur titles.

PRO-FILE
DAVIS LOVE III

Use slopes to improve your plane

Ever since he joined the PGA Tour in 1986, Davis Love III has been hailed as one of the game's most naturally talented golfers. A supreme ball striker and a very long and powerful driver, Love has won 14 tournaments on the PGA Tour, including the 1987 USPGA Championship.

However, as is the case with many gifted players who achieve success on natural talent alone, Love reached a point in 1990 where his technique was preventing him from making further improvements. Frustrated by the blocked shots he was hitting with his driver, he sought the advice of Butch Harmon during a tournament in Japan where he had played especially poorly and just made the cut.

Harmon explained that the young pro's overly steep and long backswing was causing him to hit weak and wayward shots and he asked his pupil to visualize a baseball batter's horizontal swing. He then asked Love to hit practice shots off a gentle slope with the ball slightly above his feet to flatten his excessively steep swing plane. With his new swing, Love shot 131 for the final two rounds and the pair have worked together ever since.

However, it was his final appearance at the club that inexorably linked the player and the club forever. In 1930, Jones arrived at Merion for the US Amateur Championship. Chasing an unprecedented completion of the Grand Slam, Jones swept every competitor aside on his way to a legendary victory, and then promptly retired from competitive golf at the age of 28.

Further drama would follow at Merion over the years. In 1950, Ben Hogan competed here in the US Open—his first major after recovering from a near-fatal car crash the previous year. The photograph of Hogan hitting a 1-iron to the 18th green to win the championship is arguably the most famous in golf.

The closing hole at Merion is a fitting conclusion for a major championship. At 458 yards long, the tee shot requires a blind carry of some 200 yards over an old stone quarry before the ball nestles down into the fairway over the horizon. Most players will still have a medium to long iron into a fairly narrow sloping green.

hitting hundreds of balls will not make you a better player and instead groove your existing swing flaws and make them even more difficult to eliminate.

● GROOVE A GOOD ADDRESS POSITION TO A "T"

"The top players are meticulous about the way in which they set up to the ball," says Kathy Hart-Wood, a PGA professional, "and you should be, too. Keep track of your clubface and body alignment by laying a club on the ground parallel to your target and another between your feet to monitor your ball position and shaft angle at address. Once you are in position, simply move your feet to change your ball position. With any club up to a 3-iron, the shaft of the club should be in line with the one between your feet."

● HIT OPPOSITE SHOTS IN PRACTICE

In order to avoid exaggerating a particular move in his swing, Jack Nicklaus will often hit "opposite" shots—such as the occasional draw when he is working on fading the ball— in practice.

● CHIP INTO AN UMBRELLA

To improve your feel and distance control around the greens, practice chipping into an upturned umbrella. This forces you to concentrate on a target and to plan the loft and carry of the shot in your mind.

● PRACTICE LITTLE AND OFTEN

"I do believe you should devote fifteen or twenty minutes a day to working on the basic steps of golf," advises Dick Mayer in *How To Think and Swing Like a Golf Champion*. "As a matter of fact, I'd rather see you spend a little time each day, than an hour a week … Golf is largely a matter of good habits. If you spend a little time each day, you will gradually make good habits instinctive."

● LEAVE YOUR FAVORITE CLUBS AT HOME

It is human nature to want to practice what we are already good at. To avoid this temptation, leave your favorite clubs at home when you visit the driving range and continue to use your least favorite clubs until you enjoy hitting them.

● BUILD YOURSELF A PRACTICE STATION

One of the fundamentals of good practice is ensuring that you hit every shot from a good setup position. If you are making swings with a poor grip or flawed alignment you will simply groove your bad habits. To maximize your chances of addressing the ball in an orthodox manner, lay one club on the ground parallel to your intended target and another between your feet to mark your ball position. This simple "T" shape will ensure that you hit every shot from exactly the same position.

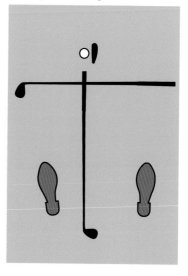

● ALWAYS AIM AT A TARGET IN PRACTICE

"At my own club or when I go eavesdropping at golf ranges in the evening," admits Tommy Armour in *Tommy Armour's ABC's of Golf*, "I see twenty players hitting balls into the wild yonder—anywhere away from the practice tee—to every one I see shooting at a definite target with a specific study in mind."

● ARRIVE EARLY FOR A GOLF LESSON

To get the maximum benefit from your golf lessons, always arrive about 10 or 15 minutes early so that you have time to warm up properly before you are due to start. Most golfers arrive at the club or the driving range at the exact time the lesson is due to start, but then waste precious minutes while they loosen up their muscles and get ready.

● FIND YOUR NATURAL RHYTHM

Many of the world's top players use a musical metronome when they practice—particularly when they are working on their putting—to help them develop and maintain their personal rhythm.

● AVOID PRACTICING IN THE RAIN

Unless it is absolutely necessary, Gary Player avoids hitting practice shots in the rain, because he believes that this can lead to bad habits, such as gripping the club too tightly in an attempt to control it, lunging at the ball and falling back onto your right side through impact in order to maintain your balance.

● MAKE YOUR REAL SWING IN FRONT OF THE PRO

Many amateur golfers try to improve their swing when the professional first asks them to hit some shots for an analysis in a lesson. This is like booking an appointment with your doctor, then pretending that there's nothing wrong with you when you get there. A golf pro needs to see your real swing in order to prescribe the correct medicine.

● WEAR STREET SHOES TO TEST YOUR BALANCE

Swinging a golf club on the carpet at home wearing street shoes tests your balance. Nick Faldo used to practice in his bare feet to improve the solidity of his leg action and his footwork during the swing.

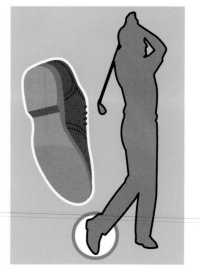

● REHEARSE HITTING ZONE FOR BETTER STRIKING

"To improve your technique through the crucial hitting area, try the prehit drill," says PGA pro, Gary Smith. "To simulate the correct delivery into the ball assume your posture and set the club in a position where it is parallel to the target line with your wrists hinged a full 90 degrees and your right elbow tucked into your side. This prehit position is what every top player is trying to achieve because from here it's almost impossible to hit a bad shot. From here, focus on the position, then swing smoothly into a three-quarter length backswing and then down and through impact."

PRACTICE IN THE WIND TO CURE HOOK OR SLICE

Practicing in a side wind will help you cure a hook or a slice. Practicing in a right-to-left wind will guard against a hook, while the opposite wind direction will help you fight a slice.

SHORT FOLLOW-THROUGH FOR POSITIVE PUTTING

A good practice putting exercise to perform is to place a club on the ground three or four inches in front of your left foot and hit some short- to-medium-length putts, focusing on curtailing your follow-through so that the putter face doesn't travel past the shaft on the floor. This will force you to become a little more aggressive through impact and will help you get the ball rolling more positively toward the target.

WORK ON MISTAKES

"I always achieve my most productive practice after an actual round," says Jack

Nicklaus in *Jack Nicklaus' Playing Lessons*. "Then the mistakes are fresh in my mind, and I can go to the practice tee and work specifically on those mistakes. Often I [write] both the fault and the correction down on paper for future reference."

PRACTICE THE SHOTS YOU NEED MOST

In *Score Better Than You Swing*, Gay Brewer tells us: "I spend more time practicing short putts, from five to 10 feet, than any other shots. It makes sense, because you're going to have more of them. You have to develop a feel on chips, pitches, and putts— by practicing."

PRACTICE WITH BETTER PLAYERS

"Competition sharpens your mind," maintains David Leadbetter in *Positive Practice*, "and adds a valuable dimension to your practice time. The short game in particular offers tremendous scope for imagination, and you should make the most of any opportunity to invent challenges—preferably against a player of similar or slightly superior ability."

THERE'S ALWAYS A CURE OR A REMEDY

"For every fault in golf there is a cure. For every bad shot there is a remedy that can produce a good one," Sam Snead assures us in *The Driver Book*.

UNDERSTAND WHY YOU ARE PRACTICING

In Jack Nicklaus' *Playing Lessons*, the great man himself tells us: "Unless you play golf purely for exercise, don't ever practice without first working out mentally why you are practicing. If you aren't clear about that, don't go out and beat 800 balls a day in the hope that a miracle will occur because, even if you do stumble across "a way", it won't last more than a matter of hours if you don't understand the reason it works."

VARY YOUR CLUBS IN PRACTICE

Try to vary your preround practice so that you use all your clubs and avoid getting too comfortable with specific irons. On one day, Greg Norman will start with the pitching wedge and then hit alternate clubs as he moves through the bag. The next day, he'll start with his sand wedge and hit only the odd-numbered clubs.

CHANGE YOUR SWING WITHOUT KNOWING IT

"If you want to change your swing, think about which end of the bay you head to," counsels Nick Bradley, a PGA professional in England. "You will nearly always find the golfers who hook the ball on the far left of the range aiming toward a target at the back right, while slicers nearly always set up on the right edge of the range and shoot to the left where there is plenty of room. If you want to get rid of a hook, do the opposite and set up on the right edge of the range and aim left, while if you want to stop slicing, set up on the left side and aim to the right. Hopefully, one day, you'll find your way to the middle!"

KEEP REGULAR STATS AND PERFORMANCE ANALYSIS

Many players keep written notes of their past performances and statistics. Nick Price, for example, has a record of many of the swing thoughts he has used in the past. Particularly when playing well, so that he can refer to them when needed in the future.

PLAY A ROUND OF GOLF ON THE RANGE

Continually working on your technique can become tiresome and eventually nonproductive. Similarly, if you know that you are not playing very well, your confidence can be adversely affected if you continue hitting poor shots. When he won the Masters in 1996, Nick Faldo had struggled with his swing all week, so, rather than focusing on his technique, he instead decided to pretend that he was playing the golf course on the range. This shifted his focus onto the task in hand and enabled him to forget about his technique.

SPLIT TIME BETWEEN TECHNIQUE AND ROUTINES

Use your practice time to develop your preshot routines as well as your swing technique. You should go through your full routine on at least 20 percent of your practice shots.

START PRACTICE WITH SHORT SHOTS

Gary Player says that you should get each of your practice sessions under way by hitting some short shots to get a feel for the clubhead and to loosen your muscles.

Swing theory
Use your natural beat **39**
Allow wrists to "give" **96**

Equipment
Think of your golf bag as a toolbox **14**
Practice in your waterproofs **213**

Setup
Use thighs to check alignment **26**
Hover putter above grass at address **121**

188

PRACTICE FUNDAMENTALS

In *My Game and Yours*, Arnold Palmer has some basic advice: "You've got to have your own clubs and a good grassy tee. You've got to take your time. You have to check your grip and remind yourself of the fundamentals. And you have to plan your shot; you have to pick out a spot and aim at it."

IMPROVE ONE CLUB AT A TIME

Sally Little tells us in *A Woman's Golf Game* by Shirli Kaskie: "You can spend the winter on an inside practice range just learning how to hit different clubs. You don't have to be outdoors to learn and you don't have to be in a hurry. Take your time. Get better at hitting each club one by one."

DON'T BE AFRAID TO SACK YOUR PRO

If your game is not improving despite regular lessons and plenty of practice, don't be afraid to tell your pro that his or her services are no longer required. Golf professionals know that they are judged on performance and will understand if you choose not to continue taking lessons from them if your handicap remains static.

USE PRACTICE TIME TO DEVELOP GOOD HABITS

Your practice should enable you to develop effective playing habits that you can take to the course. For this reason, always aim at a target when hitting practice shots. Not only will this provide you with instant feedback as to how good your swing and technique really are, but it will also make the aiming process easier when it comes to playing for real.

PRACTICE YOUR SHORT GAME "FOR REAL"

Marie Laure de Lorenzi, an ELPGA Tour professional, advises: "Whenever I practice my short game I try to make the situation as realistic as possible. I take maybe half a dozen balls and then aim to get up and down with each one. I pay as much attention to the (hopefully) short putt that I have left as I do the chip itself. Not only is this exercise a great way to simulate the on-course experience, it also gives you great feedback on the quality of your chipping and putting …"

HIT UNDERNEATH THE SCORECARD IN A BUNKER

One way to test the quality of your bunker-play technique is to place a ball either on a score card or a ten-dollar bill in the sand, and then make sure that you swing the clubhead underneath to ensure that you hit the sand and not the ball. This encourages you to take the correct length and depth of divot.

MAKE A SMALL BASKET OF BALLS LAST LONGER

When practicing at a driving range, resist the temptation to purchase the largest basket because it is likely that you will spend at least half of your time hitting shots aimlessly simply to get through the balls. Instead, purchase the smallest basket and make it last as long as the largest one by working on your preshot routine, making several practice swings in between shots and focusing intently on what you want to achieve with every shot.

STRUCTURE YOUR PUTTING PRACTICE

Dave Pelz's Putting Bible contains some very sound advice on the subject of how you should sequence your putting practice: "When you warm up before play, or go to the practice green for a true practice session, practice lag putting first, concentrating on stopping all putts from more than 35 feet close enough to make the putt a virtual tap-in. Practice putts of intermediate length, 6 to 30 feet, second and concentrate on rolling them at a speed that stops any that miss about 17 inches past the hole. Finish your practice with putts of less than 6 feet, focusing only on rolling them into the cup at a firm, brisk pace."

GET CREATIVE WHEN PRACTICING SHORT GAME

The LPGA Tour pro, Meg Mallon, continually experiments with her short game. She recommends you start by hitting five balls, opening your stance more on each shot to see how that affects height and distance. Now hit five shots, opening the clubface more on each shot. Then hit five shots, increasing the length of the swing each time while maintaining the same tempo. Finally, mix up the elements of stance, clubface, and swing length to achieve different results.

PRACTICE YOUR GAME AT HOME

Some homely advice from Chi Chi Rodriguez in *The Secrets of Power Golf*: "Simply gripping and swinging the club in the back yard is good exercise. Most sporting goods stores sell plastic golf balls which do not carry far and therefore are ideal for practice with any club, providing you have a yard. The living room rug makes a good putting green."

MAKE PRACTICE SIMULATE THE REAL GAME

"As much as possible make your practice sessions simulate the real game," Gary Wiren advises in the simply titled *Golf*. "Hit from grass when possible; use a target on all your shots; alternate the clubs, sometimes going from a wood to a short iron as you would in the playing of a hole; imagine that you are playing a particular shot on a hole at your home course; then watch the result."

AVOID COMPLACENT PUTTING PRACTICE

In his book *Golf Shotmaking*, Billy Casper writes: "Before each round I suggest you putt some four-footers to get the feel of your putter and of your stroke. Practice from as many different positions and over as many different rolls as possible. Don't just stand there and hit away at random. Take a look at the rolls and try to figure them out."

PRACTICE PUTTING WITHOUT A HOLE

"There is no finer practice for developing a reliable putting stroke than putting without a hole—just dropping a number of balls on a green or carpet and stroking them back and forth," maintains Bobby Jones in *Bobby Jones On Golf*. "Relieved of the need for finding and holding the line, the entire attention can be given to the club and the manner of swinging it."

Swing theory
Left arm guides, right hand hits **39**
Putt like a pendulum **125**

Accuracy & distance
If in doubt, aim straight **127**
Distance is more important than line **134**

190

MAKE HOLING SHORT PUTTS SECOND NATURE

In the book *A Woman's Golf Game* by Shirli Kaske, Marlene Floyd gets down to important matters: "Go to the practice putting green and practice those putts that are the really important ones, the five- and six-footers. Those are the ones that you are expected to make and that you expect yourself to make. When you don't, your confidence fades and with it your concentration. Practice them so much that when you are on the golf course, you just think of the basics."

PRACTICE IN ORDER TO BUILD CONCENTRATION

Ben Hogan always said that you should have a specific goal for each practice session, because this enables you to develop the habit of good concentration, which is an attribute that you will find useful when you actually play a round.

TRACK THE BALL TO THE HOLE ON SHORT PUTTS

"The keys to consistently holing those awkward three- or four-foot putts is getting the right line and then keeping your stroke on track," reckons Per-Ulrik Johansson, a PGA Tour professional. "On short-range putts, I like the putter to move straight back and straight through so that it has no chance to veer off line. Find a flat part of the practice putting green and then lay down two clubs either side of the hole just over a putter-width apart. Now hit some practice putts making sure that the putter doesn't touch either of the shafts on the ground. Not only will this force you to create a square path with the putter, it'll also help you with your alignment on putts from this range."

STOP WHEN YOU ACHIEVE YOUR OBJECTIVE

Jack Nicklaus believes that you can ruin your putting by practicing too much. Since your main concern on the course is the feel for distance, when you've achieved this on the putting green, you should quit practicing. Nicklaus's objective when he practiced his putting was to achieve a fluid, rhythmic feeling between his hands and the ball in a well-timed stroke. Once he achieved this seven or eight times in a row, he stopped.

ASK FOR A SHORT-GAME LESSON

The majority of shots played during a round of golf are played from within 70 yards of the green, yet very few amateurs request short-game lessons. A lesson spent pitching, chipping and putting will potentially help you save many shots and, because it is also a novelty for the pro, the lesson is likely to be far more enjoyable and interesting.

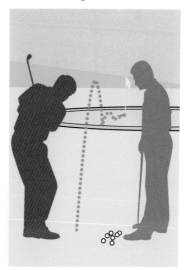

PITCH OVER A BUNKER

"The best way to practice short shots with the pitching wedge," counsels Doug Ford in *The Wedge Book*, "is to stand behind a bunker about 10 or 20 yards from the edge of the green. Then discover through trial and error just how much power it takes to get the ball to the green. Then move farther out until you reach your maximum distance for accurate shots. To determine how far a ball will roll, you should practice landing the ball on a specific spot."

AN EXAMPLE OF DEDICATION

When Seve Ballesteros was still at school he found it difficult to resist the call of golf and to concentrate on his studies. After coming home for lunch he was supposed to return to school in the afternoon, but instead he would hide his school books away and slip out to the beach with his 5-iron to practice. Better still, if there was no-one around, he would go to the far end of the golf course, out of sight, and spend all afternoon practicing.

CLOSE EYES FOR BETTER DISTANCE CONTROL

A great way to improve your feel for distance on the greens is to putt with your eyes closed. After each putt, try to guess how far the ball rolled—whether you left it short of the hole or overhit it. The feedback will help you judge the pace and distance of putts in the future.

DEVELOP POWERS OF CONCENTRATION

In *Power Golf*, Ben Hogan advises: "When I am practicing I am also trying to develop my powers of concentration. I never just walk up and hit the ball. I decide in advance how I want to hit it and where I want it to go. Try to shut out everything around you. Develop your ability to think only of how and where you want to hit the shot you are playing. If something disturbs my concentration while I am lining up a shot I start all over again."

ALWAYS PRACTICE WITH A PURPOSE

You should always have a goal for each practice session. Regardless of whether that goal is to develop a better routine, groove a particular move, or simply to improve your rhythm and tempo, you will benefit from giving your brain a specific task to focus on. Simply hitting balls without any real purpose leads to complacency and almost certainly bad habits.

DON'T REBUILD YOUR SWING BEFORE YOU PLAY

"The practice putting stroke should be exactly parallel to the intended line. That way, when you go to make your real stroke, you won't be lined up right or left of the hole," says Davis Love III in *Every Shot I Take*.

Strategy
Learn from watching playing partners' putts **128**
Always plan at least one shot ahead **156**

Club selection
Stop at a 4-iron from fairway bunkers **79**
Take more loft in low grass **102**

PRACTICE PUTTING WITH JUST ONE BALL

To enhance his sense of distance and direction and to judge slopes, grain, and speed, Lee Trevino used to practice his putting with just one ball. He claims that although you might not hole as many putts on the practice green, you'll learn a lot more from your misses and that your practice simulates the real-life situation.

RAISE RIGHT HEEL FOR BETTER BALL-STRIKING

The PGA professional, Gary Smith, says: "Allowing the right leg to straighten during the backswing is one of the most damaging swing flaws in the game, since doing so prevents you from turning correctly and causes you to lose your height—

the combination of which makes it very difficult to strike the ball cleanly and powerfully." A good way to experience what the correct backswing should feel like, he continues, "is to hit some practice shots with your right heel raised off the ground by an inch or so. This makes it virtually impossible to straighten your right leg without grounding your heel, while at the same time accentuating the feeling of a correctly flexed right knee during the backswing."

PRACTICE YOUR GREEN-READING SKILLS

Davis Love III once asked his father why some players were good at reading greens, while others weren't. His father replied that those players who were good at spotting the breaks were those who practiced reading them. He recommended that you should attempt to read a green first, then confirm or disprove your assessment by hitting a putt.

KEEP LEADING LEG STILL DURING THE STROKE

Jane Crafter and Dr. Betsy Clark have this to say in *LPGA's Guide To Every Shot*: "If you have problems moving on putts or tend to be jerky in your motion, set a club against your own target leg while putting. If the

club drops, your lower body has moved too much. Lighten up your hand pressure and continue practicing putts of various distances until the club remains steady during the stroke."

TAKE A LONG-TERM VIEW ON YOUR GAME

The PGA professional Denis Pugh advises golfers to look for long-term improvement in their game: "Most amateur golfers," he says "view the game-improvement process as a one-shot experience. Tour Pros are willing to hit poor shots in the short-term to improve their technique in the long-run, whereas most club golfers will reject a swing thought or a new technical move if it doesn't pay dividends almost immediately."

DON'T DEVOTE TOO MUCH TIME TO THE DRIVER

"Certainly you must practice a little with every club. But don't devote too much time to the driver." According to Harvey Penick in his *Little Red Golf Book*, "the driver is the most difficult club to hit, which is why they let you put the ball on a peg. The idea of practice is to improve—or at least to hold your own—and the surest way to do this is by practicing with a club that gives you good results."

Muirfield Village Ohio

18TH HOLE, PAR-4, 444 YARDS

A TEST OF STRATEGY

Set in the rolling woodlands of his home state of Ohio, Jack Nicklaus's very first golf-course design was named after the historic links of Muirfield in Scotland, the scene of the Golden Bear's first Open Championship victory. Built in 1974, Muirfield Village has developed an impressive reputation of its own, staging the 1987 Ryder Cup, as well as being the venue for Nicklaus's very own annual memorial tournament on the PGA Tour.

The historic links at Muirfield, on the East Coast of Scotland, hold many poignant memories for Jack Nicklaus. His first visit to Great Britain was in 1959, when he traveled to Muirfield as a member of the America Walker Cup side. Seven years later, he returned to win his first Open Championship and complete the missing link in his portfolio of major championship victories. It was hardly surprising then, that, when Nicklaus returned to his native Ohio to design his first golf course in 1974, a deep sense of nostalgia and history prompted him to name it Muirfield Village. The club's crest features an outline of the Open Championship Claret Jug surrounded by laurel leaves.

Nicklaus has transferred the intensity and attention to detail that he was so famous for as a player to all of his 200-plus design projects around the world. This meticulous approach is evident before you even set foot on the golf course itself. The practice range is circular, enabling the golfer to work on his or her game in a variety of different wind directions and also to allow players to practice at any time of the day without having to hit into the sun. As for

PRO-FILE
BEN HOGAN

Dig the secret out the dirt

It is often said that there was no more fearsome sight than looking into the eyes of Ben Hogan as he was preparing to play a shot. His foreboding stare seemed to intimidate other golfers and the visor of his trademark white cap was always pulled low over his face to shield his privacy.

Hogan practiced obsessively. Fellow players would complain if they were booked into the next motel room because late at night they could hear golf balls bouncing off the wall as he practiced his short game. When he awoke from a coma after his car accident, his first question was not about the condition of himself or his wife, but about how long he could remain out of action before the calluses on his hands softened up. Once, when asked to reveal the secret of his success, he famously replied: "I dug it out of the dirt."

Hogan was also one of the first players to work on the mental game. He famously once hit shots with a radio turned up full blast in order to prepare himself for playing in front of noisy galleries. On the range, Hogan always aimed at a target and his routine was to hit three fade shots, three draw shots, three high shots, and three low shots.

the course, Nicklaus continues to make alterations in an attempt to perfect the layout. The course is well balanced with an equal number of dogleg right and left holes, four par-3s and four par-5s. Nicklaus even thought about the length of the respective nines, creating a longer outward nine to give tired golfers some respite over the closing holes.

As you would expect of a course that cost some $2 million to build almost 30 years ago and with a maintenance budget of over $1 million, each hole is extremely well planned and maintained. There are plenty of very long par-4s, but the toughest of them all is the 444-yard 18th hole. An elevated tee creates an inviting downhill

drive towards an ample fairway and lures golfers into opening their shoulders. However, bunkers lurk at the right corner of the dogleg, while a long drive hit too far left can find the creek among the trees. The approach shot is uphill to a large two-tiered green surrounded by sand and huge spectator mounding that can accommodate 20,000 people.

17

Competitive Golf

There is a huge difference between playing a friendly or social round of golf and competing in a head-to-head match or a strokeplay tournament, where every shot counts and where one small mistake could cost you the match or cause you to run up a big score on a hole, thereby putting yourself out of contention in a monthly medal. The world's top golfers are used to this kind of environment and actually relish the challenge and the pressure, but the rest of us probably need some advice to help us cope with the increased mental demands of playing to win.

When every stroke counts

Competitive golf, where every single shot counts, requires a totally different mindset and attitude than a social knockabout with friends. While medal strokeplay, particularly over 36 holes, is the ultimate test of technique and consistency, the head-to-head nature of matchplay golf examines a player's ability to compete against both the golf course and the opponent. The two forms of competitive golf require different strategies and skills.

● STICK TO YOUR ROUTINE UNDER PRESSURE

The cardinal error when playing under pressure is to think that you have to change your normal routines in order to be successful. Nick Faldo says that, if you normally look at a putt from just a couple of angles, you shouldn't start reading the break from every single viewpoint just because the putt is important. Changing your routine creates unnecessary tension.

● STICK TO WHAT HAS ALREADY WORKED

The PGA European Tour professional, Colin Montgomerie, gives us the following advice: "Many amateur golfers change the way they play over the closing few holes to protect a score. That doesn't make sense to me. You should continue doing the things that have worked successfully throughout the whole round."

● YOU NEED POWER AND PRECISION TO WIN

Arnold Palmer has this advice in *My Game and Yours*: "To win, you have to hit very shot to the maximum of your capabilities, from first drive to final putt. You can't afford a lackadaisical swing. You can't afford a mistake … To win a tournament you have to hit the ball harder than your opponents: you have to have power. You have to hit it straighter: in other words, you need precision."

● PRACTICE THE SHOTS YOU KNOW YOU WILL NEED

Before playing a competitive round on a course, Annika Sorenstam will play a practice round to get a feel for the shots she will need to play and to work out where she should and shouldn't hit the ball. In some courses she has played before, she will work on specific shots well in advance so that she is fully prepared when she steps onto the first tee.

● FIND YOUR BEST WAY TO PREPARE

Arnold Palmer tells us in *My Game and Yours*: "I know from experience that the ideal way for me to prepare for a tournament is to shut out as many things aside from golf as I can. It's best that I don't meet anybody. It's best that I don't read anything. I don't want to have to think very hard about anything at all during these days—not even golf."

● REMOVE FLAG WHEN CHIPPING

"In matchplay," says Davis Love III in *Every Shot I Take*, "one thing you can do that will always get your opponent thinking is to take out the flagstick when you're chipping. Not that that's a reason to do it, but your opponent surely knows, as my father always said, 'If you think you can hole a chip shot out, take out the flagstick, because the flagstick never helped a perfect shot'."

● HIT THE SHOTS YOU KNOW YOU CAN HIT

"To avoid feeling pressured by the play of others, it's very important to play your own game," counsels Annika Sorenstam in *LPGA's Guide To Every Shot*. "By this I mean you must hit your shots and the shots that you know how to hit. Hit one shot at a time and focus on your game only. I don't really look at other players when they swing or putt, so I don't get any images of something that could interrupt my focus or composure. I just want to try to remember my good shots and focus on my game, not somebody else's."

● DON'T MAKE THE SAME MISTAKE TWICE

"The only difference between the pro and the amateur is that the pro makes fewer mistakes and only rarely will he permit himself to make the same mistake twice in a round of golf," says Dick Mayer in *How To Think and Swing Like a Golf Champion*.

● REFUSE TO BE INTIMIDATED

Tiger Woods says that the reason he never allows any other golfer to intimidate him is that he is totally convinced that he controls his own destiny.

● DON'T LOSE YOUR FOCUS

In *Golf Tips from the Stars*, Ian Baker Finch tells us: "Some people said before I won the Open Championship in 1991 that I wasn't tough enough to win a Major. But that wasn't true. I just needed to focus better, not to let outside influences bother me too much. I did learn a lot from playing with Nick Faldo in the final round when he won at St. Andrews in 1990. Then all the people inside the ropes and the dust got to me but Nick didn't seem to notice. He was doing what he had to do and he did it well. I might as well just have been a marker out there."

● MAKE YOUR OPPONENT WIN THE HOLES

""Don't give an inch," that's my philosophy to playing matchplay golf," asserts Nick Faldo in *A Swing for Life*. "Make your opponent win holes, don't give them away. If a player makes birdies and beats me head-to-head, then fine, as long as I gave 100 percent and didn't throw the game away. Never give up."

⬤ RELAX YOUR GRIP PRESSURE UNDER PRESSURE

In *The Arnold Palmer Method*, Palmer says: "There is a normal tendency when playing under pressure to increase the firmness of your grip. This is bad because a grip that is too firm encourages a jerky swing … When you feel pressure, be it on the tee or the green, relax your grip. Don't get sloppy about it, just relax a little in your hands. A relaxed grip will in turn ease tension in your wrists and forearms. You will be more likely to take the club back smoothly and put yourself in a position for a smooth, unhurried downswing."

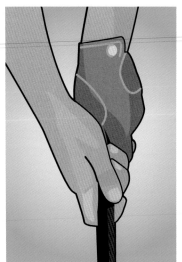

⬤ YOU AND THE COURSE ARE YOUR ONLY OPPONENTS

Jack Nicklaus has always said that one of the first lessons he learned as a professional golfer was not to view the other players in a tournament as competitors. He believes that the physical interchange between players in a head-to-head sport such as tennis doesn't exist in golf. Because he cannot influence the actions of other players, his real opponents are himself and the golf course.

⬤ RECOGNIZE YOUR WEAKNESSES

Joyce Wethered says in *The American Golfer Magazine*: "We have to recognize our weaknesses, and unless we realize them and refuse to make allow-ances for them they will catch us out every time in a crisis. When, however, we have learned them all and recognized that we are going to suffer from them always, it is worth a great deal to be able to feel amused by our own peculiar idiosyncrasies."

⬤ ACCEPTABLE GAMESMANSHIP

"Sure I grandstanded," admits Walter Hagen in *The Walter Hagen Story*. "But don't get the idea I was merely being amusing and brassy. To me that stuff was all part of my game. It helped fluster my opponent as much as it delighted the gallery and was equally important in releasing the tension from my game."

⬤ MAKE EVERY SHOT A PERSONAL CHALLENGE

Ben Hogan turned every single golf shot into a personal challenge. A good drive was not measured in yards off the tee, but by the accuracy of its position in the fairway.

⬤ IF YOU TRY HARD YOU CAN'T LOSE

In *My Golfing Reminiscences* Harold Hilton tells us: "In the first case, one can see how easy it is to throw a chance away by not trying hard from start to finish, for one never knows that the other competitors may not be doing equally indifferently. The second instance is an excellent one of the principle, "Never give up trying." By following it you cannot possibly lose anything, and you may gain."

Club selection
Wind accentuates the spin **80**
Chip with all your clubs **104**
Take your putter from the fringe **170**

Accuracy & distance
Think "thumbs up" for a better strike **34**
Double the length of swing from sand **114**

Swing theory
Slide hips to left to start downswing **39**
Faster you swing, less chance of power **68**

SUCCESS DEPENDS ON STARTING TERMS

"Of course in every match your ultimate success will depend largely upon the terms on which you have arranged to play before starting," says Horace Hutchinson in *Hints on the Game of Golf*. "The settling of these conditions is sometimes a nice matter, needing all the wisdom of the serpent in combination with the meekness of the dove. At such times you will perhaps be surprised to hear a person, who previously you believed to somewhat overrate his game, now speaking of it in terms of the greatest modesty."

LAUGH AT THE PRESSURE

Joyce Wethered tells us in *Bobby Jones and Joyce Wethered Play the Old Course*: "I know the feeling of standing on a tee with real fear in my heart, the match slipping away and the club feeling strange and useless in my hand, and yet I have fortunately been able to laugh at myself for the absurdity of such intense feelings and the perversity of one's own thoughts."

DON'T BE A PUPPET ON THE OPENING HOLES

Don't allow yourself to become a victim of nerves and apprehension on the opening holes. Dr. Bob Rotella says that you should take control of your round from the first tee and approach the opening holes with the same level of confidence as you would a hole later in the round.

DON'T LET PRESSURE CHANGE YOUR METHOD

On really important, potentially match-winning shots, it's crucial that you believe in your basic technique and don't let the pressure of the shot persuade you to start changing your method or experimenting with something new at such a critical time. Stick to your normal, consistent routine because if you try something different or new you're doubling the pressure you're under and the chances are you will blow the shot.

PLAY EACH SHOT INDIVIDUALLY

Think of a competitive round in the order of (1) playing each shot individually, (2) playing the course, and (3) playing your opponents. Reversing the series is a recipe for disaster.

REGAIN YOUR COMPOSURE AFTER A PENALTY

The PGA professional, Keith Wood, tells us: "Plenty of things go through your mind after you've hit your ball into the water and have incurred a penalty shot. Many golfers become worried that they are holding up play, embarrassed, frustrated or angry, all of which can make them speed up their play and risk making the same mistake again. If you have to take a penalty drop, make sure that you take your time playing your next shot so that you regain your composure and avoid making the same mistake twice."

DON'T LET THE SCORE AFFECT CHOICE OF SHOT

Unless you have no alternative and are in a desperate situation, never let your score dictate your choice of shot. Regardless of whether you are playing well above or below your handicap, always play the most sensible shot available to you.

PUTT BEHIND CLOSED DOORS

"When I'm putting in a tournament, to improve my concentration and focus I imagine that I'm in a room by myself with the door closed," Greg Owen, a PGA European Tour professional, says. "That way I am totally immune to any kind of outside distractions."

LAPSES CAN BE COSTLY

"Over a four-day tournament, even if every lapse costs you just one stroke, that's sixteen to twenty shots a week, and that's the difference between being the leading money winner and losing your card ..." says Tom Kite in *Golf Is Not a Game of Perfect* by Bob Rotella. "Over a career, losing concentration once in a while can mean lots of strokes."

OBSERVE YOUR OPPONENTS

Jack Nicklaus' Playing Lessons tells us how the author likes to keep his eyes open: "I never try to intrude myself on opponents, but at the same time I watch them pretty carefully any time I think I might learn something. The most obvious place is on the putting green. Simply being observant can aid you on many other shots, particularly with wind and ground conditions."

IT'S ALL IN THE MIND

"It is the mind much more than the method that makes a golf champion," says Jack Nicklaus.

ROUTINE IS YOUR ROD AND STAFF UNDER PRESSURE

Bob Rotella has this advice in his *Golf if Not a Game of Perfect calendar: 365 Anecdotes and Lessons*: "A sound preshot routine is the rod and staff of the golfer under pressure, a comfort in times of affliction and challenge. It ensures that he sets up properly, physically, and mentally. It blocks out distractions. It helps him to produce his best golf under pressure."

SHRUG OFF THE BAD DAYS

In *My Game and Yours*, Arnold Palmer tells us the secret of mastering golf for beginner and pro alike "is to cultivate a mental approach to the game which will enable you to shrug off the bad shots, shrug off the bad days, keep patient, and know in your heart that sooner or later you will be back on top."

DON'T EXPECT TO BE GIVEN SHORT PUTTS

During your preparation for an important match, spend some time holing out from within two or three feet, because you will almost certainly be asked to hole a couple of putts of this length several times during the round. Nick Faldo also recommends that you work hard on your short game since the ability to scramble pars from around the green has a demoralizing effect on an opponent.

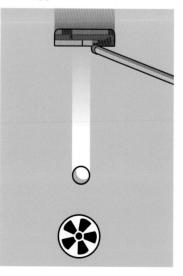

Equipment
Try before you buy **14**
Match your sand wedge to the sand **114**

Setup
Form a "Y" at address for a flexible swing **28**
Always test the sand **112**

Strategy
Use buildings to spot slopes **131**
Capitalize on the short holes **160**

PLAN IN ADVANCE LIKE A POOL PLAYER

Even the very best golfers hit only a few perfect shots during a round of golf. However, these very same players will also allow for this by determining where they want their bad shot to land so that they still have a chance to recover should they misstrike the ball. Much in the way a pool player will think one, two, three, or even more shots ahead, good golfers will always have one eye on where they want to play their next shot from.

GO INTO YOUR BUBBLE TO ESCAPE NERVES

Sweden's European Ryder Cup player Niclas Fasth says that he retreats into an imaginary bubble to help him overcome first tee nerves and to block out distractions when faced with an important shot. He also controls his nerves and reduces tension by controling his breathing.

PLAY HOLES AS IF YOUR LIFE DEPENDED ON IT

Arnold Palmer says that you should play every single shot in golf as though your life depended on a successful outcome. Once you get into the habit of not applying full concentration on every shot, you are almost certain to miss it.

INTRODUCE CHILDREN TO COMPETITION EARLY

"Get children into the right level of competition as early as they can handle it," advises Sam Snead in *The Game I Love*. "When talented youngsters don't have a chance to play with other kids of similar ability, then the danger is that they will lose interest in the game because they won't be able to tell how good they really are."

MINIMIZE YOUR BAD SHOTS

"It is not solely the capacity to make great shots that makes champions, but the essential quality of making very few bad shots …" says Tommy Armour in *How To Play Your Best Golf All The Time*. "Play the shot you've got the greatest chance of playing well, and play the shot that makes the next shot easy … Every golfer scores better when he learns his capabilities."

DON'T WORRY ABOUT BEING OUT-HIT OFF THE TEE

In match play competition, don't allow yourself to become intimidated by a longer hitter. While length off the tee can be an advantage, the shorter hitter can find the green first with an approach shot and apply pressure to his or her opponent.

IF IN DOUBT, WALK AWAY AND START AGAIN

Adopt the habit of walking away from a shot if you know that your setup or concentration is not right. Whenever you are disturbed, go through your whole preshot routine again. Greg Norman once said that in such a situation he even goes as far as placing the club back in the bag and taking it out again so that his normal routine is not disrupted in the slightest.

COPE WITH ANGER AND FEAR

Gary Wiren tells us in *Golf*: "Your two emotions most commonly displayed in the game are anger and fear. Ability to cope with these two emotions will certainly affect your success and enjoyment in golf."

KEEP THE PRESSURE ON

Nick Faldo's advice is that if you win a hole in a match and the next is a par-3, you must hit the green to continue applying pressure. He believes that if you miss the target with your tee shot, you let your opponent back into the match and the momentum gained from winning the previous hole is lost.

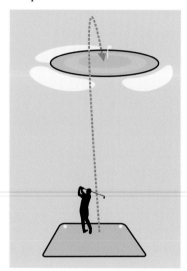

PATIENCE WINS PRIZES

"It may have become a cliché," says Jack Nicklaus in *Jack Nicklaus' Playing Lessons*, "but it is absolutely true that you cannot force a good score, and especially not a winning golf score. The best you can do in golf is to identify the most effective shot you believe you can play in any given situation and then make your very best try

to execute it. Some of those shots will come off and some of them won't and you need a great deal of patience to understand and accept that fact. If you don't—if you lack patience—then you're on the way to desperation, or at least overaggression, and that's never won any tournaments that I've been a part of."

NERVES AFFECT PUTTING THE MOST

Byron Nelson tells in *The Dogged Victims of Inexorable Fate* by Dan Jenkins: "Putting affects the nerves more than anything. I would actually get nauseated over three-footers during my prime. And there were tournaments when I couldn't keep a meal down for four days. Missing a short putt is about the most humiliating thing in the world because you're supposed to make it."

DEVELOP A KILLER INSTINCT

O. B. Keeler writes in *The American Golfer Magazine*: "Walter Hagen never steps on a golf course except to win, and to win as decisively, as crushingly, as overwhelmingly as he can. A friendly match with Walter Hagen is a match all right—but he will beat you if he can, and as much as he can."

LET YOUR OPPONENT OUT-DRIVE YOU

It is good tactics to let a player of a similar length off the tee out-drive you on a short par-4 because you will then have the opportunity to play a short iron into the green first and apply pressure. This is a match strategy that Ben Hogan often used in competition.

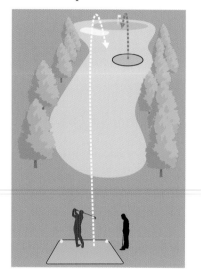

FORGET ABOUT YOUR EQUIPMENT

Arnold Palmer says that, while he will experiment with his equipment and with different clubs between tournaments, he likes to forget about them once he hits his opening tee shot and take them for granted so that he can concentrate on the important task of scoring on the course.

DON'T WAIT FOR MUSCLES TO TENSE UP

Under pressure, Lee Trevino likes to spend as little time over the ball as possible before starting his putting stroke. In the 1971 British Open at Royal Birkdale, Trevino needed to hole a four-foot putt on the last hole to win the championship. He recollects that he knocked it in so quickly that the ball hit the bottom of the hole before the TV commentator had finished talking about how the ball would break.

STAY IN THE PRESENT IN STROKEPLAY

Although it is obviously difficult not to look ahead and back during a round of competitive or social golf, Jack Nicklaus believes that you will play better if you avoid doing so. He says that the less you react emotionally to any shot, good or bad, the more chance you have of playing your normal game and not playing too cautiously or aggressively.

PLAY YOUR OWN GAME IN MATCHPLAY

It is very easy to fall into the trap of panicking and changing your game plan as soon as you fall a couple of holes behind in a match, particularly if your opponent has enjoyed a couple of pieces of good fortune along the way. Ben Hogan says you should remember that the law of averages invariably corrects itself during the round. If you start forcing your own game to catch up you risk losing more holes.

USE YOUR HANDICAP

The most effective way to win is to make the most of your handicap. Never try to impress a better player by changing your swing or trying too hard to make a good impression.

ATTACK THE COURSE STRAIGHTAWAY

"Good golfers attack a golf course right from the first tee shot in order to put themselves in command of the situation as soon as possible," says Ben Hogan in *Power Golf*.

CONCENTRATE ON THE OPENING HOLES

The first three holes of a golf match are just as important as the last three, according to Arnold Palmer. However, Palmer also says that all holes are of equal importance during a round, so avoid placing extra pressure on yourself on the first or eighteenth hole.

HIDE YOUR EMOTIONS

An opponent will receive a mental boost if he or she sees that you are annoyed or frustrated with your game or the state of the match. Keep your emotions to yourself, but don't be afraid to show your delight if you hole an important putt or make an unexpected birdie.

PLAY THE COURSE, NOT THE MAN

Most of the world's top golfers think of playing the golf course and not their fellow competitors during a strokeplay tournament. However, there will be times when you have to react to what an opponent has done, particularly during the closing holes of a competition.

The Stadium Course TPC Sawgrass, Florida

17TH HOLE, PAR-3, 132 YARDS

ULTIMATE TARGET GOLF

The TPC of Sawgrass in Jacksonville, Florida, designed by Pete Dye, was the original "stadium" course, purpose-built to accommodate thousands of spectators comfortably at a tournament. Characterized by huge mounding that surrounds the fairways and greens, sprawling water hazards, and intimidating bunkering, Sawgrass is the home of the PGA Tour and the venue for the lucrative Players' Championship, which is often regarded as the fifth major.

The par-3 17th hole at Sawgrass is the most famous short hole in the world. At 132 yards, ordinarily it would be nothing more than a flick with a 9-iron or a pitching wedge for the top players. However, since the green is surrounded by water—save for a small walkway—the hole demands concentration and accurate club selection.

As with the 12th hole at Augusta National, Tour pros dread the 17th and start to think about the tee shot long before they reach the hole because no lead is safe until it is successfully negotiated. Fans have witnessed many moments of drama since 1982, including spectacular holes-in-one and dream-shattering disasters.

In 1990, Jodie Mudd took a one-shot lead into the 17th and sensibly decided to aim at the center of the green. However, he pushed his tee shot and the ball finished right next to the hole, setting up an easy birdie that would seal his victory. In 1982, Jerry Pate birdied the hole on three out of four days to hold off Bruce Lietzke. "You're forced into being an aggressive golfer whether that's in your nature or not," says Lietzke.

Fred Couples has mastered the hole on several occasions. In

PRO-FILE

JACK NICKLAUS

Play one shot at a time

With no fewer than 18 major championship victories, two US Amateurs, and many PGA Tour titles under his belt, Jack Nicklaus remains the most successful and consistent competitor in the history of golf. Blessed with a powerful physique and an upright swing, Nicklaus dominated the professional game from the 1960s to the early 1980s. Although power was a huge part of his game, Nicklaus's main strengths were his self-belief, temperament, and mental resolve. The Golden Bear has never been too proud to admit that a great number of his victories were more the result of other players losing their nerve and playing poorly than Nicklaus himself playing spectacular golf over the closing holes. His mindset of playing to his strengths and taking one shot at a time enabled him to keep his head while all around him were losing theirs.

In strokeplay events, Nicklaus's philosophy was to focus on playing the golf course rather than concentrating on beating the other players. However, toward the end of a tournament, he would be closely aware of what his fellow competitors were doing so that he could react and change his strategy if necessary at any time.

1984, while some 98 balls found the water during the tournament, Couples parred the hole in every round. In 1996, a 30-foot birdie gave him the title again, but he will be remembered for his hole-in-one two years later.

For Davis Love III, the hole stirs up mixed emotions. He birdied the hole in the last round, when he won at Sawgrass in 1992, but his fortunes changed three years later when he was tied for the lead and needing to win to qualify for the Masters. His tee shot found the water, allowing Lee Janzen to win. The misery continued for Love in 1998, when he stood over a four-foot birdie putt, hit the ball while making a practice stroke and was subsequently disqualified for recording an incorrect score. But the ultimate moment in the island green's history came during the play-off in 1987 between Sandy Lyle and Jeff Sluman. As Sluman stood over a six-foot birdie putt to win his first title, a spectator jumped into the lake and disrupted his concentration. He missed and Lyle won on the following hole.

18

Golf Around the World

Unlike other sports, such as tennis, basketball, ice hockey, squash, and soccer—in which the players compete on exactly the same size of court week in week out—one of the most appealing aspects of golf is the variety of different courses the game is played on. From the immaculately maintained and manicured target-golf-style courses in the Arizona desert to the raw, rainy, and windswept links of Scotland and Ireland, golf is played on all continents in all weather conditions and all types of terrain. That no two courses are exactly alike or even remotely similar keeps the sport a fresh and exciting challenge for everyone.

Variety is the spice of life

Scotland may be regarded as the "home of golf", but the game is now a popular pastime around the world. As Tiger Woods, Ernie Els, and Nick Price will tell you, their willingness to travel around the world and regularly compete on different Tours, on varying styles of course, in contrasting climates, conditions, and settings is one of the secrets of success. Such experiences give them more versatility and a whole range of shotmaking options.

⬤ KEEP BALL DRY FOR AS LONG AS POSSIBLE

When putting in the rain, Greg Norman says you should keep your ball dry for as long as possible, otherwise the dimples fill with water and cause the ball to slide off the clubface at impact with very little control.

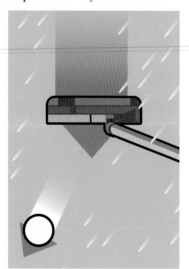

⬤ GOLF COURSES SHOULD GIVE PLEASURE

"The first purpose of any golf course should be to give pleasure, and that to the greatest number of players …" says Bobby Jones. "It will never become hopeless for the duffer nor fail to concern and interest the expert; and it will be found, like Old St. Andrews, to become more delightful the more it is studied and played."

⬤ DON'T STRETCH IN COLD WEATHER

Avoid stretching exercises in cold weather outside because your tight muscles will be susceptible to strains or tears. Warm up inside but take advice from your doctor first on how to stretch your muscles correctly.

⬤ ALLOW FOR THE GRAIN WHEN READING A GREEN

"Grain affects the break and speed of a putt," says Hank Haney in *No More Bad Shots*. "Down grain putts are faster. Into the grain, putts are slower. And cross grain putts will break more or less than usual."

⬤ SWING CLUBS TO STRETCH COLD MUSCLES

The PGA professional, Scott Canfield, says that stretching cold muscles in the winter can be dangerous for many amateur golfers. He recommends that you swing a couple of clubs together to stretch out the golfing muscles gently, while jogging on the spot standing to the side of the first tee will get the air pumping through your lungs and the blood through your veins.

Strategy
Stand well back for better view of break **131**
Play the safest shot every time **160**
Determining a tee-shot strategy **163**

Accuracy & distance
Synchronize your arms and body **35**
Longer arc equals longer drives **61**
Visualize ball running two feet past hole **121**

Swing theory
Point shaft at ball in downswing **40**
Weaken your grip for solid chipping **103**

● MATCH PUTTER LOFT TO SPEED OF GREENS

In general, many pros say that a putter with less loft is more effective on dry, fast greens, while a more lofted putter works best on slow greens.

● ALLOW EXTRA TIME FOR A WARM UP IN WINTER

One of the main reasons why many amateurs struggle to play well during the winter is that they don't warm up before they play. They stand on the first tee freezing cold and then take more holes than normal to get warm, by which time the damage to the score is already done. Take the time to make plenty of practice swings before you head to the first tee so that your muscles are loose and warm before you hit the opening tee shot.

● THINK OF SHOTS AS BREAKING PUTTS IN WIND

Hank Haney tells us in *No More Bad Shots*: "On every shot you must try to let the wind help your ball toward the hole rather than blowing your shots off line. To that end, think of your shots as breaking putts. The old theory on the greens is that every putt is straight as far as you are concerned. You simply aim for a point and let the slope and/or grain take the ball to the hole."

● LINE UP PUTTS WITHOUT BALL IN RAIN

To keep your ball dry before you putt, line up your putt with a ball marker in place instead of the ball. Wait until the very last moment before placing your ball on the green and taking your stroke.

● KEEP YOUR SHAFTS DRY

Wipe down the shaft of the club with a towel after hitting each shot, otherwise excess water will run down the length of the club onto the grip when it is replaced in the bag.

● PLAY IN SEVERAL THIN LAYERS OF CLOTHING

Although it can be very tempting to slip on a couple of heavy-duty sweaters plus a waterproof jacket to play in the bitter cold, heavy or thick items of clothing can restrict your swing. Many top golfers, including Bernhard Langer, prefer to play in several thin layers of clothing—a vest, a couple of lightweight T-shirts and a sweater—rather than one thick jumper, since this allows them to keep their mobility and freedom of movement.

● MATCH PUTTER WEIGHT TO SPEED OF GREENS

In *The Best Way To Better Golf*, Jack Nicklaus advises: "If your course has fast greens, a light putter would be best. A heavier putter, on the other hand, is usually the most appropriate on slow greens."

● KEEP HEAD, HANDS, AND FEET WARM AT ALL COSTS

The extremities of your body—your fingers, feet and head—are susceptible to the cold. Playing golf with cold hands and/or feet is a miserable experience. Invest in some golfing mittens that you can slip on in between shots and use to remove the clubs from the bag so that you avoid touching the clubhead or shaft. Thermal socks will make a huge difference to the warmth of your feet. Finally, most of your body heat is lost through your head, so a woolly hat or a cap will improve your body's insulation.

VISIT THE HOME OF GOLF

Some poetic thoughts from Dan Jenkins in *The Dogged Victims of Inexorable Fate*: "It is a special feeling, I think, that calls the golfer back to Scotland, as the sailor is called by the sea. Take me to the grave of Old Tom Morris, a voice says. Drive me around the Road Hole. Show me where the Wee Icemon chipped it in at Carnoustie. Lead me down the long, narrow 11th at Troon where Arnie made the threes. Let me hear the groans of the Spitfire ghosts at Turnberry. Carry me over the Sleepers at Prestwick. Bend me around the archery field at Muirfield. Drown me in all of these treasures of time once more in this, still another life."

SHINY GREENS ARE GRAINY GREENS

On grainy greens, the blades of grass lie flat instead of growing upright. When you are putting into the grain, the green will appear dull, while putting down-grain makes the green look shiny.

GRAIN CAN MOVE A BALL UP A SLOPE

"The most difficult thing about putting on grainy greens is judging pace," says Tony Johnstone in *Master Your Short Game*. "Down grain, a putt can be as quick as lightning, but coming back it can often be like putting into glue. Equally, if you're facing a left-to-righter and the grain is growing in sympathy, you need to allow for even more movement. I've even known grain to move the ball up a slope."

PLAY TO THE BACK OF THE GREENS IN WINTER

In the winter when the greens are very wet, don't expect much run on the ball. You can afford to be bold and carry the ball all the way to the flag. A good tip is to take a club that will enable you to hit to the back of the green, since the ball also won't fly as far in cold weather.

USE YOUR WEDGE FROM AGAINST THE COLLAR

Butch Harmon tells us in *The Four Cornerstones of Winning Golf*: "When the ball is dead against the fringe's collar, don't panic, as many amateurs do. Don't use a putter either, which is another common error made by the club-level player. Play a wedge and use this technique: Line up the clubhead's leading edge, or 'blade,' with the equator of the ball. Employ a firm-wristed putting stroke, hitting the ball where it rises above the long grass. Because of the wedge's generous, heavy flange, you'll hit the ball nice and solid, rolling it to the hole like a putt."

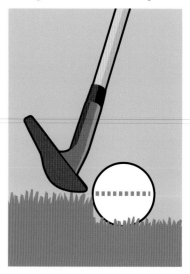

GRAIN AFFECTS BREAK THE MOST AROUND HOLE

When reading a grainy green, Lee Trevino pays special attention to the area around the hole because this is the area where the ball will break most when it is slowing down, and

Setup
Varying stance width and ball position **26**
Squat lower in the sand **111**
Play ball just ahead of chest bone **135**

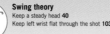

Swing theory
Keep a steady head **40**
Keep left wrist flat through the shot **103**

Equipment
Use as stiff a shaft as possible **14**
Match putter loft to speed of greens **211**

also because the grass has been trodden down to a firmer, slicker surface.

GRAIN GROWS TOWARD THE WEST

"I've found that grain on Bermuda-grass greens, such as you find in Florida and other southern areas, invariably runs toward the setting sun—to the west—so the ball pulls in that direction," reckons Lee Trevino in *Swing My Way*. "Thus cross-grain putts running north to south or south to north will dribble off to the west. Putts running east to west will roll considerably farther than those that are fighting the grain from west to east."

MAKE IT YOUR GOAL TO PUTT PAST THE HOLE

The cardinal sin during the winter is leaving the ball short of the hole. In many countries, the length of the grass on the greens will be longer than normal between October and March, and the putting surface itself is likely to be damp. Take into account the extra spike marks and irregularities in the surface, plus any possible maintenance/ drainage work being done, and you could find that the greens are very slow indeed. Make it your goal to hit every putt past

the hole from a long range. The bolder approach will pay more dividends than being tentative every time.

TAKE A POSITIVE ATTITUDE TO THE COURSE

If you make your journey to the course unhappy about having to play in poor weather conditions, this feeling will normally result in your play being apprehensive and unsatisfying. However, you will find that if you pump yourself up about the prospect of battling the cold, wind, and rain, you will trick yourself into feeling confident and give yourself an advantage over the other players in your group. Constantly tell yourself that you relish the challenge and adopt a positive body language. You'll be amazed at how quickly the negative thoughts disappear.

STRONG WINDS CAN BLOW A PUTT OFF LINE

A mild breeze is unlikely to knock a well-struck putt too far off line, but a howling wind can move the ball several inches. During the Open Championship at St. Andrews in 1995, for example, Tony Johnstone had a dead-straight three-foot putt that missed the hole by some six inches, and finished a further four feet to the right.

PLAY BALL FORWARD IN STANCE ON WET GREENS

In *The Four Cornerstones of Winning Golf*, Butch Harmon tells us: "On very slow greens, move the ball forward in your stance. This will encourage you to hit the top portion of the ball and impart overspin to it."

PRACTICE IN YOUR WATERPROOFS

Nick Faldo gives the following advice in *A Swing for Life*: "Members at Welwyn Garden City [Hertfordshire, England] used to think me mad when I would stand alone on the practice ground hitting balls in wind and rain, but you have to be prepared for any and every eventuality, and that includes swinging the club with a set of waterproofs on."

⊙ ALWAYS CARRY BALL TO
GREEN WITH CHIP SHOTS
Landing the ball first bounce on
the green when chipping is a
crucial strategy during winter.
The water from the putting
surface will often drain to the
fringes of the green and make
the area very soft underfoot. The
front part of the green is also
where most people walk onto the
putting surface, so there may be
lots of muddy footprints between
your ball and the hole. In wet
conditions, you can be more
adventurous with your chipping.
You can carry the ball through
the air more because it will stop
more quickly on the wet green.

⊙ COVER TOP OF BAG BEFORE
PUTTING UMBRELLA UP
Keep your clubs dry at all costs

and make sure that the top of
your bag is covered before you
put up an umbrella or don your
waterproofs. If you struggle to
hold your grips firmly, you won't
strike the ball cleanly.

⊙ KEEP SWING COMPACT
FROM PINE NEEDLES
"Hold the clubhead slightly
above the needles," says Butch
Harmon in *The Four
Cornerstones of Winning Golf*,
"so as not to dislodge the ball
and cost yourself a penalty
stroke. Also, carefully clear the
patches of pine needles under
your feet to secure your footing
(if you think you can without
causing the ball to move). When
you're ready to swing, keep the
backswing action compact, then
use your hands and arms to lead
the club directly into the back of
the ball."

⊙ PLACE A BET TO INCREASE
COMPETITION
Henry Cotton suggests
encouraging a competitive spirit
with your opponent by placing a
bet with them. There's no shame
in admitting to your opponent
that you are trying, he claims.

⊙ BERMUDA GRASS GIVES
YOU MORE SPIN
In his *100 Instant Golf Lessons*,
Greg Norman says: "The ball

tends to perch on the top of
Bermuda fairways and sit a bit
lower into bent and other types.
As a result, you get clean hits
and more backspin—and
sidespin—on Bermuda, but
slightly more distance on other
types of grass, where a bit of
grass gets between the clubface
and ball, reducing spin."

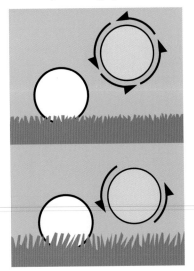

⊙ CARRY LOTS OF SMALL
TOWELS IN YOUR BAG
A golf towel can become wet and
muddy very quickly in the
winter. This makes it difficult to
clean your clubs and keep your
grips dry, while simply touching
the towel with your hands will
ensure that they remain cold and
wet. Rather than carry one large
towel, place lots of smaller ones
in your bag that you can use
throughout the round. Use one

Club selection
Hit ground same time as ball from hardpan **80**
Always land the ball on the green **102**
Restrict your pivot in wet weather **168**

Swing theory
Unwind hips, keep shoulders square **41**
Never strike the ball on the upswing **104**
Judo-chop the ball from a plugged lie **114**

Setup
Draw lines in sand to groove correct stance **111**
Stand a little open at address **124**
Look ahead of the ball at address **125**

small towel every two or three holes. It's also a good idea to have a few plastic bags handy—one for the dirty towels and gloves, the other for the clean ones.

◉ AVOID TOUCHING THE METAL ON GOLF CLUBS

In cold and wet weather, the metal parts of your clubs become icy to the touch. Continually touching the clubhead and the shaft of the club will make your hands even colder and wetter. If possible, remove the clubs from the bag before playing a shot while wearing gloves or golf mittens, then ensure that you hold the club by the grip at all times until you put it back in the bag.

◉ CONSTANTLY CHECK YOUR SPIKES

Your golf spikes can get clogged up pretty quickly when the weather is cold and wet, so constantly check to ensure that there's not too much grass wrapped around them. You need all the balance and stability you can get!

◉ TAKE AT LEAST ONE EXTRA CLUB IN COLD WEATHER

Golf balls don't fly as far through the air in the winter. The reduction in carry distance combined with the lack of roll on the ball once it hits a soggy fairway or green can make at least a one-club difference. As a general rule, always take one extra club to offset your lack of mobility and power in the cold weather, particularly on par-3s, where most of the troublesome hazards are normally found in front of the greens.

◉ STAY CLEAR OF THE SNAKES

In places such as Arizona and Florida, and some parts of Asia, it is advisable not to go thrashing around in the rough with a golf club trying to find your ball because you risk disturbing snakes. It is often preferable to leave your ball well alone if it flies into the deep rough, but if you do insist on looking for it, make sure that you tread heavily and noisily as you walk off the fairway as this will alert any snakes to your presence and they are more than likely to depart before you reach them.

◉ ALWAYS WEAR A CAP OR VISOR IN THE DESERT HEAT

You can help to avoid sunstroke when playing in very hot weather by wearing a hat or visor to protect the top of your head, which is the part of your body most susceptible to the extreme heat and most likely to burn.

◉ DRINK WATER THROUGHOUT YOUR ROUND IN DRY WEATHER

It is important to drink plenty of water before, during, and after your round of golf when playing in hot weather. Dehydration affects your body long before you begin to feel thirsty and among the effects are lack of muscle power, stamina problems, and the inability to concentrate.

◉ USE A SPRAY SUNBLOCK OR NONSTICKY LOTION

If you have to regularly apply sunblock during a round, it is a good idea to use either a spray or a nongreasy lotion. Once you get greasy sunblock on your hands it can be difficult to get off and makes holding the club correctly and firmly very difficult.

The West Course Royal Melbourne, Australia

5TH HOLE, PAR-3, 161 YARDS

BEWARE OF THE BUNKERS

Designed by Dr. Alister MacKenzie in 1931, the West course at Royal Melbourne is Australia's best-known golfing venue. Renowned for its lightning-fast greens and large bunkers, it has hosted many international events, including the 1998 President's Cup, and received praise from many of the game's greatest golfers. The composite course, made up of holes from both the East and West courses, is regularly ranked among the top five in the world.

Located in the popular sandbelt region of southern Australia, the east and west courses at Royal Melbourne boast playing conditions that are virtually perfect, all year round. The firm, sandy fairways yield plenty of long drives, yet the premium is very much on accuracy off the tee, since many of the landing areas are protected by sprawling fairway bunkers. Accurate approach play is also essential because many of the greens are also heavily guarded by sand.

While the warm climate will flatter a golfer's power off the tee, it is the quality of your approach play that dictates how well you score. In addition to the aggressive bunkering—there are well over 100 sand traps—the course's biggest defence is its lightning-fast greens. First-time visitors can spend most of their round three-putting from long range, so the smart play is to hit to the specific areas on the green that permit an uphill putt. One famous player who didn't approve of the speedy putting surfaces was Lee Trevino, who famously said: "The greens are the biggest joke since Watergate. You'd better get a picture of me going out through these gates because I won't be coming back."

However, both Nick Faldo and

PRO-FILE
ERNIE ELS

Test yourself on different courses

It's no coincidence that many of the most successful golfers in recent major championships—Tiger Woods, Vijay Singh, Nick Price, and Ernie Els—could be called "global" players. Ernie and Vijay honed their games on the European Tour before moving to America. Nick Price grew up in South Africa, then made his reputation in Europe before crossing the Atlantic to become a highly successful PGA Tour player and major winner, while Tiger plays several events each season in Europe and Asia, in addition to his forays abroad as part of the Ryder Cup, President's Cup, and World Cup teams.

Experience of playing different courses in different climates adds to players' versatility and shotmaking armoury, leaving, them better equipped to deal with any eventuality out on the golf course. The key to Ernie Els's Open Championship victory at Muirfield in 2002 was undoubtedly his third-round 71, played in torrential rain and wind. While such eminent players as Tiger Woods, David Duval, and Phil Mickelson were blown away by the ferocious weather conditions, Ernie drew on his years of experience and retained his composure as many of his challengers fell away from the top of the leader board.

Greg Norman rate this among the very best courses in the world. Norman says it is a yardstick for what constitutes a great course, while Faldo has compared the quality of the putting surfaces to those at Augusta National. "Both courses sport magnificent putting surfaces, lightning fast and full of contour," said Faldo, "but the greenside bunkers are far superior at Royal Melbourne ... the West Course at Royal Melbourne might just be the best golf course in the world, period."

The par-3 5th hole is one of the world's great short holes, requiring a well-struck iron shot across a valley to reach an angled green encircled by bunkers and also protected at the front by a steep and closely mown downslope, reminiscent of the 15th at Augusta or the 17th at Valderrama. "Given the usual glassy speed of all Royal Melbourne greens, putting from far off can be very testing indeed, particularly downhill. Three and even four putts are common for the careless or overexuberant,' said the five-times Open champion Peter Thompson.

Index

Bibliography

Armour, Tommy, *Classic Golf Tips*, Contemporary Books, 1997.

Armour, Tommy, *How To Play Your Best Golf All the Time*, Simon & Schuster, 1995.

Armour, Tommy, *Tommy Armour's ABCs of Golf*, Hodder & Stoughton, 1967.

Boros, Julius, *Swing Easy, Hit Hard*, The Lyons Press, 1994.

Brewer, Gay, *Score Better Than You Swing*, Stanley Paul, 1968.

Casper, Billy, *Golf Shotmaking with Billy Casper*, Nicholas Kaye, 1966.

Cotton, Henry, *Henry Cotton Says … Play Better Golf*, David & Charles, 1973.

Couples, Fred, *Total Shotmaking*, Collins Willow, 1993.

Daly, John, *The Killer Swing*, Collins Willow, 1993.

Eberl, George, *Golf is a Good Walk Spoiled*, Taylor Publishing, 1992.

Elliott, Bill, and Mitchell Platts, *Golf Tips from the Stars*, Hutchinson, 1993.

Els, Ernie, *How To Build a Classic Golf Swing*, Collins Willow, 1996.

Faldo, Nick, *A Swing for Life*, Weidenfeld & Nicholson, 1995.

Faldo, Nick, *Golf – The Winning Formula*, Hutchinson, 1989.

Ford, Doug, *The Wedge Book*, Nicholas Kaye, 1964.

Gallacher, Bernard, and Mark Wilson, *Teach Yourself Golf*, Hodder & Stoughton, 1988.

Gallwey, W. Timothy, *The Inner Game of Golf*, Jonathan Cape, 1981.

Galvano, Phil, *Secrets of the Perfect Swing*, Stanley Paul, 1962.

Golf Digest, Advance Publications.

Golf Magazine, AOL Time Warner.

Golf Monthly, IPC Media.

Golf Tips, Werner Publishing.

Golf For Women magazine.

Hagen, Walter, *The Walter Hagen Story*, Heinemann, 1957.

Haney, Hank, *No More Bad Shots*, Total Sports Publishing, 2001.

Harmon, Butch, *The Four Cornerstones of Winning Golf*, Simon & Schuster, 1996.

Hay, Alex, *The Mechanics of Golf*, Robert Hale, 1979.

Hilton, Harold, *My Golfing Reminiscences*, James Nisbet & Co, 1907.

Hogan, Ben, *Power Golf*, Simon & Schuster, 1994.

Horton, Tommy, *Golf: The Short Game*, Batsford Sports Books, 1970.

Huff, Byron, *Be the Target*, Contemporary Books, 1996.

Hutchinson, Horace, *Elementary Instruction Approaching*

Hutchinson, Horace, *Hints on the Game of Golf*, W. Blackwood & Sons, 1886

Irvine, Andrew, *Accumulated Golfing Hints*, Johnson Daccord, 1988.

Jacklin, Tony, and Peter Dobereiner, *Go and Play Golf*, Hutchinson, 1983.

Jacobs, John, *Golf Doctor*, Stanley Paul, 1992.

Jacobs, John, *Play Better Golf With John Jacobs*, Hutchinson, 1989.

Jenkins, Dan, *The Dogged Victims of Inexorable Fate*, Fireside, 1970.

Johnstone, Tony, *Master Your Short Game*, Triumph Books, 1996.

Jones, Bobby, *Bobby Jones On Golf*, Golf Digest Books, 1984.

Kaskie, Shirli, *A Woman's Golf Game*, Contemporary Books, 1997.

Leadbetter, David, *The Golf Swing*, Collins Willow, 1990.

Leadbetter, David, *Positive Practice*, Collins Willow, 1997.

Lewis, Beverly, *Power Driving*, Sackville Books, 1988.

Lewis, Beverly, *Golf For Women*, Sackville Books, 1989.

Love, Davis III, *Every Shot I Take*, Simon & Schuster, 1998.

Lowe, W. W., *Bedrock Principles of Golf*, Collins, 1937.

LPGA's Guide To Every Shot, Human Kinetics, 2000

Lyle, Sandy, *Golf The Lyle Way,* Hodder & Stoughton, 1988.

Mayer, Dick, *How To Think and Swing Like a Golf Champion,* Macdonald, 1959.

McCord, Gary, *Golf for Dummies,* Running Press, 2000.

McCord, Robert, *The Best Advice Ever for Golfers,* Andrew McMeel Publishing, 2001.

Miller, Johnny, *Pure Golf,* Hodder & Stoughton, 1977.

Nelson, Byron, *Winning Golf,* Taylor Publishing, 1973.

Nicklaus, Jack, *Golf My Way,* William Heinemann, 1974.

Nicklaus, Jack, *Jack Nicklaus' Lesson Tee,* Prentice Hall, 1998.

Nicklaus, Jack, *Jack Nicklaus' Playing Lessons,* Pan Books, 1993.

Nicklaus, Jack, *The Best Way To Better Golf,* Coronet Books, 1968.

Norman, Greg, *Shark Attack,* Macmillan, 1989.

Norman, Greg, *Greg Norman's 100 Instant Golf Lessons,* Pelham Books, 1992.

Novak, Joe, *Par Golf in 8 Steps,* Herbert Jenkins, 1951.

O'Connor, Christy Jr, *Golf Masterclass,* Collins Willow, 1994.

Palmer, Arnold, *My Game and Yours,* Simon & Schuster, 1984.

Palmer, Arnold, *The Arnold Palmer Method*

Pelz, Dave, *Dave Pelz's Putting Bible,* Aurum Press, 1999.

Penick, Harvey, *Little Red Golf Book,* Simon & Schuster, 1992.

Player, Gary, *Positive Golf,* Cassell, 1967.

Player, Gary, *Gary Player's Golf Book For Young People,* Simon & Schuster, 1980.

Player, Gary, *Golf Secrets,* Pelham Books, 1964.

Rees, Dai (ed. Tom Scott), *Secrets of the Golfing Greats*

Rice, Grantland, *A Close-Up of Bobby Jones: Explaining a Few of the Simpler Details That Make Up His Game.*

Rodgers, Phil, *How to Play Lower Handicap Golf,* Golf Digest Books, 1986.

Rodriguez, Chi Chi, *Secrets of Power Golf,* Pelham Books, 1968.

Rosburg, Bob, *The Putter Book,* Nicholas Kaye, 1963.

Rotella, Dr Bob, *Golf Is Not a Game of Perfect,* Simon & Schuster, 1995.

Rotella, Dr Bob, *Putting Out of Your Mind,* Simon & Schuster, 2002.

Rotella, Dr Bob, *Golf Is Not a Game of Perfect Calendar: 365 Anecdotes and Lessons,* Simon & Schuster.

Runyan, Paul, *The Short Way To Lower Scoring,* Simon & Schuster, 1979.

Saunders, Vivien, *The Golf Handbook for Women,* Three Rivers Press, 2000.

Snead, Sam, *Natural Golf,* Burke Publishing, 1954.

Snead, Sam, *The Driver Book,* Nicholas Kaye, 1963.

Snead, Sam, *The Game I Love,* Ballantine Books, 1997.

Toski, Bob, and Jim Flick, *How To Become a Complete Golfer,* Golf Digest Books, 1984.

Toski, Bob, and Davis Love Jr, *How To Feel a Real Golf Swing,* Random House, 1988.

Trevino, Lee, *Swing My Way,* Angus & Robertson, 1978.

Trevino, Lee, *The Snake in the Sand Trap and Other Tall Tales,* Stanley Paul, 1986.

Vardon, Harry, *The Complete Golfer,* Sand Sedge Publishers, 1994.

Watson, Tom, *Teach Yourself Strategic Golf,* Hodder Arnold, 1993.

Wilson, Enid, *A Gallery of Women Golfers,* Country Life, 1961.

Wilson, Mark, *The PGA European Tour Guide To Better Golf,* Pan Books, 1986.

Wiren, Gary, *Golf: Building a Solid Game,* Prentice Hall, 1991.

Woods, Earl, *Training a Tiger,* Hodder & Stoughton, 1997.

Woods, Tiger, *How I Play Golf,* Little, Brown, 2001.

Wright, Mickey, *Play Golf the Wright Way,* Taylor Publishing, 1993.

Acknowledgments

Planet Books would like to thank the following copyright holders for permission to reproduce excerpts from their titles in this book. Copyright in the customized version vests in Planet Books.

Every effort has been made to trace and identify copyright holders of material used in this book and to secure permission for reproducing it. If notified, Planet Books will be happy to rectify any omissions in future editions.

Submitted excerpts from *Dave Pelz's Putting Bible* by Dave Pelz reprinted by permission of Aurum Press. Submitted excerpts from *Golf Tips From the Stars* by Bill Elliott and Mitchell Platts reprinted by permission of Bill Elliott and Mitchell Platts. Submitted excerpt from *The Complete Golfer* by Harry Vardon reprinted by permission of Fredonia Books. Submitted excerpts from *Jack Nicklaus' Lesson Tee*, *Jack Nicklaus' Playing Lessons*, and *The Best Way to Better Golf* by Jack Nicklaus reprinted by permission of Golden Bear International. Submitted excerpts from *The Mechanics of Golf* by Alex Hay reprinted by permission of Robert Hale. Submitted excerpts from *How to Build a Classic Golf Swing* by Ernie Els and Steve Newell © (1996) (Ernie Els, Steve Newell), *Positive Practice* by David Leadbetter © (1997) (David Leadbetter), *The Killer Swing* by John Daly © (1993) (John Daly), and *Golf Masterclass* by Christy O'Connor Jr © (1994) (Christy O'Connor Jr) reprinted by permission of HarperCollins Publishers Ltd. Submitted excerpts from *Total Shotmaking: The Golfer's Guide to Low Scoring* by Fred Couples with John Andrisani, copyright © 1994 by Fred Couples and John Andirsani, reprinted by permission of HarperCollins Publishers Inc. and HarperCollins Publishers Ltd. Submitted excerpts from *The Little Red Golf Book* by Harvey Penick and Bud Shrake © (1992) (Harvey Penick, Bud Shrake) reprinted by permission of HarperCollins Publishers Ltd. and Simon & Schuster Adult Publishing Group. Submitted excerpt from *Training a Tiger* by Earl Woods, copyright © 1997 by Earl Woods, reprinted by permission of HarperCollins Publishers Inc. and Hodder and Stoughton Limited. Submitted excerpt from *Go and Play Golf* by Tony Jacklin and Peter Dobereiner (Copyright © Peter Dobereiner) reprinted by permission of A M Heath & Co. Ltd. Submitted excerpt from *Tom Watson's Strategic Golf* by Tom Watson, Nick Seitz, and illustrations by Tony Ravielli reproduced by permission of Hodder and Stoughton Limited and Atria Books, an imprint of Simon & Schuster Adult Publishing Group, copyright © 1993 by Tom Watson. Submitted excerpts from *Pure Golf* by Johnny Miller reproduced by permission of Hodder and

Stoughton Limited and Johnny Miller. Submitted excerpts from *Teach Yourself Golf* (1998) by Bernard Gallacher and Mark Wilson reprinted by permission of Hodder Arnold. Submitted excerpts from *Swing Easy, Hit Hard* by Julius Boros reprinted by permission of Lyons Press. Submitted excerpts from *Be the Target* by Byron Huff and *A Woman's Golf Game* by Shirli Kaskie reprinted by permission of The McGraw-Hill Companies. Submitted excerpt from *The Golf Handbook for Women* by Vivien Saunders © Marshall Editions reprinted by permission of Marshall Editions and Random House Inc. Submitted excerpts from *No More Bad Shots* by Hank Haney reprinted by permission of Mountain Lion Inc. Submitted excerpts from *Master Your Short Game* by Tony Johnstone (Copyright © Octopus Publishing Group 1995) reprinted by permission of Octopus Publishing Group. Submitted excerpts from *A Swing for Life* by Nick Faldo reprinted by permission of Orion Books. Submitted excerpts from *My Game and Yours* and *The Arnold Palmer Method* by Arnold Palmer reprinted by permission of Arnold Palmer Enterprises. Submitted excerpts from *Greg Norman's 100 Instant Golf Lessons: One Hundred Ways to Shave Strokes Off Your Golf Game* by Greg Norman with George Peper, copyright © 1993 by Great White Shark Enterprises Inc., reprinted by permission of The Penguin Group (UK) and Simon and Schuster Adult Publishing Group. Submitted excerpts from *The Game I Love* by Sam Snead reprinted by permission of Random House, Inc. Submitted excerpts from *Score Better Than You Swing* by Gay Brewer, published by Stanley Paul, reprinted by permission of The Random House Group Ltd. Submitted excerpts from *Play Better Golf* with John Jacobs, published by Hutchinson, reprinted by permission of The Random House Group Ltd. Submitted excerpts from *Golf My Way* by Jack Nicklaus reprinted by permission of The Random House Group Ltd. (published by William Heinemann) and Simon and Schuster Adult Publishing Group. Submitted excerpts from *Golf is a Good Walk Spoiled* by Geoge Eberl, *Winning Golf* by Nelson Byron, and *Play Golf the Wright Way* by Mickey Wright, published by Taylor Publishing, an imprint of Rowman & Littlefield Publishing Group, reprinted by permission of Rowman & Littlefield Publishing Group. Submitted excerpts from *Tommy Armour's ABCs of Golf* by Tommy Armour, copyright © 1967 by Thomas D. Armour, copyright renewed © 1995 by John Armour, reprinted with permission of Simon and Schuster Adult Publishing. Submitted excerpts from *How To Play Your Best Golf All the Time* by Tommy Armour, copyright © 1953 by Thomas D. Armour, copyright renewed © 1981

by John Armour and Benjamin Andrews, reprinted with permission of Simon and Schuster Adult Publishing Group. Submitted excerpts from *The Walter Hagen Story* by Walter Hagen reprinted with permission of Simon and Schuster Adult Publishing Group. Submitted excerpts from *The Four Cornerstones of Winning Golf* by Claude "Butch" Harmon, Jr. and John Andrisani, copyright © 1996 by Claude Harmon, Jr. and John Andrisani, reprinted with permission of Simon and Schuster Adult Publishing Group. Submitted excerpts from *The Dogged Victims of Inexorable Fate* by Dan Jenkins, copyright © 1970 by Dan Jenkins, reprinted with permission of Simon and Schuster Adult Publishing Group. Submitted excerpts from *Every Shot I Take: Lessons Learnt About Golf, Life and a Father's Love* by Davis Love III, copyright © 1997 by Davis Love III and Michael Bamberger, reprinted with permission of Simon and Schuster Adult Publishing Group. Submitted excerpts from *Golf is Not a Game of Perfect* by Bob Rotella, copyright © 1995 by Robert J. Rotella, reprinted with permission of Simon and Schuster Adult Publishing Group. Submitted excerpts from *Putting Out of Your Mind* by Bob Rotella with Bob Cullen, copyright © 2001 by Robert J. Rotella. Submitted excerpts from *Golf is Not a Game of Perfect: 365 Anecdotes and Lessons* by Bob Rotella (NY: Simon & Schuster, 2001) reprinted with permission of Simon and Schuster Adult Publishing Group. Submitted excerpts from *How to Become a Complete Golfer* by Bob Toski, Jim Flick, and Larry Dennis reprinted with permission of Atria Books, an imprint of Simon & Schuster Adult Publishing Group, copyright © 1978 Golf Digest, Inc. Submitted excerpts from *Play Lower Handicap Golf* by Phil Rodgers and Al Barkow reprinted with permission of Atria Books, an imprint of Simon & Schuster Adult Publishing Group, copyright © 1986 Phil Rodgers.

PICTURE CREDITS
All photographs supplied by Mark Newcombe/ Visions in Golf except: p.31 Pebble Beach, Robert Walker/Visions In Golf; p.49 Cypress Point, Tom Treick/Visions In Golf; p.55 Muirfield, Eric Hepworth/Visions In Golf; p.63 Carnoustie, Eric Hepworth/Visions In Golf; p.91 Pinehurst No.2, Robert Walker/Visions In Golf; p.117 Pine Valley, Robert Walker/Visions In Golf; p.149 Southern Hills, Michael Cohen/ Visions In Golf; p.173 Ballybunion, Eric Hepworth/Visions In Golf; p.195 Muirfield Village, Robert Walker/Visions in Golf; p.217 Royal Melbourne, David Scaletti/Visions In Golf.